Idalee Wolf Vonk

GROWING IN STATURE

*52 Junior Worship Programs
with object lessons, stories,
playlets, and poems*

THE STANDARD PUBLISHING COMPANY
CINCINNATI, OHIO
2913

© MCMLI
THE STANDARD PUBLISHING COMPANY
Printed in U. S. A.

TO BIBLE-SCHOOL TEACHERS
AND WORKERS EVERYWHERE WHO
GIVE GENEROUSLY OF THEIR TIME
AND TALENTS THAT CHILDREN
MAY BE BROUGHT TO CHRIST.

*"And Jesus increased in wisdom
and stature, and in favour
with God and man."—
Luke 2:52.*

CONTENTS

Program	Page
January	
1. SHARING	7
2. SPEAKING THE TRUTH	12
3. ACTING THE TRUTH	16
4. PURITY	21
February	
5. KINDNESS	26
6. FORGIVING	31
7. OVERCOMING DIFFICULTIES	36
8. HELPING OTHERS	41
March	
9. PEACE	46
10. LEARNING MORE OF GOD'S WORD	51
11. WORK	57
12. COURAGE	61
April	
13. GIVING THANKS	66
14. REVERENCE	71
15. FAITH	77
16. SINCERITY	81
May	
17. OVERCOMING PREJUDICES	85
18. GENTLENESS	90
19. PRAYER	95
20. SPREADING HAPPINESS	100
June	
21. LOYALTY TO FRIENDS	105
22. MEEKNESS	110
23. PATIENCE	115
24. LOVE	119
July	
25. TRUSTWORTHINESS	124
26. SELF-CONTROL	128
27. GROWING STRONG (Taking Care of Our Bodies)	134
28. CO-OPERATION	139

CONTENTS

Program — Page

August

29. Overcoming Jealousy and Envy 144
30. Faithfulness to God 149
31. Perseverance 153
32. Honesty 158

September

33. Fair Play 163
34. Assuming Responsibilities 168
35. Choosing the Right 174
36. Being a Good Example 178

October

37. Appreciation 183
38. Doing Our Part 187
39. Self-denial 191
40. Obedience 197

November

41. Humbleness of Mind 202
42. Serving Others 206
43. Serving God 211
44. Joy 216

December

45. The Shepherds Who Heard a Message 221
46. The Wise-men Who Followed the Star 226
47. God's Gift to the World 232
48. Keeping Christmas All Year 237

Special-day Programs

49. Easter 241
50. Mother's Day 245
51. Father's Day 249
52. Missions 252

SERVICE NO. 1—JANUARY

Growing in Stature Through—

SHARING

Freely ye have received, freely give.—Matthew 10: 8b.

Prelude: Have a student quartet sing "The Touch of His Hand On Mine."

Call to Worship: Do you want to know your Saviour?
Do you want to learn His Word?
If you do, then come and worship—
Worship Christ, the risen Lord.

Song of Praise: "Why Should He Love Me So?"

Thoughts on the Theme: (*An object lesson by one of the students.*)*

(Provide the student with a knife, a paper bag, and two apples—a luscious-looking red one and one badly rotted. Place the rotted apple inside the paper bag.)

Both John and Larry helped Mr. Wilson clean his basement one Saturday afternoon. In addition to a shiny quarter, Mr. Wilson gave each of them a beautiful, luscious-looking red apple when all the work was done. On the way home, Larry thought, "I don't feel like eating an apple right now; but if I take it home, Mary will be sure to see it. Then I'll have to share it with her! I know what I'll do! I'll hide the apple inside my jacket. When I get to my room, I'll put it in a paper bag and hide it in my closet. Then I'll eat it later when I am alone." So Larry hid his beautiful red apple in this paper bag. (Holds up the paper bag with the rotted apple in it.)

On the way home John admired his apple and then opened his mouth wide to take a big bite. Then he changed his mind. "No," he thought, "I'll not eat it now. This is the nicest apple I have seen for a long time. I shall take it home and give Mother half." As soon as John arrived home, he cut the apple in half. (Cut the apple in half. Then later cut it into fourths.) Just as he was giving mother half, Jane and her friend, Barbara, came home from skating. "Oh, what a beautiful apple!" Jane cried. "Are there more?"

---

* The *Object Lessons* to be presented by the students and the short talks under *Adult Leader* (see page 11) should be enlarged upon as presented. Lack of space necessitated their presentation here as briefly as possible. While preparing the object lessons, the students should be coached by one of the teachers, because this part of every service is intended to help develop leadership in the students. If the book is used for young children, the teacher will have to give the object lessons.

7

"No, Jane," mother replied. "Mr. Wilson gave this one to John, and he gave this half to me. You may have half of my piece." Mother picked up the knife and cut her half in two.

"And you may have half of mine, Barbara," John said.

Because John shared, four people enjoyed one apple.

In the meantime, Larry's apple lay hidden in a paper bag on the floor of his closet. Several days later, when he was alone in his room, he decided to eat his apple. When he took it from the bag he was greatly disappointed, for this is how it looked—(display rotted apple).

Because Larry was selfish and did not want to share, he cheated even himself. More than that, he wasted the beautiful, luscious red apple. The more we share, the more people we make happy, and the greater are our own blessings. But when we are selfish, we really cheat ourselves out of the joy that comes from sharing; and many times, like Larry, we waste the very things we think we are saving for ourselves.

*Story:** SHARE WHAT YOU HAVE.

It all started one quiet winter's evening as old Mr. Walters sat beside his open fireplace, reading a book of poetry. Suddenly he leaned closer to the lamp and read aloud,

>"If you truly love Jesus,
>   Then do not delay;
>   Go share what you have
>   With some one today."

His eyes wandered from the book, and for a long time he sat watching the flames leap and fall across the burning log. Then he slowly and carefully looked around his little cottage. What did he own that would make some one else happy? What did he own that some one else could use or would like to have? Suddenly, his eyes caught the gleam of a large kettle with a brightly polished copper bottom. It was an exceptionally big kettle—just right for the canning Mrs. Browning always did for her large family.

That kettle had always meant a great deal to Mr. Walters, for it had belonged to his grandmother. It was the only thing he owned that any one ever needed or borrowed. Yes, it would have to be the prize kettle with the copper bottom. So, early the next morning, Mr. Walters tiptoed across Mrs. Browning's snow-covered porch. He

---

* Read the stories aloud several times before you read them to the class, so they can be read with as much expression as possible.

SHARING

Adult Leader:

This is the beginning of a new year. Last year's calendars are no longer useful to us, so we replace them with new ones. As we throw away our old calendars, let us try to throw away all our bad habits. Let us begin this new year determined to try harder in every way to grow in stature so as to be a blessing to God and a credit to our homes and to our Saviour.

But throwing away our bad habits is not enough. As we throw them away, we must form good habits and make them an active part of our daily lives. We have been thinking about one of the habits most important to every Christian—the habit of sharing with others. Here is a calendar which will help us all year to remember to share or to give our best to Christ. (Have various students read from their Bibles the verses listed on the calendar poster. Encourage the students to discuss each verse as it is read.)

January—Deuteronomy 16:17.
February—Psalm 41:1.
March—Matthew 6:19-21.
April—Mark 10:21.
May—Luke 6:38.
June—Luke 11:41.
July—Acts 20:35.
August—Romans 12:20.
September—2 Corinthians 9:6, 7.
October—Colossians 4:1.
November—1 Thessalonians 5:18.
December—1 Timothy 6:17, 18.

The purpose of the handwork is to provide the means for the children to make some object which, when taken home, will act as a reminder of a lesson which they have learned at Bible school. Too much of the limited Bible-school time should not be devoted to the handwork, so you may wish to make all patterns and have all tracing done before the Bible-school period. In some instances, the objects could even be cut out of the colored paper so that only the pasting and lettering need be done during the handwork period. This preliminary work could be done at a monthly departmental teachers' meeting by the various teachers, or at the monthly class meeting by the students, or at a special meeting of teachers and students arranged for the sole purpose of getting a month's handwork ready for use. The posters should be displayed for a longer time than just the one Sunday when the lesson is taught. Use them throughout the Junior Department as permanent posters [using cellophane tape to attach them to the walls], or share them with other departments of the Bible school.

(Instructions for making the calendar poster and individual posters are found in the companion book, *Patterns for 52 Visual Lessons.*)

Benediction.

SERVICE NO. 2—JANUARY

Growing in Stature Through—

SPEAKING THE TRUTH

Wherefore putting away lying, speak every man truth with his neighbour.—Ephesians 4:25a.

Prelude: Play softly "Holy, Holy, Holy."

Call to Worship:

Leader: *Lord, who shall abide in thy tabernacle? who shall dwell in thy holy hill?*

Group: *He that walketh uprightly, and worketh righteousness, and speaketh the truth in his heart* (Psalm 15:1, 2).

Hymn of Praise: "Wonderful Saviour."

Thoughts on the Theme: (*An object lesson presented by one of the students.*)

(Equip the student with as large a magnifying glass as you can find and he can safely handle. In a large group he will have to hold the glass in front of a piece of newsprint so all can see. In a small group, the magnifying glass and the newsprint can be passed around for individual inspection.)

Here are a magnifying glass and a piece of newspaper. We can read the newspaper without a magnifying glass, but sometimes the print is very small. When we try to read it rapidly, we are apt to make mistakes because we can not see clearly. If we hold the magnifying glass in front of the printed page, the letters become much larger and clearer. The glass does not change the sentences nor give the letters different shapes nor change the meaning of the words. The magnifying glass merely makes each letter look clearer, so we can read the words correctly.

Speaking the truth is just like using a magnifying glass. It does not change what has happened. It merely makes the happenings clearer and more easily understood by all. When we speak the truth, the story is always the same.

Story: THE DAY JIM TOLD A LIE.

Jim stood in the produce department of the super market, staring at one bag of potatoes and then at one piled across the aisle. Both bags held ten pounds. Both were filled with the kind of potatoes

Mrs. Bailey wanted, but there was a large sign over one pile which said, "*This week's special;* 10 *lbs. Idaho potatoes* 49c." Only forty-nine cents! Mrs. Bailey always used the fifty-nine-cent potatoes. These special ones were ten cents cheaper. Mrs. Bailey always gave Jim a dime when he ran an errand for her. That would make twenty cents—just enough for a ticket to the basketball game scheduled tomorrow after school.

Until yesterday, Jim had saved the last twenty cents of his allowance for this game which promised to be the most exciting one of the season. On the way home from school the other fellows decided to stop at the corner drugstore for a double-dip chocolate sundae with nuts and a juicy red cherry. Jim could never resist a double-dip chocolate sundae. All the while he ate it he told himself he really did not want to see the game anyway. But that was yesterday. Now that the sundae was forgotten and the game so close at hand, Jim was anxious to somehow get twenty cents for a ticket.

Anyway, he told himself, as he carried the ten pounds of special potatoes around the paved walk to Mrs. Bailey's kitchen door, she would never know the difference. His cheeks felt suddenly hot and the room seemed extremely stuffy as Mrs. Bailey placed fifteen cents in his hand and said, "That was a heavy load today, Jim. The potatoes alone weighed ten pounds. It is well worth an extra nickel."

Everything seemed to go wrong that evening and the next day. His homework problems, which had always seemed so simple, now were too difficult to figure. Forty-nine, fifteen, and twenty seemed to be in his mind constantly, and made the problems confusing. When he tried to concentrate on writing a theme for English, he could think of nothing but potatoes or basketball games or super markets.

The next morning Jim was not a bit hungry at breakfast. And all day at school everything went wrong. To make matters worse, the classrooms seemed stuffy—just like Mrs. Bailey's kitchen.

When the dismissal bell finally rang, there was a wild, hilarious rush for the gymnasium. Jim got as far as the ticket window. His stomach felt so queer and his head so dizzy he knew he would never enjoy the game. Without a word to his friends, he suddenly turned and hurried down the hall to the side exit. The closer he came to Mrs. Bailey's home the clearer his head became. There was no use, he told himself. He would never be himself again until he had confessed what he had done. And that was not going to be easy. Mrs. Bailey had always been so kind and so generous. He hated himself for telling a lie. It was wrong, and he knew it. He had been taught at home and at Bible school always to speak the truth.

As he turned the last corner, he stopped abruptly. Mrs. Bailey was passing through her gate. She saw him and smiled as she gaily waved.

"Hello, Jim! Isn't this a beautiful day? I just need a loaf of bread, so I thought I would go to the super market myself to be out in this wonderful sunshine."

For a moment, Jim was too startled to speak. What if he had gone to that game! What if Mrs. Bailey had gone to the super market before he had arrived! What if she had seen for herself the potatoes marked forty-nine cents! Surely she would remember that he had said they were fifty-nine! And his lying about the clerk forgetting to put the cash-register tabulation slip in the bag with the groceries! She would remember that, too. Surely she would never trust him again.

"Mrs. Bailey," Jim began as he tried to moisten his dry lips with his equally dry tongue. "I—I—I lied to you yesterday. And it has been bothering me ever since." Then he told Mrs. Bailey about the double-dip chocolate sundae and the basketball game and the special potatoes for only forty-nine cents.

"Jim," she said, "I have always trusted you completely. If I had gone to the super market today and had seen the potatoes, I would have realized what you had done. From that moment on I would not have trusted you, because you had lied to me. But your coming this way and confessing makes me want to continue to trust you as I have always done. Come along, Jim," she added in her usual friendly way. "Maybe I'll buy more than a loaf of bread, now that you can carry my shopping home for me. And I want to stop in the drugstore. I, too, am very fond of double-dip chocolate sundaes!"

Prayer Hymn: "Into My Heart."

Prayer (by the teacher).

Prayer Response: Sing softly the first verse of "Have Thine Own Way, Lord."

Offertory Service:

Jesus said, "Give, and it shall be given unto you; good measure, pressed down, and shaken together, and running over, . . . for with the same measure that ye mete withal it shall be measured to you again" (Luke 6:38).

(Play softly "Give of Your Best to Your Master" while the offering is taken. Have a short prayer by one of the students.)

SPEAKING THE TRUTH

Adult Leader:

When we wish to take a trip, the first thing we must decide is where we want to go. Then, after having decided upon our destination, we must find out which roads are the best for us to travel. If it is a long journey and we do not know the way, we get a reliable road map. Then we study it carefully to find out which are the safest and best roads and which will provide for us the most beauty as we travel along.

Our lifetime spent here on earth is very much like taking a long journey. Our destination is the heavenly home which Jesus promised to us. The first thing we must do to be sure we shall some day reach heaven is to get started on the right road. We must find the right road map and then follow it carefully.

But some people have not learned how to read the road map, and so they get started off in the wrong direction. (Display poster figure No. 1.) Perhaps they start down the road called *greed*. That leads them to the road called *hatred*. If they turn left, they reach the *path of sin*. If they turn right, they come upon the road called *jealousy*. That road will lead them either to *envy, fear, spite,* or *loneliness*. Again this road will lead them either to the *path of sin* or to *thoughtlessness, unhappiness, shame,* or *sadness*. (Follow along other paths on the poster map.)

But Christian boys and girls and men and women will follow another road map—their Bibles. Let us turn to Psalm 25:10 and learn what roads or paths will lead us to the Lord. (Use poster figure No. 2, and have a pupil read the verse as you conclude. The patterns for the posters and individual road maps will be found in the companion book, *Patterns for 52 Visual Lessons.**)

The path of mercy and the path of truth—those are the paths of the Lord's. If we follow these two paths every day, they shall surely take us to the Lord. But other paths, such as selfishness, envy, untruth, deceit lead all who travel on them farther and farther away from God.

Benediction.

**Patterns for 52 Visual Lessons* contains patterns for the children to use in making posters to illustrate each lesson in *Growing in Stature.*

SERVICE NO. 3—JANUARY

Growing in Stature Through—

ACTING THE TRUTH

But if ye have bitter envying and strife in your hearts, glory not, and lie not against the truth.—James 3:14.

Prelude: Sing "More About Jesus" as a solo or a duet.

Call to Worship:

> More about Jesus—come, learn more today.
> More about Jesus—come, worship and pray.
> More about Jesus—come, tell Him your love,
> And thank Him for blessings received from above.

Hymn of Praise: "I'm Trusting My All in His Hands."

Thoughts on the Theme: (*An object lesson presented by one of the students.*)

(Provide the student with a soft rubber ball which he and another boy will toss between them before the group while he explains the first paragraph.)

As you see, John and I are playing toss. Everything will go along fine, and we shall enjoy the game as long as we both toss the ball the right way. If for some reason I toss the ball backwards over my head, or if I pretend to be tossing it to John, but instead I toss it to the side, it would spoil the game. John would soon learn he could not trust me, for I would be pretending to be playing in the right way, but I would not actually be doing so. In other words, I would be acting a lie. Soon nobody would want to play with me.

That is just what happens to us when we act a lie. When we try to cover up our wrongs by pretending we are doing the right thing, we are deceiving those about us. Our family and friends will soon learn we can not be trusted, and soon we shall find ourselves all alone.

The psalmist prayed, "Deliver my soul, O Lord, from lying lips, and from a deceitful tongue" (Psalm 120:2). If we pray like the psalmist and then speak only the truth, we will be sure to act the truth at all times.

Story: IT ALL BEGAN WITH A THOUGHT.

As Mary Lou stepped off the bus in the Rockport terminal, she felt that a whole new world had been opened to her. Until now she had lived on a farm. She had ridden in a county school bus with all the other farm children. She had carried her lunch in a little tin kit that had a thermos bottle fastened in the lid. After school she had helped with the chores and always fed the chickens, rain or shine. None of the other children seemed to mind, but to Mary Lou living anywhere but in a big city was a terrible handicap. Now that she was ready for high school, it was decided best for her to live with Aunt Jane and Uncle Harry in the big and exciting city of Rockport.

"I'll never tell any one I've lived on a farm," she thought as she alighted from the bus. "I'll pretend I've always lived in a big city, and in a big house with an iron fence all around it, and a swinging front gate."

That is how it all began—just as a thought as Mary Lou got off the bus. But before September was over, Mary Lou found herself in the middle of what seemed a hopeless tangle of lies. She had not meant it to happen like that, but somehow the first lie called for the second; the second called for the third. Before she fully realized what was happening, she was acting and telling lies all day at school. By the end of September she had not only told her school friends and classmates that she had always lived in Chicago, but that the family chauffeur had driven her to and from a private school in a big, shiny car. By the end of October the large brick house, which she described to the girls as her home, had acquired a swimming pool and a tennis court.

At first, Mary Lou voluntarily talked a great deal about her home and former school friends, for she was anxious that no one would even suspect she had lived on a farm. But now Mary Lou only spoke of such things in answer to the questions the girls constantly asked. She had to concentrate so hard on remembering all the tales she had told, she could not study her lessons well. And it was so hard to keep from talking about her sisters and brothers. Whenever she thought of them, she felt ashamed—as if she had disowned them.

"How can I ever get out of this terrible mess?" she would constantly wonder. "I can not go to the girls and tell them I have been lying! I could never do that! Oh, how can I ever get out of this?"

Then one day, the week before the spring recess, something very unexpected happened which brought the unhappy matter to a hurried climax.

"I have a big surprise for you, Mary Lou," Aunt Jane announced that morning at the breakfast table. When Aunt Jane was happy (as she usually was), her eyes sparkled and her face seemed all aglow. That morning she seemed to beam more than usual.

Mary Lou did not think much about Aunt Jane's remark, because other important things were filling her thoughts. It was the day before the spring vacation began. Shortened classes were scheduled in order to have the entire afternoon free for an operetta in which all grades and departments were participating. Mary Lou had been selected to sing one of the leading roles. Parents, relatives, and friends of the students were invited, and a large crowd was expected. Mary Lou had gone into great detail to explain to every one why neither her mother nor her father could attend.

The afternoon finally came, and Mary Lou lived the hours as if in a dream. She had sung solos for Bible-school and church entertainments since she was in the Primary Department. But this was the first time she had had such a leading part. As soon as the performance was over, her friends gathered in an excited group, all telling her at once how beautifully she had sung. Then she was suddenly conscious that her name was being called.

"Mr. Wellington wants you on the stage, Mary Lou!" some one called. Before she realized what was happening, the group had edged her back onto the stage, where the principal stood waiting for her. After a few words of praise, Mr. Wellington said:

"And now, Mary Lou, we have a big surprise for you. We wanted to be sure your mother and father and your brothers and sisters could all be here this afternoon, so we arranged special transportation for them. There they are!" he exclaimed, pointing happily to the third row in the middle aisle. Mary Lou could never remember actually leaving the stage. The rest of the afternoon seemed confused and blurred in her memory. She remembered the wild applause of the audience. She also remembered introducing her family to some of her teachers and classmates—which ones, she did not remember. Then followed the big, beautiful dinner Aunt Jane had prepared. And finally the late trip back to the farm with her family.

It was wonderful to be with her family again! She had not fully realized how much she had missed her brothers and sisters. She found herself enjoying the chores she had hated before. The days passed by quickly. But at night she would lie awake for a long time, thinking about her school friends. How could she ever face them after all the lies she had told? Of course, they all knew the truth by now. Why had she ever started telling and acting such lies? Why should she have been ashamed of her home and her family? Surely, the girls would never want to see her again.

Then one afternoon, when the spring vacation was almost over, a letter arrived from Lila Bixby, the class president. Mary Lou's cheeks became hot and her lips dry as she hurriedly opened the envelope. She felt certain she knew the message before she read it. Surely, it could only be asking her not to return. Then her eyes grew big and suddenly filled with tears.

"Dear Mary Lou," the letter began. "Lucky you! I have just returned from a meeting of the class officers and every one of us sat wishing we were you. Imagine being on a farm this glorious spring weather, instead of in a stuffy old city with nothing but sidewalks and streetcar tracks.

"We were planning the end-of-the-year picnic for our class and thought it would be wonderful if we could have it on your farm. Do you think your parents would consent? Please assure them we would take very good care of everyth—"

Mary Lou could read no more. Tears were running down her cheeks. That night, as she knelt by her bed to say her prayers, her eyes were again wet with tears. "I am so ashamed, dear God," she whispered. "I am not worthy of such great love. Forgive me, and help me to always speak and act the truth hereafter."

Prayer Hymn: Sing softly the first verse of "More Love to Thee" before the prayer. Sing the second verse softly as a prayer response.

Prayer (by the teacher).

Offertory Service:

Every good gift and every perfect gift is from above, and cometh down from the Father (James 1:17a).

God has given generously to each of us. He has blessed us richly. He has sent down to us from above many good and perfect gifts. When we bring our gifts to Him, we are but returning a small part of the many wonderful gifts He has given to us.

(Play softly "His Wondrous Love" while the offering is taken. Conclude with a short dedicatory prayer by one of the students.)

Adult Leader:

What is a puppet? (Have various students explain their idea of a puppet.) Yes, a puppet is a little figure made of wood, cloth, or sometimes paper, which has strings attached to its hands, feet, and head. The puppet moves according to the way these strings are pulled. It can not move any part of its body alone. It performs or acts just according to the way the person pulling the strings wants it to.

Have you ever thought that lies can make puppets out of real people? When we pretend to be something which we are not, or pretend to be doing something which we are not doing, then we are just puppets. These little dolls seem to be moving and walking about, but when you look closely you find they can not move unless some one pulls the strings. And even then they can only move certain ways. They have not the freedom of doing as they wish. When we act lies, we can only move certain ways. We can not do as we wish, for lies are like the puppet strings. We can only move the way the strings (or lies) move us. But when we speak the truth, we are able to move in all directions, for truth always gives us freedom. (Directions for making a poster puppet and individual paper puppets are given in *Patterns for 52 Visual Lessons.*)

Benediction.

SERVICE NO. 4—JANUARY

Growing in Stature Through—

PURITY

Be thou an example of the believers, in word, in conversation, in charity, in spirit, in faith, in purity.—1 Timothy 4:12b.

Prelude: If possible, use "In the Garden" as an instrumental number by one of the students. Otherwise, have it sung as a duet.

Call to Worship:

Leader:
>What kind of law is the law of the Lord?
>And what of His testimony?
>What kind of statutes are the statutes of the Lord?
>And what of His commandments?
>And who can tell of the fear of the Lord,
>And of His judgments?

Group: *The law of the Lord is perfect, converting the soul: the testimony of the Lord is sure, making wise the simple. The statutes of the Lord are right, rejoicing the heart: the commandment of the Lord is pure, enlightening the eyes. The fear of the Lord is clean, enduring for ever: the judgments of the Lord are true and righteous altogether* (Psalm 19:7-9).

Hymn of Praise: "Safe in the Arms of Jesus."

Thoughts on the Theme: (An object lesson presented by one of the students.)

(Provide the student with a filled fountain pen and two pieces of theme paper, one covered with neatly written handwriting, the other written in a careless, messy fashion with uneven lines and misshaped letters.)

Here we have two pieces of theme paper. They are exactly the same size. They are made of the very same materials. Before they were used they looked exactly alike. Now, as you see, they look quite different. They are so unlike, we could scarcely mistake one for the other. If you were asked to choose one of them, I am sure most of you would choose this one, because the handwriting is so clear and neat.

These two sheets of theme paper are just like us. We are all made alike, yet we each have a certain look about us that is completely different from any one else. When we live clean, pure lives and form clean, pure habits, we are like this neatly written sheet. When we have unclean habits, and therefore let our lives become unclean, we are like this sheet. Just as people would rather choose the neatly written sheet, so would they rather be with some one who tries to follow pure habits.

It would not take much to spoil this neatly written sheet. All we would have to do is to put a few ink blots on it, like this. (Shake the fountain pen hard over the sheet so that the sheet has some ink blots across the writing.) A few bad habits can spoil the purity of our lives just as quickly. Now when I hold this sheet before you, you no longer see the neat handwriting. The first thing you see are these ink blots. The first thing others see in us are our bad habits.

Jesus said, "Blessed are the pure in heart: for they shall see God" (Matthew 5:8). The only way we can keep our hearts pure is to keep our habits pure. That means speaking pure words, thinking pure thoughts, and doing pure deeds.

Story: YOUNG TIMOTHY.

(Or *How Leslie Went to College.*)

Ever since the day Leslie accepted Christ as his Saviour and was baptized with ten other boys from the Junior Department, he wanted to become a minister. On winter nights he would lie quietly in bed, listening to the trees swaying as the forceful north wind whistled through their leafless branches.

"That is what I want to do," he would think. "I want to sway people like the wind sways the trees. I want to be mighty like the north wind and sway people to follow Christ."

Leslie studied hard at school. He knew that in order to be a minister he would have to go to college. There was no way for Leslie to know the great disappointment that awaited him. A week after his high-school graduation his mother became ill. The doctor came regularly all summer. Then one day he said:

"Mrs. Richards will never get well in this climate. She must go to California."

Mr. Richards looked across the table at Leslie. This meant leaving their friends and relatives. This meant going to a strange place. This meant finding new work in a distant state. And, without being told, Leslie knew that it meant no college for him.

Shortly after Leslie arrived in California, he found work as a longshoreman on one of the many docks. His job was to help load and unload the ships which carried cargo from all parts of the world to this busy harbor. Leslie was the youngest longshoreman on that particular dock. The rest were older men, some of whom had been sailors on fishing schooners. They were quite different from Leslie. Their manners were rough. They spoke in loud, coarse voices. And often they swore at each other. There was not much time for talking during the morning hours. When the noon whistle blew, the men all gathered in the shade provided by one of the warehouse buildings. While they were eating their lunches they would talk and laugh loudly with each other in their usual rough way. Leslie had joined the group hesitatingly. When the foreman said, "Come along, kid; we eat now," he felt as if he should. But they were *so* different! As Leslie sat listening to their rough language filled with swearing and unclean words, his appetite dwindled. He forgot where he was and that he was not only the newest member of the group, but also the youngest by far. He seemed to hear the north wind whistling through the leafless trees. He could never remember exactly what he said to the men that day, but he could never forget the way they looked at him. When he finished, there was a moment of silence. Then the foreman said, "It's all right, kid. We'll try to remember never to swear when you are around. No one ever talked to us like this before. Kid, you should have been a preacher."

During the weeks that followed it was obvious that the men were all trying to be their very best whenever Leslie was around. Often during their lunch hours, as they sat in the shade of the warehouse, some one would ask a question about the Bible or about God or about Jesus. Leslie would try to answer them the best way he could. They always sat and listened to every word he said. Then one day old Mike, who had the reputation of being the roughest, hardest longshoreman anywhere along the West Coast, surprised every one by saying, "I like to sit and listen to you talk, son. You make me want to know more about Christ. Can't you teach us all about Him— a little at a time every day while we sit here eating our lunch?" That is how it happened that Leslie taught what we might call a "Men's Bible Class" every day from twelve to one during the months that followed.

When summer came, Leslie had finished teaching the men the life of Christ and was telling them about the missionary journeys of the apostle Paul. He told them of Silas and Barnabas and young Timothy. The day Leslie read them the first epistle which Paul wrote to Timothy, old Mike suddenly stopped him, saying, "Read that again!"

"Let no man despise thy youth," Leslie read, "but be thou an example of the believers, in word, in conversation, in charity, in spirit, in faith, in purity" (1 Timothy 4:12).

Perhaps that verse started old Mike thinking. Or perhaps that verse made old Mike sure that what he had been thinking was the thing to do. Leslie never knew. But the next day at noon old Mike stood up and cleared his throat. The rest of the men sat smiling and watching Leslie as if they were waiting for a big surprise. Mike's roughened, gnarled hand was shaking as he offered Leslie a large, fat envelope.

"Take it, son," he said. "It's to you from all of us. There's enough in here to see you through your first year at college. And by that time we'll have filled another one for you. We want to make a preacher out of you, boy—a preacher who can do for hundreds what you have done for us few. If you don't mind, we're going to call you young Timothy—*our* young Timothy."

As Leslie stood speechless among his fellow workers, he felt like a little boy again. He suddenly seemed to be far away across the country, listening to the trees swaying as the strong north wind whistled through their leafless branches.

"That is what I want to do," he said softly. "I want to sway people like the wind sways the trees. I want to be mighty like the north wind and sway people to follow Christ."

Prayer Hymn: Sing softly the first verse of "Have Thine Own Way, Lord."

Prayer (by the teacher).

Offertory Service:
(Sing "Fairest Lord Jesus" while the offering is taken.)

Dedicatory Prayer:

>Bless these gifts so freely given,
>Bless them in the work they do,
>So that others now in darkness
>May receive Thy blessings, too.
>In Jesus' name we pray. Amen.

Adult Leader:

(If snow is available, make this an object lesson by using a container of clean, white snow and a smaller portion of soot taken from a furnace or stove. Display them separately. Then mix them as you develop the following thoughts.)

One of the wonders of nature and beauties of the winter season is snow. When it falls to earth from heaven, it is pure, white, and spotless. It covers the earth like a huge white rug. It remains white and clean as long as it is kept by itself, but soon soot or coal dust comes along and mixes with it. No longer is it white and pure, but now it turns black and unsightly.

Our lives are much like the new-fallen snow. As long as we love Jesus and follow His teachings, our lives will remain pure and clean. But when we forget Christ and sin, either by impure words, impure thoughts, or impure acts, then our lives become black and dirty, like the snow all mixed with soot and coal dust.

When the soot and coal dust once blacken the snow, it will never be white again. Without Christ our lives would be much like that, for when we once sinned, there would be no way to purify our souls and hearts again.

In Psalm 51 we read, "Wash me, and I shall be whiter than snow" (verse 7b). No one but Jesus can wash the sin from our lives and make us whiter than snow. But we must do our part. We must give Him our love as He has given us His. We must follow His teachings in everything we do all the time. And we must try in every way possible to keep our lives pure and clean.

(Directions for making a snowflake poster and snowflake blotters are given in *Patterns for 52 Visual Lessons*.)

Benediction.

SERVICE NO. 5—JANUARY

Growing in Stature Through—

KINDNESS

Be ye kind one to another.—Ephesians 4: 32a.

Prelude: Solo by one of the Juniors, "Do a Deed of Kindness."

Call to Worship:

> *Praise the Lord, all ye nations: praise him, all ye people.*
> *For his merciful kindness is great toward us: and the truth of the Lord endureth for ever. Praise ye the Lord* (Psalm 117).

Hymn of Praise: "I Know Whom I Have Believed."

Thoughts on the Theme: (An object lesson by one of the students.)

(Provide the student with a magnet—a small horseshoe magnet or a small tack hammer with a magnet end—and a small assortment of nails, pins, hairpins, needles, and so on.)

All of you know what a magnet is and how it draws certain metals to it. Whenever we hold a magnet near nails or pins, they instantly cling to it. When we hold the magnet, it seems very small and insignificant. Yet it has a great deal of power.

Being kind is like having a magnetic power just like this horseshoe (or hammer). The more kindness we show others, the more others will be drawn to us. As these nails are being drawn to this magnet, so others will be drawn to us through our kind words and deeds.

Story: BIGHEARTED BESS.

There was great excitement in the Hardy, Summerfield, and Bronson families the day Great-aunt Jessica's letter arrived. Just having Great-aunt Jessica visit her relatives in Parkersburg would have been exciting enough, but she had written the reason for her trip—to "get re-acquainted with all my relatives and to select one of my young great-nieces to accompany me on a trip to California during the coming summer vacation."

No one in Parkersburg had seen Great-aunt Jessica since she had moved to Maine some twenty years before. None of the children in the Hardy, Summerfield, and Bronson families had ever seen her. To them she was like a good fairy who remembered every one's birthday and who always sent a beautiful Christmas gift for each of her relatives. And, of course, every one knew that Great-aunt Jessica was **extremely wealthy.**

In her letter, Great-aunt Jessica requested all members of the three branches of the family to meet together at 4:30 p.m. at the Summerfield home, since it was the closest to the train depot. She would not have time for a lengthy visit, she said, so she requested that every one arrive promptly. But that was not the only reason Mrs. Hardy, Mrs. Summerfield, and Mrs. Bronson cautioned their children that morning against loitering on the way home from school. They well remembered how impatient Great-aunt Jessica always was with any form of tardiness or delay.

Sally and Ann Bronson, Jessica, Loretta, and Myra Summerfield, Natalie and Elizabeth (Bess) Hardy all attended Franklin High. As previously arranged, they all hurried to the main entrance as soon as school was dismissed. Together they boarded the first bus leaving for downtown, where they had to transfer to a bus passing the Summerfield home. It was necessary to walk three squares downtown in order to board the second bus. The seven cousins walked along in high spirits. Their topic of conversation was, of course, Great-aunt Jessica and who, in their opinions, would be chosen to accompany her to California.

"I'm the eldest of all Great-aunt Jessica's great-nieces," Sally declared, with a cheerful giggle, "so *I* should be the one to go with her."

"But *I* am the only one who was named for her!" laughed Jessica. "Surely that should mean something!"

"I look more like Great-aunt Jessica looked when she was our age," Natalie reminded them. "Therefore, *I* should be the one to go."

"Oh, but I am sure Great-aunt Jessica will choose me," Loretta said gaily, "just because I am *not* the eldest, and I do *not* look like her, and I was *not* named after her. I'll send all of you postcards along the way!"

They all laughed as they hurried along.

"How about you, Bess?" Myra asked. "Isn't Great-aunt Jessica going to choose you?"

Bess was trying to keep pace with her cousins and look over her shoulder at the same time. "I'm sorry," she said hurriedly; "I wasn't listening."

"What is so interesting back there?" Sally inquired as they all paused to glance back at the corner they just passed.

"It's that little lady," Bess explained, "the one all dressed in gray with that pale-blue feather in her hat. She looks so forlorn—like she is upset about something."

"There she goes again!" Natalie said impatiently. "No wonder all the girls at school call her 'bighearted Bess'! She is always concerned about somebody else. Come along, Bess. Mother will be displeased if we are late. There is nothing wrong with that little old lady."

"She is probably just waiting for a friend," suggested Ann.

"No," Bess said firmly. "She is upset about something. Maybe I can help her. Walk ahead. I'll catch up with you."

She hurried back to the little old lady. "Pardon me," she said in her usual manner, which always seemed sincere, pleasant, and sweet. "I could not help noticing you have been standing here a few minutes. Is there anything I can do for you?"

"Oh, thank you! Thank you!" cried the dainty little old lady. "How kind of you! I am so grateful! Of all the stupid things for me to do! A half hour ago I broke my glasses, and without them I am quite lost. I can not see clearly six feet in front of me without them, let alone traffic lights on the opposite corners! My glasses won't be ready until tomorrow noon, and already I have a throbbing headache!"

"I shall be glad to help you in any way I can," Bess said quickly. "Here, hold onto my arm. Now, where would you like to go?" She glanced over her shoulder, but her cousins and her sister were out of sight.

"First I should like to go somewhere for a cup of coffee. Breaking my glasses has upset me considerably. If I can sit quietly for a few moments and have a cup of coffee, I think I shall feel much better. Then I should like to go to the postoffice to buy stamps and mail several letters. Then I should like to take a taxi to the place I am going. I shall be ever so grateful if you can help me. But, my dear, are you sure you have the time to spare?"

"Oh, certainly!" Bess assured her as she turned and led the little old lady to the quiet coffee shop she and her mother often visited.

After telling the driver where to take her, the little old lady sighed deeply and relaxed against the back seat of the taxi. But just for a moment. Then she gave a startled exclamation and sat bolt upright. Why, she had forgotten to ask the girl's name! When the girl refused to be paid for her time and kindness, she should have asked her to write her name and address on a slip of paper. Then she could have sent her a gift when she arrived home. "Breaking my glasses has certainly upset me!" thought the little old lady. "It is so unlike me to be so thoughtless."

Several children were looking out of each front window of the Summerfield home, eagerly watching for both Great-aunt Jessica and Bess.

"I surely hope Bess gets here first!" exclaimed young Peter.

KINDNESS

"So do I!" cried Bobby and Jimmy excitedly at the same time.

"A taxi!" cried Lawrence. Every one strained forward to get a first glimpse of Great-aunt Jessica. When a dainty little old lady in gray with a light-blue feather in her hat stepped from the cab, all the teen-age cousins gasped.

"Why, she is the little old lady Bess stopped to help!" whispered Sally, in a strained voice. Just then the Hardy's family car pulled up in front of the house, and Bess and her father got out.

"It is certainly lucky for me you came along right then, Dad!" Bess exclaimed. The little old lady paused halfway down the walk and turned around quickly.

"My dear!" she cried as Bess gave a surprised, but delighted, exclamation at seeing her again. "I would remember that pleasant voice anywhere! I am Great-aunt Jessica. Surely you are not one of my own great-nieces?"

"Yes, I am!" Bess cried. "I am Bess—Elizabeth Hardy. Why, Great-aunt Jessica! I have been afraid that I would be the last one to meet you! And to think that I have been the first!"

Great-aunt Jessica took Bess' arm once more, and together they continued down the walk. "Won't it be pleasant walking down the streets of San Francisco and Los Angeles just like this—the two of us?" she asked happily. "But let us keep it a secret until after dinner."

Prayer Hymn: Sing softly the first verse of "Sweet Hour of Prayer."
Sing the last verse as a prayer response.

Prayer (by the teacher).

Offertory Service:

> Students: *What shall I render unto the Lord for all his benefits toward me?* (Psalm 116: 12).
> Leader: *Upon the first day of the week let every one of you lay by him in store, as God hath prospered him* (1 Corinthians 16: 2a).

(Play softly "There Shall Be Showers of Blessings." Conclude with a short prayer by one of the students.)

Adult Leader:

In the beginning, when God created the world, He also created the seasons. Each season brings to us many beauties and wonders of nature. One of winter's wonders (and certainly one of its beauties) is the snow. All of you, I am sure, have found great delight playing outdoors in the snow—going sledding, throwing snowballs, or making a snow man. If you have made a snow man, then you know how a great big snowball (big enough to be the snow man's body) was once a snowball small enough to hold in your hand. The more you rolled the snowball the more snow clung to it, and the larger it became.

Doing kindnesses for others is just like making a huge snowball. We start out with just a little word spoken kindly. As it rolls along it not only gathers other kind words, but also friendly smiles. When we speak kind words, we are sure to receive friendly smiles in return. So our snowball called kindness grows bigger. As the kind words and friendly smiles roll along, they not only gather other kind words and friendly smiles, but they also find helping hands. When we speak kind words and give friendly smiles, we become eager to help those about us. So our ball grows bigger and bigger. As the kind words, friendly smiles, and helping hands roll along, they not only gather other kind words, friendly smiles, and helping hands, but they also gather good deeds. And so our ball grows bigger with other good deeds.

(For directions to make a snowball poster and individual snow men, see *Patterns for 52 Visual Lessons*.)

Benediction.

SERVICE NO. 6—FEBRUARY

Growing in Stature Through—

FORGIVING

And be ye kind one to another, tenderhearted, forgiving one another, even as God for Christ's sake hath forgiven you.—Ephesians 4:32.

Prelude: Have a quartet (two altos and two sopranos) sing "Just When I Need Him Most."

Call to Worship:

Come, let us worship and bow down: let us kneel before the Lord our maker (Psalm 95:6).

But if, as you kneel before God, you remember that your brother has ought against you, then go, forgive your brother or ask forgiveness. Then return to the altar of God and offer your gift (Adapted from Matthew 5:23, 24).

Hymn of Praise: "I Need Jesus."

Thoughts on the Theme: (An object lesson by one of the students.)

(Provide the student with an eraser and three pieces of white typing paper. Write in large letters on each sheet, " 'Forgive, and ye shall be forgiven.' Luke 6:37c." Use an indelible pencil for writing the first, a hard lead pencil for writing the second, and a soft-lead pencil that erases easily and completely for writing the third.)

Jesus said, "Forgive and ye shall be forgiven." Jesus did not say that we should forgive if we felt like doing so. Jesus did not say forgive, but do not forget. Jesus said *forgive*—that means for us to forgive every one and with our whole heart—if we in turn expect God to forgive our sins. When we forgive completely, it is like erasing the happening completely from our minds and our hearts.

The letters on this sheet of paper were written with an indelible pencil. No matter how hard I try to erase the letters, they remain clear and bold. I can not use this sheet of paper again, for no matter what I write on it, these indelible letters will always show through. That is what happens in our life when we refuse to forgive some one who has wronged us. We shall never be able to help that person, because our unwillingness to forgive will fill our mind with unkind thoughts which will keep us from doing kind, Christian deeds.

Let us see what happens to this sheet of paper when I try to erase the letters. (Erase the letters written with the hard lead pencil.)

As you see, some of the writing erased, but we still can plainly see the outline of the letters. In fact, we still can read the sentence, although it is somewhat fainter than it was. That is like the person who says, "I will forgive, but I will never forget." On the surface it seems as if he has forgiven and forgotten the happening, but underneath he feels unkind toward the person he pretends to forgive.

Now, when I erase the letters from this sheet of paper, they all disappear completely. The sheet of paper is perfectly clean—so clean that it can be used again. That is like the person who forgives completely. And in forgiving completely, he also forgets completely. It is as if the happening never occurred. His mind and thoughts are so clean he can start all over as if nothing ever happened. That is what Jesus meant when He said, "Forgive, and ye shall be forgiven."

Story: HOW THE TIGER LILY AND THE ONION CAME TO BE.

Once upon a time, when the world was young, a large bed of lilies graced one edge of a beautiful, spacious garden. They were tall and stately lilies—all spotlessly white.

"How happy the lilies always are," the rambling rose said to the morning-glory early one day. "They seem so peaceful and so friendly." "They stand so straight and prim," said the morning-glory. "They look like little white soldiers guarding the edge of the brook."

But at that very moment there was trouble in the lily bed. A very mischievous little lily grew so close to the water's edge her feet were often wet. But she loved the water. Every chance she could, she bowed very low and filled her deep lily cup with water from the brook. She thought it very cool and refreshing, but to the grouchy lily growing closer to the path, it felt like a cold, chilling rain. At least so she said, for every time the mischievous little lily had her cup full of water, she would sprinkle the grouchy lily. On that particular morning, the one lily was especially mischievous, and the other lily especially grouchy. So, when she was sprinkled the third time, the grouchy lily shouted in anger:

"This is the last straw! I have asked you many times to stop sprinkling that cold, chilling water on me and to leave me alone! But you will not listen, so I shall tell Mother Nature when she passes through the garden this afternoon!"

The mischievous little lily stood erect. "Tell Mother Nature!" she cried. "Oh, no! Please not that! I am sorry I teased you. Truly, I am. And I promise I shall never tease you again!"

The grouchy lily turned stiffly away. "That is what you always say," she said, "but you break your promise every time. Now it is too late. I shall tell Mother Nature just as soon as I see her."

"Oh, no! Please! Please!" begged the mischievous lily. "I am sorry. Forgive me. Please forgive me, and I promise—I give you my word—that I shall never, never tease you again."

"Forgive you after all you have done to me?" cried the grouchy lily, indignantly. "Look! I am still dripping wet. And it is the third time this morning!"

"I know I have done wrong," begged the mischievous little lily. "But I am sorry. Please forgive me!"

But the grouchy lily would not. One by one the other lilies pleaded and begged for the mischievous little lily, but the grouchy one refused to listen.

How unhappy the poor little lily was the rest of the morning! She had done wrong. She knew it. And she would never, never do it again. Oh, why had she been so mischievous? What if the grouchy lily really told Mother Nature! She hung her head low in fear and shame. Mother Nature had been so wonderful to them. She had dressed them in such beautiful, pure-white dresses. She had given them the choice spot in the garden. And then she felt Mother Nature smiling at them over the garden wall.

Mother Nature always seemed to know when there was any trouble among the flowers or trees or bushes in the big, beautiful garden. She came directly to the lily bed, smiling at the roses and patting the pansies as she passed by. She stood among the lilies, looking at one and then another. Finally, she saw the mischievous little lily, her head drooping in fear and shame.

"What is wrong among my lilies today?" Mother Nature asked kindly. But no one answered. A deep hush had settled upon the entire garden. Finally, the grouchy lily pointed an accusing finger at the mischievous one and said hatefully, "She has been acting up again. She sprinkled me three times this morning with cold, chilling water from that babbling brook."

"But I am sorry!" the mischievous lily said quickly. "I told you I am sorry. I promise I shall never do it again."

"You have told me that before," the grouchy lily snapped angrily.

"But I mean it this time. Honestly, I will never sprinkle water on you again. Please forgive me!"

The grouchy lily lifted her head high and said, "I told you, it is too late."

"But she is sorry," Mother Nature said gently. "She has asked you to forgive her."

"I shall never forgive her," the grouchy lily said with deep feeling.

"But she is truly sorry," Mother Nature repeated in her gentle way. "She has asked your forgiveness."

The grouchy lily only stood more erect and held her head higher. "I shall never forgive her," she repeated firmly.

"I shall give you until sundown to think it over," Mother Nature said. Then she smiled and passed on to the iris bed.

What hours of pleading followed! All the lilies pleaded and reasoned and begged the grouchy lily to forgive the mischievous one. But she would not listen. "I shall never forgive her," was all she would say.

Then the sun began to sink lower and lower behind the purple hills in the west. Every flower in the garden held his breath as Mother Nature passed through the gate.

"My dear," Mother Nature said gently to the grouchy lily, "will you accept the apologies and forgive the mischievous lily?"

"I shall never forgive her," was the stubborn reply.

"When we are unwilling to forgive, our hearts become filled with hatred and bitterness," Mother Nature said gently. "We are no longer beautiful. We ruin ourselves with our own bitterness, stubbornness, and hatred. In time, you shall see." Then Mother Nature turned to the mischievous lily and said, "Because you can not control your desire to tease, and because you have often broken your word, you shall no longer be dressed in pure white. There shall be a spot on your dress for every time you have teased or broken a promise." Then Mother Nature smiled and said good night to all the flowers in the big garden.

The next morning two gardeners came down the path with their rakes and hoes.

"Look at the new kind of lily!" cried the first gardener, pointing to the mischievous one. "A speckled orange one!"

"Its colors remind me of a tiger," said the second.

"That's what we shall call it!" exclaimed the first gardener. "A tiger lily."

Then he bent low, sniffing the air. "What is that?" he asked, with a puzzled frown. "What smells so strong right in the middle of this bed of fragrant lilies?"

"It smells rather bitter," said the second. "Here. It must be this weed. I've never seen anything like it. Just three long, thin stems."

"Pull it out!" cried the first gardener. "It does not belong in a bed of lilies!"

This knife and fork represent another great difficulty we had to overcome. It took several years of patient training on the part of our mother and several years of practice on our own part before we learned to first feed ourselves and then eat properly.

Learning to write was another great difficulty we had to overcome. Probably all of you remember the first time you tried to write with a pen and ink. It turned out to be quite a messy business, because it seemed such a terribly hard thing to do. Again, we only learned to write neatly with pen and ink after we practiced many hours. If we had not stuck to it, we still could not use pen and ink properly.

Before we could play any game, we had to overcome certain difficulties. When we tried to catch a baseball the first time, we were not very successful. But we kept trying and kept practicing until we could bat it, catch it, and throw it.

We can do these things so easily now, it is hard to imagine they ever represented difficulties in our lives. That is what will eventually happen to all those things which now seem difficult. If we continue to earnestly try, we shall overcome our present difficulties. Then, later on, we shall look back on them, as we do these represented ones, and smile at ourselves for ever thinking them hard to do.

Story: THE STORY OF FANNY CROSBY.

To many of us, the very thought of complete blindness suggests difficulties too great to overcome. Yet one of America's greatest hymn writers could never remember seeing even the light of day. Fanny Crosby lost her sight when she was but six weeks old.

On March 24, 1823, she was born into a very humble home in Southeast, N. Y. She was an extremely happy child, even though she could not run about and play with the other children. Whenever any one pitied her because of her blindness, she would lift her head high, smile happily, and always make a gay reply. When she was eight years old, she wrote a little poem which not only tells of her happy, determined spirit, but also shows that even at a young age she was gifted poetically:

> O what a happy soul am I!
> Although I can not see,
> I am resolved that in this world
> Contented I will be.
>
> How many blessings I enjoy,
> That other people don't;
> To weep and sigh because I'm blind,
> I can not. and I won't!

When she was fifteen years old she went to New York City to enroll in the Institution for the Blind. It did not take her long to develop her unusual gift for writing verse. At first, she wrote only popular songs—one of which brought her $3,000 in royalties.

When Fanny Crosby was forty-one years old she met W. B. Bradbury, the famous composer. Knowing of her remarkable talent, he asked her to write a hymn. And so Fanny Crosby wrote her first hymn, which began:

> We are going, we are going,
> To a home beyond the skies,
> Where the fields are robed in beauty,
> And the sunlight never dies.

As she wrote these words she suddenly felt that at last she had found her real mission in life. From that moment until her death in 1915, a steady stream of beautiful hymns flowed from her busy pen. It is estimated that Fanny Crosby wrote all of 8,000 hymns and songs. Some of our most beautiful and most beloved hymns were written by this blind poet. She wrote "Pass Me Not, O Gentle Saviour," "Sweet Hour of Prayer," "Safe in the Arms of Jesus," "All the Way My Saviour Leads Me," "Jesus Is Tenderly Calling Thee Home," "I Am Thine, O Lord," "Rescue the Perishing," "Speed Away," "Blessed Assurance, Jesus Is Mine," "Jesus, Keep Me Near the Cross," "Saved by Grace," "Holy Is the Lord," "Praise Him! Praise Him!" "To the Work," "My Saviour First of All," "He Hideth My Soul," "Tell Me the Story of Jesus," "'Tis the Blessed Hour of Prayer."

Never once throughout her whole life did Fanny Crosby allow her blindness to cause her any gloom or unhappiness. She often wrote, "I am the happiest creature in all the land."

A Scotch minister once said to her, "I think it is a great pity that the Master, when He showered so many gifts upon you, did not give you sight."

Fanny held her head high as she said, "If at birth I had been able to make one petition to my Creator, it would have been that I should be made blind."

The Scotch minister showed great surprise. "Why?" he asked in amazement.

"Because, when I get to heaven, the first face that shall gladden my sight will be that of my Saviour," Fanny Crosby replied.

Fanny Crosby's earnest prayer was that she might win a million souls for Christ. Many people believe her prayer was answered, for her hymns have done much to awaken the love for Christ in the hearts of those who heard or sang them.

OVERCOMING DIFFICULTIES

Overcoming difficulties! Succeeding despite a great handicap! Can you think of a more inspiring example than Fanny Jane Crosby, the blind poet from New York?

Prayer Hymn: Sing softly the first verse of "Safe in the Arms of Jesus."

Prayer (by the teacher).

Offertory Service:

No matter how many difficulties we feel we have in our lives, we can always look about us and find others who are truly faced with more difficulties and greater handicaps than ourselves. We can always find many things for which to be grateful. One of the ways by which we can show how grateful we are is through sharing what we have so that God's kingdom may continue to grow strong here on earth.

Freely ye have received, freely give (Matthew 10:8b).

(Play softly "All the Way My Saviour Leads Me." Conclude with brief prayers by several students.)

Adult Leader:

The apostle Paul had some physical infirmity or handicap. We do not know exactly what it was. Some believe his one leg was crippled, which gave him constant trouble. Some believe his back was injured. Whatever the handicap was, Paul was referring to it when he wrote in his second letter to the Corinthians, "Therefore I take pleasure in infirmities, in reproaches, in necessities, in presecutions, in distresses for Christ's sake: *for when I am weak, then am I strong.*"

"When I am weak, then am I strong." What did Paul mean? How can any one be strong when he is weak?

Sometimes when we are physically strong, we forget what a wonderful blessing health is. We feel so able and so capable ourselves, that we do not trust in God for help as we should. We feel we can manage very well alone, and so we forget all about God. But when we are ill and weak, we find strength in prayer. We find new courage when we put our faith and trust in God. That is what Paul meant. Being weak physically made him strong spiritually. Paul overcame his handicaps and difficulties through prayer and through faith in God.

Some of our great American heroes followed Paul's example. This month we celebrate the birthdays of Abraham Lincoln and George Washington, two of our presidents who overcame great difficulties through prayer.

The colonies had very little money to spend on an army. They had not been organized under a national head at the outbreak of the

Revolutionary War. Washington and his men faced severe hardships and found great difficulties blocking them at every turn. Their winter at Valley Forge was almost too much to bear. Food was scarce. Their scant clothing had been worn thin from long and constant wear. Some of the men had to tie their shoes onto their feet with ropes; some had no shoes at all. When they walked, their bleeding feet left red footprints in the deep snow. Then Washington was missed. His men looked for him, but no one remembered seeing him for some time. When they searched for him they found him kneeling on the frozen snow, his clothing clutched tightly about him to keep out the sharp, piercing wind. Washington had gone off alone to pray.

The life of Abraham Lincoln is a wonderful story of how a courageous and ambitious boy overcame many great handicaps until he became the President of these United States. Lincoln not only prayed constantly throughout his whole life, but he faithfully read his Bible. More than that, Lincoln remembered what he read and put the teachings of Christ to work in his life. We find his letters, his speeches, and his conversations filled with Biblical quotations.

To the brave and the faithful, handicaps and difficulties are not immovable obstacles blocking the way. They are steppingstones to make the individuals stronger and to help them climb higher. A successful man turns difficulties into blessings.

(Show the poster on "Signs of Greatness" and direct the making of Lincoln log booklets, both found in *Patterns for 52 Visual Lessons*.)

Benediction.

SERVICE NO. 8—FEBRUARY

Growing in Stature Through—

HELPING OTHERS

And great multitudes came unto him, having with them those that were lame, blind, dumb, maimed, and many others, and cast them down at Jesus' feet; and he healed them.—Matthew 15:30.

Prelude: Use "The Lord Is My Shepherd" as an instrumental or vocal duet.

Call to Worship:

> Let us join together in this worship hour
> To sing songs of praise,
> To bring our gifts,
> And to pray unto the risen Lord.

Hymn of Praise: "Do a Deed of Kindness."

Thoughts on the Theme: (An object lesson by one of the students.)

(Provide the student with a wheel large enough for the spokes, hub, and rim to be clearly seen by all.)

As you see, this wheel has many spokes. They are all held together by the hub, which forms the center of the wheel. There is a definite place for each spoke in the hub. Sometimes these spokes get broken along the way or become loose and come out. When that happens, the whole wheel becomes weaker in that part because of the missing spoke. No other spoke can take its place or do its work.

The opposite end of each spoke has a definite place in the rim. Here again, when the spoke is missing, there is a vacant place in the rim, and the space between the rim and the hub is made weaker because of the missing spoke.

The world in which we live is like the rim of this wheel. God's love is like the hub. And we are like the spokes. The only way God's love can be brought to earth is through us—through the lives we live. The best way we can show God's love is by helping others. Jesus taught us to love each other—that means to help each other. When we fail to do this, we are like broken spokes. We no longer connect God's love with the earth. Just as no other spoke can do the work of the broken one, so no one else can help others for us. So when we fail to help others, we not only break the connection between God's love and the world, but (like the broken spoke) the kingdom of God is made weaker because we fail to do our part to keep it strong.

Story: THE STORY OF SNUBBY AND CHUBBY.

Snubby and Chubby were two little frisky brown squirrels who lived in the big trees in the woods behind Tommy's house. Snubby lived in the oak tree. He chose that tree because it was the largest and most beautiful. And Snubby always chose the best for himself. Chubby lived across the lilac bush from him, in a young maple tree.

Chubby was a busy little thing. He scurried here and there all day long, doing his own work and helping every one else at the same time. As soon as any squirrel was in difficulty, he would run as fast as he could to Chubby's young maple tree. Some days there was a steady stream of little squirrels scampering up the maple's slender trunk, all wanting Chubby's advice or comfort or encouraging words or his help. As soon as Chubby heard that any squirrel was ill, he would select the choice nuts from his plentiful store and carry them to the ailing one. Yes, indeed, Chubby was a busy, popular little squirrel whom every one loved.

Now, Snubby was just the opposite. As I told you before, he always selected the best for himself. And he always *kept* the best for himself. "I have enough work of my own," he would say. "Why should I neglect mine to help some one else? Let the other squirrels take care of themselves the way I do!"

When news came to him that Fluffy was in bed with a terrible cold, he merely grunted and said, "Huh. He should have known better than to stay out in the rain!"

When the strong wintry winds uprooted the old elm tree and ruined Brownie's home and all his supplies, Chubby hurried to him, saying, "Come live with me until the warm spring sun shines again. Then you can build yourself another home." But Snubby only grunted and said, "Huh. He was lucky it didn't happen before this. I could have told him that tree was too old to have strong roots."

When the dogs chased little Crunchy and one of them almost caught him by sinking sharp claws into his hind leg, Chubby nursed him back to health. All the other squirrels came to see Crunchy every day and brought him choice tidbits. That is, all but Snubby. He merely grunted and said, "Huh. Any one foolish enough to be caught by a dog deserves nothing more!"

Then spring came to the wood behind Tommy's house. The ice and snow melted. Frisky little breezes, who had been afraid to come out while the wintry winds were blowing, now played and sang all day long. Soon the tiny wildflowers appeared. And then the little green leaves. Once again the wood was beautifully dressed in gay spring clothes.

Then one day a group of workmen arrived with queer-looking things. Some of them seemed like long sticks with sharp pieces of metal fastened to one end. Other things looked like very long pieces of metal with handles at each end, and one whole edge of sharp points. "They look like teeth," Chubby said to the frightened little group who had crowded into his tiny home.

The men seemed to look at each tree very carefully; that is, each of the big trees. They did not even notice the young maple. One of the men took a piece of chalk from his pocket and made two marks on the trunks of some of the trees. Chubby leaned out of his nest to be sure. "They put a mark on the big oak tree!" he cried. "Poor Snubby! I wonder what that means?"

Chubby and all the other little squirrels were soon to discover what that mark meant. For the men began to cut down the big oak tree! When the tree finally fell to the ground with a loud crash, Chubby jumped up and down crying, "Oh, Snubby, Snubby! Poor little Snubby."

And poor little Snubby it was! For he was without a home and not a nut to his name! At first the other squirrels said, "It serves him right. He has never helped any one in his life. He has always taken the very best and kept it for himself. When we are ill or in trouble, he just grunts and says unkind things. Now let him find out what it means to be without friends!"

But Chubby shook his head. "No," he said. "As soon as the men leave the wood we must go and find Snubby. We must comfort him and help him. I shall bring him here, and he shall live with me until he finds another home. And let each of us share our nuts with him. Snubby has never known the joy that comes from helping others. Perhaps this is the way he will learn."

Tommy, of course, did not know such a thing had happened in the big wood behind his house. Tommy seldom played in the wood, for he never seemed to have the time. He always made his bed, hung up his clothing, and tidied his room before he went to school. When he returned in the afternoon, he ran errands for his mother and for old Mrs. Walters, who lived across the road. Then he took his baby sister for a ride in her stroller. Just before dinner he usually went bike riding with Jerry and Bill, or went kite flying with them. After dinner he always dried the dishes for Mother.

"I like to help others," he always said. "It makes me feel happy inside."

I wonder which squirrel Tommy was like—Snubby or Chubby?

Prayer Hymn: Sing softly "Bow Down Thine Ear."

Prayer (by the teacher).

Offertory Service:

(Read in unison the following. Then have one of the students explain the meaning.)

"*Upon the first day of the week let every one of you lay by him in store, as God hath prospered him*" (1 Corinthians 16:2a).

(Play "Why Should He Love Me So" while the offering is taken. Conclude with a short dedicatory prayer by one of the students.)

Adult Leader:

After the apostle Paul's conversion on the road to Damascus, he spent all his time traveling from city to city establishing churches. He met with the followers of Christ in Corinth or Thessalonica, and he remained a while teaching them more about Christ and His commandments. Then he moved on to the next city and organized a church there.

But Paul did not forget the new churches. He could not visit them as he would like to have done. So he did the next best thing— he wrote them letters. These letters are a part of our New Testament.

Through these letters Paul tried to teach the people more about Christ and about the way Christ wanted them to live. He wrote a great deal about loving each other and about helping each other. He reminded the people again and again that the best way to show their love for Christ, who had died for them, was through serving each other. In Paul's letters to the Romans he wrote, "Be kindly affectioned one to another with brotherly love." In his first letter to the Corinthians, Paul wrote, "Love never faileth" (1 Corinthians 13:8). In his second letter to the Corinthians, Paul told the people to help each other and to share with the needy "to prove the sincerity of your love" (2 Corinthians 8:1-8).

(Conclude by having various students locate and read the verses of Scripture suggested on the face of the clock, as shown in the poster for today. Paste the little hand so that it will always point to the great commandments [Matthew 22:37-39]. Fasten the large hand on with a brad and move it around the clock as each verse is read and discussed. Explain how serving and helping others are ways in which we can obey this great commandment, and by obeying it show God how much we really love Him. These are the Scriptures to be read: Matthew 20:26-28; 22:37-39; 25:40; John 13:34; Romans 12:10; 13:8, 10; 15:1, 2; Galatians 6:2, 10; Colossians 3:17; Hebrews 13:1, 2. The pattern for the poster and individual clocks may be found in *Patterns for 52 Visual Lessons.*)

Benediction.

SERVICE NO. 9—MARCH

Growing in Stature Through—

PEACE

As much as lieth in you, live peaceably with all men.—Romans 12:18b.

Prelude: "It Is Well With My Soul." Continue to play softly during the call to worship.

Call to Worship:

> All is well with our soul when we love Christ, our Saviour.
> All is well with our soul when we trust and obey.
> All is well with our soul when we follow His footsteps.
> Let us bow and give thanks. Let us worship and pray.

Hymn of Praise: "Wonderful Peace."

Thoughts on the Theme: (*An object lesson by one of the students.*)

(Provide the student with a vegetable or cereal bowl and a hammer. Use an old discarded dish, but one that is still in good condition, and therefore useful. Be sure it is light weight enough for the student to easily break it with the hammer.)

Here is a vegetable bowl. As long as it is used on the table for serving food, then washed and dried and stacked away, it will go on being useful for a long time. But if some one should come along with this hammer and hit the bowl like this (break the dish with a blow), it would no longer be lovely to look at or useful to use. It would be nothing but a pile of broken pieces, just as you see before you now.

Peace is like this bowl before it was broken, when it was lovely to look at, when it could be used many times each day, when it served and helped people. This hammer is jealousy, hatred, spite, greed, desire for power and fame. All these things can destroy peace—unkind words, arguments, unwillingness to co-operate or to do our part. Just as this hammer ruined this bowl, so these things ruin peace.

We were wasteful in our object lesson this morning. We wasted a perfectly good bowl. Destroyers of peace are always wasteful. War is a terrible destroyer of peace. A war costs many times more than it would take to clothe and feed all the poor and hungry people all over the world. Those things in our everyday life that ruin peace are all wasteful. They cost friendships, they cost happiness, and they waste many precious hours.

We could glue this bowl together again. It would take a long time to fit the pieces in their proper places. It would take a great deal of patience to glue them so they hold fast. But no matter how carefully the pieces were fitted and glued together, we could always see each place where it was broken.

After a war, nations have to patch their ruined towns and buildings and homes. When two people quarrel, it takes much time and patience and understanding to patch their broken friendship. A patched bowl is never so good as a perfect one. So it is with friendships. A patched friendship is never so beautiful as one that has never been ruined by a quarrel.

Story: MY MOM, A CHAMPION PEACEMAKER.

"It makes no difference if he is a smart aleck," Mom said. "This quarreling must stop. Do you understand, son?"

"Yes, Mom," I answered over my bowl of cereal. "But all the kids hate him, and so do I."

"Thomas Mitchell!" Mom said severely as she buttered my toast. "Any more of such talk and you shall spend the morning upstairs in your room!"

I was about to say that just because Butch looked like a fifteen-year-old instead of thirteen like the rest of us, he thought he could bully all the fellows in the neighborhood. But I happened to remember that it was Saturday, so I said under my breath (and I am ashamed of it now), "Well, I still hate him."

Butch was a funny kid. He never seemed happy unless he was fighting. It didn't make any difference to him whom he fought or why. He could pick an argument with any one. And he was always spoiling things, just the way he ruined our baseball practice game. When we left the vacant lot that Saturday morning, we were all pretty angry and plenty disgusted with Butch.

"Come to my back yard," I said as I led the way down the street. "Let's talk this over."

We often talked things over under the big maple tree in our back yard. It was shady and quiet, and there was always a breeze even on the hottest days. The ten of us were just comfortably spread out on the grass when Butch came slowly down the driveway wearing his usual sneering grin. He stopped halfway down the drive and stood with his legs apart, as he always did when he was ready to pick a fight. For a moment every one was silent. Then Joe slowly and deliberately reached for the baseball bat nearest him.

"I'm going to let him have it this time," he said under his breath.

"Same here," said David, as he picked up a rock in each hand.

"He's asking for it," Bruce muttered as he reached for one of the branches which had been broken during the storm the night before.

Butch continued down the drive slowly. No one said a word. Just as Butch reached the end of the driveway, the back door opened and Mom stepped out to shake her dustmop.

"Why, Thomas!" she exclaimed. "What a lovely surprise! I had no idea you were bringing all the boys to help clean up the back lawn. Last night's storm really blew the branches off the trees!" She was looking at Bruce and Harry and Mack. They were all still holding fast to the branches. "Just pile all the fallen limbs behind the garage," Mom said gaily. "My, but it is kind of you boys to come and help like this! Why, you are even straightening the rocks around my flower beds!" She was looking at Pete and Arnold and Leroy, who stood with a rock in each hand. "Isn't that wonderful? Butch, stand over here and finish shaking the dust mop for me, please. I might as well pick a few roses while I am out here. I just finished baking a big platter of chocolate-nut cookies. As soon as you finish, every one come in and we'll lunch on fresh cookies and lemonade."

She hummed merrily as she picked a couple of roses. Then she suddenly opened the back door. "Come along, Butch," she said. "I need you to help me make the lemonade." She gently nudged Butch indoors.

Well, what could we do? I looked at the boys. The boys looked at me. Then we started to clean the back lawn. My eyes almost popped out when we entered the kitchen a little while later and I saw Butch tied inside one of Mom's aprons, pouring lemonade into the glasses.

"I like to do things like this," he was telling my Mom. "I never have a chance at home."

"Oh?" Mom said in her friendly way. "Have you sisters who do such things?"

"I live with my grandparents," Butch said. "They are both old and don't do much fussing around the house."

"Well now, Butch, you must come more often."

Then we crowded around the table and drank lemonade and ate and ate cookies. Mom sat down with us. She sat between Butch and Joe. She got us talking and laughing. Mom can do that so easily. Then she said:

"Now, boys, I want you to do better with your baseball team this year than you did last. There is no reason why you can't win every game. You must practice harder than you did last year. And I think you need a manager."

"A manager!" we all echoed.

PEACE

"Yes," Mom went on, "a manager. Some one to take care of things for you. To arrange the games. To see that all of you boys come out for practice. And to see that the other teams play fair. I think Butch would make a fine manager."

"BUTCH!" we all yelled together.

"Yes, Butch," Mom went on calmly, just as if she hadn't noticed a thing. "How about it, Butch? Would you like to be the manager?"

"Oh, gee!" Butch said. "Oh, whiz! The manager! Oh, boy, that would be great!"

I looked at Butch. What was wrong with him? I thought. He looked so different. He didn't look as big as I thought he was. Why, he was a nice-looking kid when he wasn't sneering. And he seemed—well, he seemed just like the rest of us. I looked at Joe. He raised his left eyebrow. That was our O. K. signal. So I said:

"That might be a good idea, Mom. I guess we do need a manager."

"Fine!" Mom said. "Every Saturday morning after your practice game, I want all of you to come here for lunch. That will give us a chance to talk things over and see how everything is coming along. Butch and I are going to make champs out of you!"

All the boys noticed the change in Butch. You could tell the way they talked to him—just like he had always been one of us. I looked at Mom. Gosh, she's wonderful. She'll make champs out of us, I thought. She's such a champ herself—a champion peacemaker.

Prayer Hymn: Before the prayer sing the first two verses of "My Prayer." Sing the third as the prayer response.

Prayer (by the teacher).

Offertory Service:

(Play softly "This Is My Father's World" while the Scripture is read, while the offering is taken, and while a student concludes with a prayer.)

Every good gift and every perfect gift is from above, and cometh down from the Father (James 1:17a).

Adult Leader: (Refer to poster as you develop the following thoughts.)

All of you know the proverb, "A stitch in time saves nine." If we mend a tear in a garment right away, we save ourselves much work. Sometimes we even save the garment from being completely ruined. In order to mend a tear, there are certain things we need—a needle, pins, thread, and scissors. Without using these we can not mend the tear, so it becomes larger. And before we realize it, the tear is so large the garment is ruined and must be discarded.

In the same way, one kind word can save nine angry ones. When a tear appears in a friendship, we must take care of it immediately. If we do not, the tear (or quarrel) will grow bigger, and soon will ruin the friendship completely. But there are certain things we need to repair the torn friendship. First of all we need love. It is like the needle that sews the torn pieces together. Then we need understanding. That is like the thread, for without love, understanding would be useless. Then we need the willingness to forgive. That is like the scissors, for it makes all the unhappy events disappear, just as the scissors cut away all the frayed edges.

(For directions for making a "Stitch in Time" poster and individual prevention folders, see *Patterns for 52 Visual Lessons*.)

Benediction.

SERVICE NO. 10—MARCH

Growing in Stature Through—

LEARNING MORE OF GOD'S WORD

Study to shew thyself approved unto God, a workman that needeth not to be ashamed, rightly dividing the word of truth.—
2 Timothy 2:15.

Prelude: "Tell Me the Old, Old Story," sung by a quartet.

Call to Worship:

O Lord—
Thy word is a lamp unto my feet, and a light unto my path (Psalm 119:105).
Give me understanding, that I may learn thy commandments (Psalm 119:73b).

Hymn of Praise: "Wonderful Words of Life."

Thoughts on the Theme: (*An object lesson by one of the students.*)

(Provide the student with a sponge and a bowl of water.)

A sponge is a very useful article to have around all the time. But it must be a *good* sponge. If it is not a genuine sponge, but one made of cheap materials which are hard and stiff, it can not absorb much water. When a genuine sponge is placed in a bowl of water, it will absorb the water, just as this sponge is doing now. I put it into the bowl dry. Now I take it from the bowl, and it is filled with water. In fact, it has absorbed so much water that it now weighs more and is larger than it was before I put it into the bowl. I can squeeze all the water from the sponge slowly, like this. Or I can squeeze all the water from the sponge in a hurry by pressing it hard and quickly —like this. Now it is lighter in weight. And it is smaller in size. But all I have to do to again fill it with all the water it can hold, is to put it back into the bowl of water.

We are like this sponge. God's Word—or our Bible—is like this bowl of water. If we do not learn God's Word our minds are empty. We are like the dry sponge. For without the knowledge of God's Word we can not be useful. All we had to do to fill the sponge was to drop it into this bowl of water. All we have to do to fill our minds and our hearts with the life and teachings of Christ is to read our Bibles.

Usually when our lives are running smoothly we forget God's Word and do not call upon Him as we do when we are troubled. We are then like the sponge squeezed hard and quickly so all the water leaves it in a hurry.

When the sponge was dry it was smaller and lighter. When it was filled with water it was larger and heavier. When we are without the knowledge of God's Word we can not influence others. Whatever we say does not carry much weight. But when we know God's Word we can influence others to do the right and to live for Christ. People will look to us for comfort and advice. We shall be like the sponge filled with water.

At the very beginning, I said the sponge must be a *good* sponge to be useful. We must be *good* Christians in order to be useful in the kingdom of God.

Story: ALLIE MAE'S BIBLE.

Until Allie Mae was ten years old she had never gone to church. She had never gone to Bible school. In fact, she had not even seen a Bible. Her family lived deep in the mountains of Tennessee. In the summer she lived in fairyland beauty. Maples and oaks, chestnut and elm trees gracefully swayed all day long as the breezes played hide and seek on the mountain tops. Cool little mountain streams trickled here and there over smooth boulders or wound their way between moss-covered banks. But the summer was so short on the top of those mountains! And autumns and winters and springs were so long!

There were no roads to Sunset Peak, as the mountain top was called on which Allie Mae lived, just narrow, winding footpaths. Twice a year—early summer and just before the first snowfall—Allie Mae's father made a trip to Bartlettsville, the nearest town, to buy the necessary supplies. He rode his mule over the mountain trails to the blacksmith's shop at the fork of the road. That was an overnight trip. The following morning the smithy would drive him in his rattling little coupe to Bartlettsville. And that was an overnight trip. After the limited supplies were bought, it was back to the smithy's house by nightfall. The next morning at sunrise the supplies were packed on the mule. Long after sundown Mr. Jarvis would arrive at the log-cabin door to be greeted by Allie Mae and her mother. The fall and spring rains made the narrow, winding path too slippery for safe footing for the mule. Winter snow and ice made such a trip completely impossible. So Allie Mae lived in a very small world on the top of Sunset Peak.

One day Jim McCully stopped overnight at Allie Mae's home. He lived a good half day's journey farther up the trail. A sudden rainstorm forced him to spend the night at the Jarvis' log cabin. Jim had wonderful news to tell. Every one in town was talking about a new road which was to be built from Bartlettsville all the way up to the very top of Sunset Peak! The state was going to build a park up there or a resort or a sanitarium—Jim McCully could not remember what. But he was sure of one thing—the new road would go right by the Jarvis log cabin, and by his, too!

"That's mighty fine news, Jim!" Mrs. Jarvis cried. "Now maybe our younguns kin git off to school and git some larnin'."

That night Allie Mae was too excited to sleep. She kept thinking of the possibility of going to school. She had never gone to school, neither had her mother nor her father, nor their parents before them. For generations they had been mountain folk, living in the same log cabins on Sunset Peak and doing things the same way. Allie Mae wondered what it would be like to go to school.

The coming weeks were filled with excitement for her. She sat for hours on the big overhanging rock and watched the road crew at work. They were building such a wonderful road! So wide and so smooth! They had such big machines and such a large crew of workmen that the road was soon paved far beyond their tract of land.

Early one morning a car drove along the new road and stopped right in front of their cabin. Allie Mae was too frightened even to move. She had never been so close to a car before! Then a man and a woman got out. When they started to walk up the path, Allie Mae ran into the house so fast she stubbed her bare toe. She had never been so close to strangers before, either. They frightened her. But the man had a gentle voice and a kind face, and the woman smiled sweetly. Allie Mae soon ventured out from behind her mother's big apron.

"I am Mr. Newark," the gentle voice was saying, "and this is Mrs. Newark. We are ministers of God's Word and we want to invite you folk to come and worship with us tomorrow morning. We shall meet in the clearing between your cabin and the one down the road. Perhaps by the time autumn comes we can build a church. But while the weather is warm and pleasant we shall worship and learn of God's Word out of doors."

Mrs. Jarvis dried her hands on her big apron. Her eyes were wide with surprise.

"God's Word ain't for folk the likes of us," she said. "We ain't got no larnin'."

"God's Word is for every one," the gentle voice said. "Mrs. Newark is going to start a school and will teach all of you how to read and write. Then every one on Sunset Peak—old and young—will have learning. And every one will be able to read God's Word."

The next morning the Jarvis family was the first to arrive at the clearing. "We don't want to miss a thing," Mr. Jarvis had said as they walked along the new road. It was all so wonderful! When every one had arrived, Mr. Newark opened what Allie Mae thought was a black box. But it was not a box at all, for it had legs and white keys. Mrs. Newark made beautiful sounds come from it. Mr. Newark sang a song. Then he taught it to them, and they sang while Mrs. Newark played.

"Praise God from whom all blessings flow," they sang. "Praise Him, all creatures here below; Praise Him above, ye heav'nly host; Praise Father, Son, and Holy Ghost."

"Let's sing it agin!" cried Mr. Jarvis. So they sang it again. "Let's sing it agin!" cried Mrs. Browning. So they sang it again, and again, and again, until the hills seemed to echo their joyous praise. The singing was wonderful! These people had never heard such a song before.

Then Mr. Newark read to them from a book. "Thy word is a lamp unto my feet, and a light unto my path," he read. "Give me understanding, that I may learn thy commandments." Then he read about a little baby who was born in a stable behind an inn. He read about shepherds and about Wise-men who came bringing gifts. He read how Jesus grew in wisdom and in stature. He read on and on, for each time he closed the Book some one cried, "Read some more!" No one had ever before told them such wonderful things as these.

But the most beautiful day for Allie Mae was when she read the twenty-third Psalm before the whole congregation. "As soon as you learn to read," Mr. Newark had said, "we shall give you a Bible to take home and keep for your very own." Allie Mae was the very first one to receive a Bible. A Bible all her own! A Bible she could read every day! A Bible telling her the beautiful story of Jesus!

Prayer Hymn: Sing softly the first verse of "Sweet Hour of Prayer" before the prayer, and the second verse as the response.

Prayer:

Our loving Father which art in heaven, we thank Thee for the Bible which reveals to us Thy Word and tells us the beautiful story of Jesus. We are grateful for the blessings of living in these United States, where we can read and study the Bible at all times. We pray for all those in faraway lands who have never had the privilege of learning about Thee. We know how empty their lives must be, for without Thee and Thy wonderful love our lives would truly be empty.

We pray for a deeper understanding as we read our Bibles. We pray for more wisdom and understanding as we study Thy Word, so that we may live better lives, influencing others to follow Christ.

Forgive our sins, we pray. Bless us so that we may see opportunities about us each day to show our love for Thee by serving and helping others. In Jesus' name we pray. Amen.

Offertory Service:

(Play "Trust and Obey" softly while the following poem is read, while the offering is taken, and the dedicatory prayer is offered by one of the students:)

> The Bible teaches how to live.
> It also teaches how to give.
> So if we try in every way
> To be like Jesus every day,
> We must obey His Word on living,
> And likewise show our love through giving.

Adult Leader:

William Romaine, an English minister who lived in the eighteenth century, wrote, "The longer you read the Bible the more you will like it; it will grow sweeter and sweeter; and the more you get into the spirit of it the more you will get into the spirit of Christ."

Thomas Jefferson said he truly believed the sincere and earnest study of the Bible will "make better citizens, better fathers, and better husbands."

Daniel Webster said, "I have read the Bible through many times, and now make it a practice to read it through once every year."

Patrick Henry said the Bible "is a Book worth all other books which were ever printed."

Great men down through history have found time to read and study their Bibles. David Livingstone wrote, "All that I am I owe to Jesus Christ, revealed to me in His divine Book."

Let us turn to our Bibles and find some things for ourselves concerning God's Word. Let us find the answers to these questions: Is the Word of God true? Is the Word of God pure? Is it right? Does it have power? How long will the Word of God remain? (Have various students locate and read the following Scripture verses from their Bibles. As they read the verse, turn the pages of the book attached to the poster suggested in *Patterns for 52 Visual Lessons*.)

Psalm 119:160.
Proverbs 30:5.
Psalm 33:4.
Hebrews 4:12.
Psalm 119:105.
Colossians 3:16.
Ephesians 6:17.
Isaiah 40:8.
1 Peter 1:25.

Benediction.

May God's Word dwell in your hearts and be a lamp unto your feet and a light unto your path, now and for evermore. Amen.

SERVICE NO. 11—MARCH

Growing in Stature Through—

WORK

Let every man prove his own work, and then shall he have rejoicing in himself alone, and not in another.—Galatians 6:4.

Prelude: "Work, for the Night Is Coming."

Call to Worship:

It is written—
*Every man's work shall be made manifest: for the day shall declare it, because it shall be revealed by fire; and the fire shall try every man's work of what sort it is.
If any man's work abide which he hath built thereupon, he shall receive a reward* (1 Corinthians 3:13, 14).

Come, let us worship God through songs and prayer. Let us learn more of His Word.

Hymn of Praise: "Help Me Find My Place."

Thoughts on the Theme: (An object lesson by one of the students.)

(Provide the student with a string of pearls of graduated size.)

Each of these pearls has a particular place on this string. These little ones are all grouped together near the clasp. The closer to the center, the larger the pearls. And here, in the very center, we find the largest pearl on the string.

The beauty of this string lies in each pearl being in its proper place. If we broke the string and then restrung the pearls without first arranging them according to size, much of the beauty would be lost. We would have big beads and little beads mixed together. Instead of adding to the beauty of each other, they would rather detract from the beauty of each other.

We are much like these pearls. Some of us are very small. These pearls near the clasp are like the babies and little folk in the Beginner and Primary departments. There is a definite place for them. They add much beauty to the world, and they are the happiest when they are all playing together. Juniors and Intermediates are like these pearls. We are developing in size, but are not fully grown. The adults would be like these pearls—the largest ones on the string. Just as every pearl has a definite place on the string, so every one of us has a definite place in this world. We have a certain job to do. One pearl can not take the place of another pearl. They each have their own place on the string which no other pearl can fill. Each one of us has certain work to do. No one else can do that work for us. When we fail to do our work, it is like taking away one of the pearls and leaving an empty place on the string. When we will not do the work given to us, but want to do the work of adults, then we are like a little pearl trying to take the place of a big one. As we grow and develop, we move along, and some day we fill important places, in just the way the big pearls are placed in the very center of this string.

Story: NOT ASHAMED TO WORK.

When Mr. Bernard offered him a job weeding at the golf course every Saturday morning, Allen was almost speechless for joy. Of course he would accept it! Of course he could arrange to be there by eight-thirty every Saturday morning! Of course he could work straight through until noon! Imagine a break like that! A chance to earn some money every week! Why, he would earn enough for a new bicycle in no time. He quickened his already lively pace and started whistling a jolly tune.

Suddenly, Allen stopped abruptly. The Highland Golf Course! That was where Dwight Nelson went every Saturday. He, of course, went to play golf, not to pull weeds. Allen groaned. Why hadn't he thought of that when Mr. Bernard offered him the job? It was no disgrace to spend Saturday mornings pulling weeds, but Dwight Nelson was about the last person Allen wanted to know about it.

Dwight lived in the big brick house with rolling lawns and a gardener to take care of the flower beds. Every one at Central High wanted to be a special friend to Dwight, he was such a good sport and genuine fellow. He did not seem to chum with any one in particular, though. He always seemed to be too busy with other things to attend many of the Sophomore-class activities. For instance, two weeks ago the class went on a Saturday hike, but Dwight could not go along because he always spent Saturday mornings at the Highland Golf Course. Allen was disgusted with himself. He should have remembered that.

Allen spent the next two days debating whether or not he should call Mr. Bernard and tell him to get some one else for the weeding job. He simply could not let Dwight see him doing such work. Dwight had always acted especially friendly toward him. And every one at Central High looked up to Dwight—partly because his father was the mayor. But every time Allen decided to call Mr. Bernard, the bicycle in Benson's Sporting Goods window flashed through his mind.

"Park your bike in the rack behind the clubhouse," Mr. Bernard called as Allen arrived at the golf course shortly before eight-thirty the next morning.

Allen lingered a moment near the rack, admiring a brand-new bike parked there with several other ones. What a beauty! Allen examined it more closely. Just like the one in Benson's window! Then he hurried to Mr. Bernard.

"We'll weed on the other side of the footbridge," Mr. Bernard said. "You'll find my helper over there. Tell him you are the new fellow I told him about. He will show you what to do. I'll be coming along later."

It was a beautiful spring morning. Allen threw back his shoulders and held his head high as he took a deep breath of the crisp, refreshing air. It should be almost fun working outdoors on a morning like this. Suddenly, he thought of Dwight and glanced quickly over his shoulder. It was too early for Dwight. But he had better be on the lookout all morning. If he saw Dwight first, he could probably keep Dwight from seeing him. Then he stopped abruptly. Dwight was standing no more than six feet away, with a broad grin on his tanned face.

"Hi, Allen," he said in a friendly way. "I didn't know you were the new weeder."

Allen's face turned red. "Well, I—that is—"

"If I had known it," Dwight went on, not noticing Allen's confusion, "we could have come out together. At least we can go home together—or are you just working until noon?"

Allen swallowed hard. Bicycle from town with Dwight Nelson! With the mayor's son!

"I'm—I'm just working until noon," he stammered.

"That's too bad," Dwight said. "I work all day Saturday."

"You *work* here?" Allen almost shouted the words.

"Every other day after school and all day Saturday. That is how I earned the money for my new bicycle. Did you see it up there? Isn't it a beauty?"

"Yes," Allen said, rather dazed. "Yes, I saw it. It is a beauty. Just like the one I want—like the one in Benson's window."

"Too bad you aren't working all day," Dwight said. "You could ride it home tonight."

"Maybe I could work all day," Allen said eagerly. "Do you think Mr. Bernard would want me to?"

"I know he would," Dwight assured him. "Two of the fellows

did not show up last night and we are behind in our work this week. I guess Mr. Bernard wants you to weed with me. He always has two of us work together. There's nothing to it. You can just watch me a few minutes. Then start over there."

Allen watched. Imagine that, he thought! Dwight Nelson working *here*—the mayor's son a weeder at the Highland Golf Course, and earning his own bicycle just the way I am! I surely have a lot to learn. Since Wednesday, I have been afraid that Dwight Nelson would see me working. And all the while Dwight Nelson was out here working in most of his free time. I guess that is what makes him such a swell fellow. He works hard. And he is not ashamed of it.

Prayer Hymn: "Bow Down Thine Ear."

Prayer (by the teacher).

Offertory Service:

(Tell the parable of the talents as recorded in Matthew 25:14-30.

Conclude with the thought that what we share with others multiplies and becomes blessings. What we keep or hoard for ourselves will eventually be taken from us.

Play softly "It Pays to Serve Jesus" while the offering is taken and while one of the students offers a brief prayer of thanks.)

Adult Leader:

(Use the windmill poster as you develop the following thoughts.)

March is known as the windy month. Wind, we know, can be destructive—as it is during a wind storm or tornado. But wind can also be useful—as it is when it turns the arms of a windmill.

When we drive out into the country, we find metal windmills on many farms. They are used primarily for pumping water. Without wind a windmill is absolutely useless. These arms turn only when the wind blows. Whatever work the windmill is supposed to do can not be done unless the arms turn—or unless the wind blows.

We are like this windmill. We each have definite jobs to do, but we are useless as long as our arms remain idle. It takes wind to put these arms into motion and make a windmill useful. It takes the desire to work to put our arms into motion and make us useful.

(The poster and patterns for pinwheels can be found in *Patterns for 52 Visual Lessons.*)

Benediction.

SERVICE NO. 12—MARCH

Growing in Stature Through—

COURAGE

Be of good courage, and he shall strengthen your heart, all ye that hope in the Lord.—Psalm 31:24.

Prelude: Use "Master, the Tempest Is Raging," as a duet by two of the students.

Call to Worship:

The Lord is my light and my salvation; whom shall I fear? the Lord is the strength of my life; of whom shall I be afraid?
Wait on the Lord: be of good courage, and he shall strengthen thine heart: wait, I say, on the Lord (Psalm 27:1, 14).

Hymn of Praise: "Onward, Christian Soldiers."

Thoughts on the Theme: (*An object lesson by one of the students.*)

(Provide the student with a lighted candle securely fastened in a candleholder and a piece of paper to be used as a fan. Assign this lesson to one of the older students so there will be no chance of an accident.)

In our science classes we are told that fire needs air in order to burn. Yet too much air blowing directly upon a candle will put out the flame. On the other hand, if we were to put a jar over this lighted candle, the flame would go out; but this time it would be because there was not enough air.

When I fan a distance away from the candle, it has no effect upon the flame. But the closer I fan to the candle, the more the flame flickers. And the harder I fan, the more the flame flickers. If I fan close enough and hard enough, the flame will go out. The candle will not burn again until I hold a lighted match to its wick.

We are much like this candle. Our courage is like the flame. How brightly we shine depends upon how much courage we have. Troubles, difficulties, hardships, handicaps, and daily problems are like the fan disturbing the air around us. When they are small and far away from us, we can go right on burning brightly, for our courage is too strong for them to disturb. But the bigger the problems or the troubles and the closer they come to us, the more courage it takes to keep going. Once in a while a problem will come along that will seem too big for us, and we will feel we have not enough courage to go on. It is like the hard and close fanning that put out the candle's flame. We had to put a lighted match to the wick in order for the candle to burn brightly again. God is like the lighted match, for He alone can renew our courage and give us added strength to carry on in a useful way once again.

Story: A KITE, SIX SHIRTS, AND A MUD PUDDLE.

Donald had been delivering Mr. Fields' carefully ironed dress shirts ever since his mother began laundering them for the fine old gentleman who lived in the big brick house at the end of State Street. Every one in Millersburg knew the reputation Mr. Fields had for being extremely fussy about the washing and ironing of his shirts. In fact, that is why Donald's mother had been laundering them for Mr. Fields for the past six months. It happened this way:

Donald's eldest brother, Ben, worked as Mr. Fields' gardener during the summer vacation. One morning, Ben overheard Mr. Fields vigorously scolding the laundryman because his shirts had not been delivered at the promised time.

"A fine thing!" exclaimed Mr. Fields. "I need a shirt for a special affair this evening. And you tell me you can not deliver one until tomorrow afternoon!"

Mr. Fields became very excited. Ben, working near by, was so alarmed for him that he said the first thing that came to his mind.

"My mother will be glad to launder a shirt for you, Mr. Fields. If I take one to her right away, I am sure she will have it ready for you by six o'clock tonight."

The shirt was so beautifully washed and ironed that Mr. Fields offered to pay Donald's mother very generously if she would take care of all his shirts for him. It was an opportunity to earn a little extra money for Ben's last year at college, so she gladly accepted. Now Donald walked along carrying the precious shirts as carefully as if he were handling a priceless piece of the most delicate china.

As soon as he turned onto State Street, Donald saw the group of boys standing almost directly across the street from Mr. Fields' wrought-iron gates. Even at a distance it was not hard to figure out what they were doing. Little Jimmy Bailey was crying. The kite which Donald saw him flying earlier in the afternoon was dangling from one of the topmost branches of the big elm tree. The four older boys were teasing him. One of them pulled off Jimmy's little beanie with a spinning pinwheel attached and roughly mussed his hair. When Jimmy grabbed for his beanie, the older boy threw it over his head to another who stood near a mud puddle.

"A crybaby! That's what you are! Nothing but a crybaby!"

Donald slowed down to take a good look at the four boys. They were all older than he. He did not know any of them.

"Get my kite down!" Jimmy sobbed, as he frantically tried to grab his beanie. "You took my kite away from me! Now it's way high up in the tree!"

"Crybabies shouldn't fly kites," one of the older boys teased. "And they shouldn't wear beanies either!" With that he threw Jimmy's red felt beanie in the highest branch he could. This made Jimmy sob harder than ever. Donald moistened his lips twice before he had the courage to speak. Four bigger boys against him. But this was not right.

"Cut it out, fellows," Don said, trying hard not to appear nervous.

"Cut what out?" one of the boys sneered. "And who is telling *us* what to do?"

"Cut out teasing Jimmy," Donald said boldly. "And *I* am telling you. You fellows should be ashamed of yourselves, picking on a little kid like Jimmy! Get his kite down for him. And his beanie!"

"And what happens if we don't get the kite and the beanie?"

"Then I will get them."

"Yeah? You and who else?"

"Nobody else. I'll do it alone."

"Well, we're not getting them down. Now let's see you try."

Donald's head was swimming. Four big fellows against him. But this was not right. Jimmy was such a little kid. There was going to be trouble, he felt sure. But he could not desert Jimmy now. Without any hesitation he laid the bundle of shirts neatly wrapped in brown paper on the pavement and started to climb the tree with surprising quickness.

"Try to come down!" shouted the one who had thrown the beanie into the tree. "Just try to come down!"

But Donald made no reply. He could almost reach the kite now.

"Aw, leave him alone," the biggest boy growled. "It will take him a week to get the kite down."

"But he made this his business. Now let's finish it."

"Aw, leave him alone," the biggest boy said again as he turned and started down the street. The rest followed, but the boy who wanted to cause more trouble paused beside the bundle of shirts long enough to give it a hard kick. Donald nearly fell out of the tree as he saw the wrapping paper split and Mr. Fields' fine dress shirts drop in the middle of the mud puddle.

Before little Jimmy started home, he turned his tear-stained face up to Donald and said, "Thanks, Donald. I'm going to try to be just like you when I grow up." But Donald felt anything but happy as he lifted the shirts out of the soft, slimy mud.

His first impulse was to get home as fast as possible. Mother would understand, but how could he explain to Mr. Fields? He took a few hurried steps and then stopped. He looked over his shoulder at the big red house across the street. He just remembered. Mr. Fields had called that afternoon to say he was going out of town on the late night plane. It was almost five o'clock now. Even if he hurried right home and his mother washed the shirts, they would not be dry enough to iron until morning.

He felt as if his legs would not hold him up until he reached the big front door. The cement walk from the street to the porch had never seemed so long. His hand trembled a little as he reached for the knocker, but the door opened before he touched it.

"Come in, Donald," Mr. Fields said. "I saw the whole thing from the upstairs window." Then he reached into his pocket and drew out the amount of money he always paid for his shirts. Donald's eyes opened wide as Mr. Fields handed it to him and said as he always did, "Give this to your mother, Donald, and tell her thanks for another splendid job on my shirts. And will you please take these six shirts home as my next laundry order? Tell your mother I have postponed my trip until next week. Also tell her that I am sorry there is so much mud on these shirts, but if she wants to know how it got there, to ask a mighty brave young fellow."

Donald wanted to laugh and cry at once. He wanted to say something special to Mr. Fields, but his tongue felt too big and his lips too dry. And his head seemed to be spinning with whirling thoughts. He stood there looking up into Mr. Fields' face just as little Jimmy had looked into his. All he could stammer was, "Thanks, Mr. Fields. I'm going to try to be just like you when I grow up."

Prayer Hymn: Sing softly the first verse of "My Faith Looks Up to Thee."

Prayer (by the teacher).

Offertory Service:

Whatsoever a man soweth, that shall he also reap (Galatians 6: 7b).

He which soweth sparingly shall reap also sparingly; and he which soweth bountifully shall reap also bountifully (2 Corinthians 9: 6).

Whatever you give, the same shall be given unto you. If you give just a little, then you shall receive just a little. But if you give generously, then you shall receive generous blessings in return.

Every man according as he purposeth in his heart, so let him give; not grudgingly, or of necessity: for God loveth a cheerful giver (2 Corinthians 9:7).

(Play softly "O Jesus, Thou Art Standing," while the offering is taken and during a brief prayer by one of the students.)

Adult Leader:

I am sure all of you remember the stories of King Arthur and his Knights of the Round Table. When the knights went off to fight for a cause they felt was right, they would dress in the king's armor. They would wear helmets to protect their heads, and metal guards around their loins. They would strap on breastplates. They would carry swords and shields. The king's seal was stamped on everything they wore, so that the enemies could tell at a glance they belonged to King Arthur's court. It took brave knights with a great deal of courage to win battles, so King Arthur gave his men the very best armor to wear as a protection against the enemies.

Today it takes brave and courageous Christians to face the many enemies of righteousness. But God does not expect us to fight hard and win battles against such enemies as unfairness, selfishness, thoughtlessness, indifference, ignorance, or unkindness without being properly protected. He has given us complete suits of armor to wear, and each piece is plainly marked so the enemies can tell immediately that we belong to God's army.

Let us turn to the sixth chapter of Ephesians and learn more about the armor that God has provided for us. (Have various students read verses 13 through 17. Discuss each verse separately as read. Refer to the shield poster which is described in *Patterns for 52 Visual Lessons*. Patterns are also given for miniature shields.)

Benediction.

SERVICE NO. 13—APRIL

Growing in Stature Through—

GIVING THANKS

O give thanks unto the Lord, for he is good: for his mercy endureth for ever.—Psalm 107:1.

Prelude: "O Worship the King."

Call to Worship:

> Great is the Lord, and greatly to be praised; and his greatness is unsearchable.
> The Lord is gracious, and full of compassion; slow to anger, and of great mercy.
> The Lord is good to all: and his tender mercies are over all his works
>   (Psalm 145:3, 8, 9).
> Come, let us worship the Lord.

Hymn of Praise: "Count Your Blessings."

Thoughts on the Theme: (*An object lesson by one of the students.*)

(Provide the student with a patchwork quilt. Any size will do.)

When we look at this quilt, the first things that catch our eyes are the many brightly colored patches. Just looking at the quilt hurriedly, we see many of them, but if we took the time to look at the whole quilt very closely, we would find more and more patches.

This patchwork quilt is like our lives. The patches are like the blessings God gives to us. When we think of God's blessings, we always think of certain ones first—like clothing, food, our homes, our parents, brothers and sisters, friends, schools, churches, the Bible, and the great blessing of Jesus. The longer we look at this quilt the more patches we see. The longer we look at our lives the more blessings we find—health, the blessings of sight, speech and hearing, healthy bodies, the sun, rain, winds, trees, flowers, birds, the seasons. We could go on and on listing blessings, our lives are so full of them. Just like counting the patches, it surely would take us a long time to count every blessing God has given to us. The bigger the quilt (the older we grow) the more pieces (blessings) there are.

Story: A DOSE OF HER OWN MEDICINE.

The plans were for all the girls to meet at the church and go to Leta's home in a group for the monthly meeting of the class.

"It looks as if we are all here," Joyce said as Doris and Anna Louise arrived.

"Here's hoping we have a better meeting than we had last month," Arleen said, linking her arm through Georgette's as the girls started toward the bus stop.

"But definitely!" exclaimed Phyllis. "The Girls' Club was off to a good start before Leta joined. Now all we do is to listen to her complain about everything."

"The sad part is that Leta is really a very nice girl," Mary Jo added. "She could be twice as popular if she stopped complaining and was a little cheerful once in a while."

"I wish there was some way we could help her without offending her," Wilma said.

"Let's give her a dose of her own medicine," Alberta laughed in her jolly way. "That should cure her."

"A dose of her own medicine? Say! That is a wonderful idea!" exclaimed Beverly. She was president of the club. "That is just what Leta needs. She is really a lovely girl and is talented in many ways. If she fully realized what a terrible habit she has developed, I am sure she would change."

"It is just that Leta is never grateful!" Melissa said. "She can look at a perfectly wonderful blessing and find something unpleasant about it or wish for something else."

"Yes, Leta is never satisfied. She is never thankful. I think Alberta's suggestion is a good one. Why don't we try it out in the meeting tonight?"

"Let's!" cried the girls all at once.

"This is an excellent chance," Beverly said as the girls gathered around her so every one could hear. "We are all here but Leta, so we all know about it. Here comes our bus. Now remember, as soon as we enter Leta's home, let's all begin to complain. Complain about everything. Do not smile or laugh. No matter what is suggested or what is done, be unhappy about it. We'll try to hold out the whole evening or until something happens which gives us an opportunity to explain to Leta."

"Hello!" Leta called as she opened the front door to admit the girls. "I've had such a terrible—"

"So have we!" Jo Ann cut in abruptly.

"What a terrible ride!" said Wilma.

"We thought we would never get here!" complained Joyce, putting on a long face.

"The ride was so long and so rough," Phyllis whined.

"Really, the ride made me quite ill," Arleen said, holding her head and side.

"It was so hot and stuffy in that bus," Georgette scowled.

"It has been that way all week. Unbearable," sighed Anna Louise.

Frances was the last girl in. "You look lovely tonight, Leta," she said. "Only the left side of your hair is all mussed."

Leta smiled weakly and immediately began patting her hair. She had been wholly unprepared for such a somber entry. The girls usually laughed and jested with each other all the time.

"Sit down," she said with a nervous gesture. "Sit down."

Mary Jo sank into one of the soft chairs. She sprang up instantly, saying, 'This chair is too soft. It makes my legs go to sleep."

"I'll trade with you," Nanette said quickly. "This chair is too hard. It makes my back ache."

And so the meeting of groans and complaints began.

The girls almost cheered when Leta said, "It can't be as bad as all that," after listening to the girls complain about a new project they were considering. As the meeting progressed it was obvious to the girls that Leta was trying her best to get them out of their assumed depressed mood. Finally, Beverly read a letter she had received from Mrs. Wilson, complimenting the girls on their plans to begin a church library. Enclosed with her letter was a check for ten dollars, to be used for purchasing books. It was extremely hard for the girls to hide their excitement when they heard the news. Ten dollars! What a generous gift! How like Mrs. Wilson! She was always doing something wonderful for some one! They must write her immediately, expressing their sincere thanks. But aloud they said:

"Just ten dollars? Why, she could afford twice as much."

"Now I guess we'll have to write a letter to thank her."

"If only we had the books bought. It will be such a job selecting them."

"Why didn't she send books instead? It would have saved us a lot of work."

Leta sat speechless, staring at the girls. Then she jumped to her feet, exclaiming:

"Why, girls! Whatever is wrong with you tonight? This is a wonderful gift! How kind and thoughtful of Mrs. Wilson to send it to us! We should be so grateful! We should be thankful!"

Alberta gave a shrill scream and tossed her hanky into the air. "Hurrah! Hurrah!" she cried. "It worked!"

"Leta is cured!" Doris cried joyously. "Cured by her own medicine!"

Such talking and laughing as followed! Beverly rapped the gavel on the table for order. Then she explained to the bewildered Leta why they had pretended to be so displeased with everything. Leta's eyes grew wide with astonishment.

"You mean I have been like that?" she gasped. "Oh, girls, have I really been like that?"

"At times you have been worse," Linda said. "That is why we wanted you to see yourself as others see you."

"Why didn't you tell me sooner?" Leta asked unhappily. "Please, *please* tell me if I am ever like that again."

More talking and laughing followed. Beverly rapped again for order.

"Girls," she said, "I would suggest that we start this meeting all over. Let us go out on the porch, and when Leta comes to the door, we shall be our old selves once again."

"All but me," Leta said sincerely. "From now on I shall try to be a new person."

Prayer Hymn: First verse of "Draw Me Nearer."

Prayer (by the teacher).

Offertory Service:

Jesus said, "Take heed, and beware of covetousness: for a man's life consisteth not in the abundance of the things which he possesseth" (Luke 12:15). "It is more blessed to give than to receive" (Acts 20:35b).

(Play "Blessed Assurance" while the offering is taken. Conclude with a brief dedicatory prayer by one of the students.)

Adult Leader:

(Display the suggested poster described in *Patterns for 52 Visual Lessons,* but have only one flower placed in the center of the bowl. Add the other flowers and leaves as you develop the following thoughts:)

Flowers are one of the beautiful blessings of springtime. We look forward each year to our gardens awakening, when the warm sun shines once again. Not only do we enjoy flowers blooming in our gardens, but we also like to cut some and enjoy their beauty and fragrance indoors. But one bloom placed all alone in a bowl looks out of place. It is just as lovely as it was out in the garden, but something is missing.

That is the way we would be without God's love. We would feel lost and alone in this big world. All we have to do to bring out the beauty of this flower is to surround it with other flowers. All we need to do to bring out the beauty of our lives is to surround ourselves with God's love.

As we fill this bowl with flowers, let us think more about giving thanks. The more we give thanks, the more we feel God's love about us. (Have various students read the Scripture written on the stem of each flower. Discuss each verse as read. Then place the flower in the bowl. The Scriptures to be read are: 1 Chronicles 23:30; 29:13; Luke 17:11-16; 2 Corinthians 9:15; Ephesians 1:16; 5:20; Colossians 1:3; 1 Thessalonians 5:18; Hebrews 13:15.

Now we have a bowl filled with flowers—or a life filled with thanks for blessings received. But the bowl still looks a little empty. No matter how thankful we are, our lives are still incomplete unless we express our thanks to God through prayer. These leaves will fill in the bare spots and add the finishing touches to our bouquet. Prayers will fill in the empty spots in our lives and add the finishing touch to our expression of thanks.

(Have the students make flower pots according to the directions given in the book mentioned above.)

Benediction.

SERVICE NO. 14—APRIL

Growing in Stature Through—

REVERENCE

O come, let us worship and bow down: let us kneel before the Lord our maker.—Psalm 95:6.

Prelude: Play softly several times, "The Lord Is in His Holy Temple." Then have students stand and sing it. Have them remain standing through the call to worship.

Call to Worship:

>*I was glad when they said unto me,*
>*Let us go into the house of the Lord* (Psalm 122:1).
>For
>*The Lord is in his holy temple: let all the earth keep silence before him* (Habakkuk 2:20).

Hymn of Praise: "Holy Is the Lord."

Thoughts on the Theme: (*An object lesson by one of the students.*)

>(Prop a flashlight on a table in front of the group so that the light can be seen by all without shining in any one's eyes, or use any kind of desk light. Provide the student with an assortment of paper ranging from very thin transparent tissue or onion-skin paper to a piece of heavy, black poster paper.)

Perhaps you have never thought that there is more than one way to enter a church. But there are as many ways to enter a church as there are people entering it. This is what I mean:

Here we have a constant, steady light. When we hold this piece of cardboard in front of it, we completely hide the light. The cardboard is so thick that even though we are holding it directly in front of the bulb, the light can not pass through it. We can try these other pieces one by one. But while they are thinner than the cardboard, they are still too heavy for the light to shine through. But when we hold this piece of white typing paper before the bulb, we can begin to see the light. This piece of lighter-weight paper gives us a little more light. And finally, when we hold this very thin, transparent paper before the bulb, the light shines through brightly.

This light is like the Spirit of God. It is always present. It is always brightly shining for us. These pieces of cardboard and paper are like people entering a church. Some people enter the church with minds so heavy and dark with personal thoughts that the light of God can not shine through. They have not learned to put all worldly thoughts out of their minds when they enter church. Therefore, their worldly thoughts become like this piece of stiff cardboard between them and the Spirit of God. Some people go to church to please others. Some go because their friends go. Some people go to church, but do not enter into the worship program in any way. They sit and let their minds wander, or plan for things during the coming week. Some people go to church and sleep through the service. Some whisper through the service. Some read. These people are all like the pieces of paper which are not so thick as the cardboard, but which still keep out the light.

But the people who go to church because they love God and wish to worship Him, and who enter the church reverently, and who join in every part of the service are the ones who find the Spirit of God. They are like this thin, transparent paper. Their minds are so free from worldly thoughts and so ready for the Spirit of God that His light finds no difficulty entering into their hearts.

Story: GOD'S FACTORY.

Mr. Cyrus sat behind his huge mahogany desk and toyed idly with a pencil. He was a big man with short, thick hair that was graying at the temples. His shoulders were broad and muscular. When he stood, he towered over six feet. He swung his tilted swivel chair around and sat facing the window. He seemed to have forgotten Mr. Dudley, who was seated across the polished desk, eagerly awaiting his reply. But, then, Mr. Cyrus was used to having people wait for him and on him all day. After all, he was the owner of the Cyrus mills and factories and most of the modest cottages that housed the millworkers in Cyrusville. Finally, he swung around and faced Mr. Dudley, still waiting in his quiet, patient way.

"Well, now, Mr. Dudley," he began slowly, as if carefully choosing each word. "I am not at all convinced that the millworkers need a church; that is, a church building. Two years ago, at your suggestion, I agreed to let the vacant building on Pine Street be used for a mission. It has proved adequate these two years. Let things remain as they are for the time being."

"But the one-room store building is no longer big enough, Mr. Cyrus," the young minister repeated. "We have long outgrown that one room. The millworkers are liberal in their giving, but it will handicap the work greatly if we try to assume the responsibility of building a church now. But if you would be willing to help—"

"Let things remain as they are," Mr. Cyrus repeated. He arose as he spoke, indicating that the interview was over. Mr. Dudley also arose.

"You are a businessman, Mr. Cyrus," he said earnestly. "Surely, you would not pass up a good deal. The mission has grown by leaps and bounds. The millworkers need the gospel just the way you need the millworkers. Better workers mean better business for you. Please do not consider this matter closed until you have at least investigated for yourself. Come to either of our Sunday services or to any of our midweek services. Then make your decision."

Mr. Cyrus hesitated a moment. It was hard for even Mr. Cyrus to say "No" to a young minister as earnest and as sincere as Mr. Dudley.

"Well, then, all right," Mr. Cyrus said as he offered the minister his hand. "I shall arrange a trip to the mission in the very near future. We shall let the matter ride until then."

Mr. Dudley drove home full of hope. Surely, when Mr. Cyrus saw for himself how packed the one-room mission was every service and how sincere and eager the people were to help with the work, he would consent to help build a new church. After all, the promise of a visit to the mission was all he could expect out of an interview with Mr. Cyrus. It was Saturday morning. He would spend the entire afternoon and evening reviewing the sermons for tomorrow's services. Everything must be the very best, just in case Mr. Cyrus was prsent.

But Mr. Cyrus was never one to leave any unfinished business for even a day. At eleven-thirty he rang for his secretary. "I am going to the Pine Street Mission," he said. "If anything important arises, you can reach me there." He intended to inspect the building alone, so he was surprised when a freckled-faced boy about twelve years old opened the door for him.

"I saw you get out of your car, sir," the boy said. "I am Jerry Walters."

"How do you do, Jerry," Mr. Cyprus said with his usual curt nod. "I am Mr. Cyrus."

"Yes, I know," the boy said quickly. "You build factories."

Mr. Cyrus smiled. "Do you come here to church?" he asked.

"Oh, yes, sir," came the quick reply. "And Bible school, too. Just about everybody comes here."

"What brings you here today?" Mr. Cyrus asked.

"We take turns cleaning the mission every Saturday afternoon.

The Junior Department cleans it this month. I didn't have anything to do at home, so I came early. The rest of the kids and the teachers will be here soon."

"Oh?" said Mr. Cyrus, raising his eyebrows and glancing around the small vestibule set off from the main room by pieces of wallboard. "Let's take a look around."

As he passed through the doorway Jerry said in a nervous, strained voice, "If you please, sir—we always take off our hats when we go in there."

Mr. Cyrus raised his eyebrows again and hastily removed his soft, light-gray felt hat. "That's right," he said in a very light tone, trying to make Jerry feel at ease once more. "We are always supposed to take off our hats when we enter a house."

"Especially God's house," came the quick reply.

Mr. Cyrus glanced at Jerry as they made their way down the center aisle. "Where do you sit, Jerry?" he asked, just to keep up the conversation. Perhaps that was why Jerry's reply was such a surprise.

"I usually stand outside that window," Jerry replied in a matter-of-fact way as he pointed to the center window on the west wall.

"Why do you stand outside?" Mr. Cyrus asked quickly. "Why don't you come in and sit down?"

"There is never room for children at the morning services," Jerry explained. "The adults come in first. Then the young people. The girls stand around the back, and the little kids sit in the aisle. We boys stand around the windows on the outside. Some of the men do, too. It seems like there is less room inside all the time."

They were standing in front of the small, raised platform built across the far end of the room. Mr. Cyrus leaned against the plain, oblong table in front of the pulpit as he glanced critically around the large room. Jerry moistened his lips twice before he had the courage to speak. Then his voice sounded strained and a little frightened.

"Please, sir, that is the communion table. We never lean against it."

Mr. Cyrus stepped away quickly. "Oh?" was all he managed to say. Jerry felt very uncomfortable. Maybe he should not have said that to Mr. Cyrus. After all, Mr. Cyrus was so rich and so important. But Mr. Dudley always said—then his eyes caught sight of the picture of the Good Shepherd thumbtacked to the wall behind the pulpit.

"See that picture?" he asked quickly, trying to change the subject. When Mr. Cyrus nodded, he continued, "We pretend it is a stained-glass window with the sunlight shining through. We are going to have a stained-glass window like that when we have a church some day."

"A stained-glass window with the sunlight shining through," Mr. Cyrus repeated aloud. To himself he added, How like that young preacher! He had changed this empty, bare storeroom into a sanctuary with nothing to work with but—but—but reverence!

"So you would like to build a new church," Mr. Cyrus said as he turned and started toward the door. "I might do a little building here myself."

Jerry stopped abruptly and looked up at Mr. Cyrus with wide eyes. "Here?" he asked. "You are going to build something right here?"

"Right here and maybe on the lot next door and the lot behind," Mr. Cyrus said, smiling down at the thin little fellow.

"You build factories," Jerry said in an accusing tone. "You build lots of factories. Are you going to build a factory here?"

Mr. Cyrus was ready to laugh. Then he changed his mind. "Am I going to build a factory?" he repeated. "Well, now, maybe I am. Factories turn out fine products. God's factories should turn out fine men and women. Let's find Mr. Dudley and see what he thinks about building one of God's factories right on this very spot."

Prayer Hymn: The Doxology sung softly.

Prayer (by the teacher).

Offertory Service:

God has given many gifts to each of us. The gifts He has given to you may be different than the gifts He has given to me. But each one of us receives countless blessings every day. Therefore, each one of us should return to God a just portion of the gifts He has given to us, so that the work of His kingdom will go forward.

Every man shall give as he is able, according to the blessing of the Lord thy God which he hath given thee (Deuteronomy 16:17).

(Play softly "Near the Cross" while the offering is taken. Conclude with sentence prayers by students.)

Adult Leader:

(Display the poster of church bell and belfry described in *Patterns for 52 Visual Lessons*. Open the bells to swinging position as you refer to the Scripture verses on each: Psalms 29:2; 34:3; 95:1, 2; 96:6; 100:4.

Who can quote for us the first Commandment? (Exodus 20:2, 3).

In this commandment God tells us to worship no other gods but Him. Our God is the only true and living God. There are other religions in the world (especially in the Far East) which worship false gods, not the true God. Some people worship a prophet who lived centuries ago, named Mohammed. Some of the Chinese worship an image or statue called Buddha. But these are not the true and living God.

God has commanded us to worship Him, and Him alone. That means we should give Him all our love and all our devotion. If we do this, then we shall revere His name and have reverence for His house of worship.

What does "revere His name" mean? And how can we have reverence for His house of worship?

Let us turn to Exodus 20:7 and find the answer to the first question. To revere the name of God means to use it only with the greatest respect. Whenever we hear any one say, "My God!" or "For God's sake!" or "For Christ's sake!" they are breaking the third Commandment: "Thou shalt not take the name of the Lord thy God in vain; for the Lord will not hold him guiltless that taketh his name in vain."

Now, how can we have reverence for God's house?

If we were invited to visit the king in Buckingham Palace, we would approach the palace in awe. We would walk quietly through the halls to the throne room, admiring everything we saw, but not touching or soiling a thing. We would not dream of slamming a door or sliding down a hall or throwing a book upon the floor. And when we entered the room where the king's throne stands, if we spoke at all it would be in a soft, hushed whisper. When we enter a church, which is God's palace, we should feel and show even greater reverence, for God is greater and more powerful than any king.

(Swing open the bells on the poster and have the students locate and read the various verses. Discuss each as read. Always encourage all students to participate. It is important training in the development of personal expression as well as leadership. Have the students make "Praise ye the Lord" bells.)

Benediction.

SERVICE NO. 15—APRIL

Growing in Stature Through—

FAITH

Now faith is the substance of things hoped for, the evidence of things not seen.—Hebrews 11:1.

Prelude: "Faith of Our Fathers" played as an instrumental solo.

Call to Worship: (By two students.)

> First: *When Jesus was entered into Capernaum, there came unto him a centurion, beseeching him, and saying, Lord, my servant lieth at home sick of the palsy, grievously tormented.*
>
> Second: *And Jesus saith unto him, I will come and heal him.*
>
> First: *The centurion answered and said, Lord, I am not worthy that thou shouldest come under my roof: but speak the word only, and my servant shall be healed.*
>
> Second: *When Jesus heard it, he marvelled, and said to them that followed, Verily I say unto you, I have not found so great faith, no, not in Israel* (Matthew 8:5-8, 10).

Hymn of Praise: "My Faith Looks Up to Thee."

Thoughts on the Theme: (An object lesson by one of the students.)

(Provide the student with a dress box securely tied with a piece of string).

Let us pretend you went to a department store to buy yourself a new spring dress or a new spring suit. There were many dresses and suits on the display racks. There were dresses made of all kinds of materials, in all colors, and all sizes. After you look them all over carefully, you choose one which you feel is just right for you. "I should like to buy this dress," you say. But the saleslady shakes her head. Instead of taking from the rack the dress you have chosen, she hands you this box, all carefully tied with this string. "Here is a much better dress," she says. "It is more beautiful. It will look more becoming on you. It is made of better material, so it will last longer."

Now if you are willing to put aside the dress or the suit you have chosen for yourself, and take the one which the saleslady *says* is inside this box without opening the box to see for yourself, you are showing complete faith in the saleslady's word.

God offers us many promises in much the same way. We can not actually see them. We can not actually feel them. But through the Bible God *says* they are for us. If we are willing to put aside those things which we choose for ourselves and which we think are the best for ourselves and take God's Word instead, we are showing complete faith in God.

Story: GOD WILL PROVIDE.

As a boy and young man, Malcolm Sawyer had seen much hardship. He was born on a small farm in the rockiest part of Ohio. The land was so hilly and the soil so poor his father struggled hard to provide a living for the family. Supplies were often low and money scarce. When Malcolm or any of his sisters or brothers questioned how the family would ever manage to live through the latter part of the winter and the early spring, until the first planting was ready for harvest, their parents would always answer, "God will provide."

Now, Malcolm sat at the head of a makeshift table, repeating those same words to his sons and daughter.

"But this is all the food we have, Malcolm," his wife said quietly. "There is not even a crust of bread left. In fact, there is hardly enough food to satisfy all of us at this meal."

Malcolm looked at Prudence and repeated, "God will provide," so sincerely that no one questioned further.

It had been a long, hard journey from southern Ohio across the stretches of open plain to the Mississippi River. Then more plains until the rugged Rockies loomed before them like a giant monster challenging the rest of the way. At the end of each day, the limited supply of food was noticeably smaller. Now they sat on squatty little nail kegs around a table made of thin slats of wood nailed together and resting on wooden sawhorses. There was not much room in a covered wagon for such things as tables and chairs.

All afternoon Malcolm laughed and talked gaily to his sons and to little Miriam as he guided the horses along the seemingly endless trail. There was never a doubt in his mind but that surely God would provide for them that night as He had always done in the past. At sundown, the weary horses were unharnessed and fed. Once again the thin slats of wood were brought out of the covered wagon and placed on the sawhorses. Then the family gathered round it, sitting on the sturdy little kegs as they had done for every meal all along the way. Only this meal was different from the rest. Often the table held but a scant portion for each. Tonight it was bare. But Malcolm folded his hands and bowed his head in his usual manner.

"Dear God," he prayed, "the way has been long and hard. Yet

Thou hast been with us every mile. How can we ever question such loving care? We thank Thee for all Thou hast provided. We thank Thee for the food—"

Just then a sound more like an echo than a shout disturbed the quietness of the evening hour. A long, low object was moving toward them. Malcolm stood his full height and peered into the gathering shadows.

"It is another covered wagon!" he exclaimed, "drawn by four sturdy oxen, and a man is walking along carrying something. It is a bag, a large bag. I see a woman walking a few paces ahead of him near the oxen, holding her hand high over her head. Now she is waving. She is carrying something, too. It is a basket covered with a cloth."

Now the wagon was close enough for even little Miriam to see. The pioneer woman was so close Prudence could see her plain brown homespun, so like her own simple dress. A cheerful cry of "Welcome! Welcome!" came from those inside the wagon and those walking along beside the oxen.

"Welcome, indeed!" cried the pioneer woman. "We bring you the Welcome Wagon which goes forward to greet every new family traveling over this trail. We welcome you into our settlement!"

It seemed to the children that people kept coming out of the covered wagon, carrying boxes and sacks and baskets. Some of the women gathered around Prudence or patted the children's heads while the men shook hands with Malcolm. The rest of the women placed more food on the table taken from baskets and boxes than Malcolm's family had seen for several months. Malcolm looked at Prudence and then at his sons. He did not have to speak the words. They all knew what he was thinking.

"Come," said Malcolm, trying hard to keep his voice steady. "Let us give thanks to God for ever providing for those who have faith in Him."

Prayer Hymn: Sing softly the first verse of "I Need Thee Every Hour" as the prayer hymn. Sing second verse as prayer response.

Prayer (by the teacher).

Offertory Service:

(Sing the first verse of "I Gave My Life for Thee." Continue to play this hymn softly while the offering is taken and during the dedicatory prayer offered by one of the students.)

The gift of God is eternal life through Jesus Christ our Lord (Romans 6:23b).

> What a wonderful gift God has given to men—
> To send His own Son from above.
> Let us thank Him through prayers and thank Him through deeds
> And thank Him through offerings of love.

Freely ye have received, freely give (Matthew 10: 8b).

Adult Leader:

(Display the umbrella poster suggested in *Patterns for 52 Visual Lessons,* and refer to it as you develop the following thoughts.)

It is a good idea to keep an umbrella handy during these spring days which are filled with sudden April showers. For an umbrella will keep us dry. If we go out in the rain without an umbrella, we, of course, have nothing to protect us. Therefore, we get wet. Often we suffer because we catch cold. Now, the smaller the umbrella we hold over us, the less protection we have; or, in other words, the bigger the umbrella, the more protection we shall have and the dryer we shall stay.

Faith in God is like an umbrella. When we have but little faith, it is like holding a very small umbrella over our heads and expecting to keep dry while we are out in a hard April shower. The greater the faith we have, the more protection we shall have against such things as doubt, fear, weaknesses, uncertainty, and worry.

In Paul's first letter to the Romans (verse 17) he wrote, "The just shall live by faith." What do you suppose Paul meant? How can we live by faith? If we live by faith, will we ever worry? Will we ever be fearful that things will not turn out for the best? (As long as time permits, lead the group in a discussion suggested by the above questions. Have the students make umbrellas—patterns are given in the book mentioned above.)

Benediction.

SERVICE NO. 16—APRIL

Growing in Stature Through—

SINCERITY

Grace be with all them that love our Lord Jesus Christ in sincerity.— Ephesians 6:24.

Prelude: Use "Give Me Your Heart" as a solo or an instrumental number.

Call to Worship:

Come, let us learn the law of the Lord.
Let us worship Him with a whole heart, for—
Blessed are the undefiled in the way, who walk in the law of the Lord.
Blessed are they that keep his testimonies, and that seek him with the whole heart (Psalm 119:1, 2).

Hymn of Praise: "Let Jesus Come Into Your Heart."

Thoughts on the Theme: (An object lesson by one of the students.)

(Provide the student with two alarm clocks. Have the one set accurately and the other about twenty minutes slow.)

All of us know how important it is to have a clock we can depend upon to tell us the correct time both day and night. A clock that loses time might cause us to miss a train or a bus. It might cause us to be late for school. In fact, we can get into all kinds of difficulties by depending upon a clock that does not tell us the exact hour.

If we had this clock in the kitchen and this clock in the living room, it would not take us long to discover that the living-room clock is always slow, whereas the kitchen clock is always exact. For a while we might look at the living-room clock and then allow a little extra time, knowing it was always slow. But we could never be sure how much extra time we would have to allow. Soon we would pay no attention to the living-room clock. We would always look at the kitchen clock whenever we wanted to know the time of day.

People who are insincere are like this clock. They are not true. They can not be trusted. Soon others will discover they are not what they seem to be, and will not care to be with them. But those who are sincere in what they say and do are like this clock that can always be trusted because it is true to the hour.

A Statement of Purpose (by a student):

I hope I shall always possess firmness and virtue enough to maintain, what I consider the most enviable of all titles, the character of an "honest man."—*Washington.*

Story: LEARNING THE HARD WAY.

The first time Homer Wendell rang the fire alarm every member of the volunteer department dropped whatever work he was doing and came immediately. Clyde Barkley, owner of the general store, was the first to arrive.

"Where's the fire, Homer?" he cried, springing from his delivery truck. "Is it your house?"

Homer leaned leisurely against the pole supporting the fire-alarm bell.

"There's no fire," he grinned. "I just wanted to see if every one would come."

One by one the men arrived in great haste. No one had much to say, although many found it hard to keep quiet. "He is a newcomer to Millersdale," they said among themselves. "He doesn't know how sincere and loyal we are to each other. Let's not hold this against him. He just did not know."

As Boyd Young, the postal clerk, drove off, he said firmly, though still smiling and friendly, "Well, now you know, Homer, that when the fire alarm sounds, every one comes right away. Better not try it again."

About a month later, the alarm sounded again in the middle of a busy Saturday morning. Every man listened to be sure. Two rings and a pause. Two rings and a pause. That was the Wendell ring. Several men hesitated, but only for a minute. Homer had fooled them once. Surely he would not do it a second time. But when the men arrived, there was Homer leaning leisurely against the alarm pole.

"You don't know how funny you look," he laughed gaily. "Things have been so dead around here lately, I thought I would put a little life into this town."

Constable Watkins frowned. "I don't see anything funny about this, Homer," he scowled.

"Neither do I!" Jack Fisher, the druggist, said roughly. "This is Saturday morning. My store is full of customers."

"The same here!" There was real disgust in Clyde Barkley's voice. "Everybody comes to town on Saturday. We haven't time for such nonsense."

"Ah, be a good sport," laughed Homer. "This is more fun than I've had all month." But the men who returned to their work that busy Saturday morning did not think so.

About two weeks later, a gentle spring rain turned into a severe electrical storm. Great blinding flashes of lightning seemed to rip the heavens apart. One of the most violent bolts hit the Wendell home, and, like a giant lighted match, set fire to the left wing. Homer grabbed young Peter, and Mrs. Wendell picked up Pat. They raced from the burning house to the fire alarm. The alarm sounded weird as it rang out through the storm. At the first sound of the alarm every man on the volunteer department leaped to his feet. Then they stopped. Two rings and a pause. Two rings and a pause. That was the Wendell ring. What a crazy sense of humor Homer had! Did he really think they would come rushing to his house in such a storm just to hear him laugh and tell them how funny they looked? One by one the men settled down in their respective homes, certain that Homer was again trying to have some fun.

When the storm finally ended, word of the Wendell fire spread throughout the whole of Millersdale in less than an hour. People hurried from all directions bringing food, clothing, and bedding. The men from the volunteer squad stood around Homer with shaking heads and few words.

"It would be different if I had not heard the alarm," Jack Fisher said. "But I heard it plain as day. I started out, then I decided you were only fooling again."

"I heard it, too," Boyd Young said, and he lowered his eyes. "This is the first time I did not come at once."

"We should have come anyway," Constable Watkins said uneasily. "We could have saved some of your things. This is the first time we failed to do our duty."

But Homer shook his head. "It's all my fault," he said sadly. "You had no way of knowing that I was sincere this time. I guess I had to learn my lesson the hard way. Sincerity and loyalty go together. I can not expect my friends to be loyal if I am insincere."

Prayer Hymn: "Open My Eyes That I May See."

Prayer (by the teacher).

Offertory Service:

> Leader: *Lay not up for yourselves treasures upon earth, where moth and rust doth corrupt, and where thieves break through and steal:*
>
> Students: *But lay up for yourselves treasures in heaven, where neither*

moth nor rust doth corrupt, and where thieves do not break through nor steal:

All: *For where your treasure is, there will your heart be also* (Matthew 6:19-21).

(Play softly "My Saviour First of All" while the offering is taken and during the short dedicatory prayer by one of the students.)

Adult Leader:

(Refer to the suggested palette poster in *Patterns for 52 Visual Lessons* as you develop the following thoughts:)

These days we give much thought to colors. When we are redecorating our homes, we study color charts and color wheels in an effort to get all our colors to harmonize. We usually choose one main color and then try to have all other colors to blend or harmonize with it. Even when we plan a new spring outfit we give colors careful thought. We select only the ones we wear well or which are becoming to us.

There are certain colors which become a Christian. These colors are found in the Christian's color wheel—our Bible. Today we are studying an important color—sincerity. Some of the other colors which we have studied in previous lessons are patience, meekness, loyalty, purity, and faith. Of course, there are many more, some of which we shall study in the weeks to come. A Christian is known by his colors. It would be foolish for us to buy a dress or suit of a color that does not look well on us. It is just as foolish for us to think we can be Christians and not wear the colors found in God's Word.

(Have the students make individual color palettes, as found in the book mentioned above.)

Benediction.

SERVICE NO. 17—MAY

Growing in Stature Through—

OVERCOMING PREJUDICES

Grudge not one against another, brethren, lest ye be condemned . . .
—James 5:9.

Prelude: Have a quartet (two sopranos and two altos) sing " 'Whosoever' Meaneth Me."

Call to Worship:

Come, all who love the Lord.
It matters not your class, your color, or how much of earthly wealth you count as yours.
Come and worship if your heart is true and filled with love and thankfulness.
For this is all that matters in the eyes of God.
Come and let us praise a just and loving Father.

Hymn of Praise: "Whosoever Will."

Thoughts on the Theme: (*An object lesson by one of the students.*)

(Provide the student with a vase of assorted fall flowers.)

Any bouquet of flowers is interesting, because no two flowers are exactly alike. Let us look at this bouquet closely and count the different colors—yellow, red, blue, green, orange, purple. Also, no two flowers have the same shape. Some have long petals, some short; some grow tall, some grow on short stems; some bloom over a long period, some bloom for a very short time. Some are very popular and every one knows them by name. Some are not grown in every garden, and few people know much about them.

These flowers are just like the various races of the earth. Each race is of a different color. Each race has physical characteristics different from any other race. We are a taller race than the Chinese or Japanese. Their eyes are more slanted than ours. The Indians and Negroes have characteristics which are different from the Chinese or Japanese or from the white race. But just as God created all the flowers, He also created all the races of men.

These flowers are also like the many peoples of the earth—the Russians, the English, the Germans, the French, the Italians, the Greeks, the Jews, the Arabs, the Poles, the Americans. Just as these flowers grow differently, so the peoples of the earth live differently. Some of these flowers grow better on the east side of the house, some on the west. Some need the early morning sun. Some thrive if planted where they will have the hotter early afternoon sun. Some must be watered every day. Some can get along very well if watered once a week. If we tried to force all these flowers to grow the same way, some would die. Each flower has its own particular needs, just as each race and nationality has its own particular needs. We can not force others to live just exactly as we live, any more than we can force all of these flowers to grow exactly alike.

This vase is holding all these different flowers closely together. If I take them from the vase, hold them here on the table, and then withdraw my hand, they fall, each going in a different direction. This vase is like God's love. Just as it holds all kinds of flowers closely together, so God's love holds all races and all nationalities closely together. But when God's love is removed, then the close bonds between countries, races, and nationalities are broken.

Story: MR. GORIZIA'S SPECIAL LOAD.

"What I tell you boys? What I tell you?" cried fat, little Mr. Gorizia,* rubbing his chubby hands together and almost jumping up and down in excitement. "What I tell you? I haul pretty special load! No? Pretty special load! That you! You pretty special load! Hop in! Jump in! Truck clean as kitchen table. Plenty room. Plenty benches! Get in and we go!"

The whole group had been awkwardly quiet since Mr. Gorizia's big truck pulled up in front of the school. They were going to Bloomington Woods, about thirty miles from town. Grace's father always used his big truck for such affairs, but he was unexpectedly called out of town. Up until three o'clock on Friday it looked as if there would be no picnic the next day. Then Miss Matthews announced that another truck had been offered, so they would all meet in front of the school at nine o'clock the next morning as originally planned. They were too excited that the picnic would not be postponed to even wonder whose truck would be used.

Mr. Gorizia's fruit store was just around the corner from the school. Almost all of the students from Miss Matthews' class passed it on the way home. That is how they saw Mr. Gorizia, hose in hand, scrubbing his truck. Some of the boys thought it fun to shout smart remarks every time they passed, especially if Mr. Gorizia or any of his family was about. They were the same boys who called Tony Gorizia a Dago whenever he tried to join their groups at school.

---

* Pronounced Gō-rēt'-sē-ȧ.

Wesley, James, Arthur, and Fred were the ringleaders. So, as they passed Mr. Gorizia that Friday, they shouted rude remarks about him to each other. Then Arthur said:

"It's about time you cleaned that dirty old truck of yours."

Mr. Gorizia smiled in his usual friendly manner and waved. "Yes, 'bout time," he chuckled. Nothing ever seemed to make Mr. Gorizia lose his happy smile or his jolly chuckle.

"Why are you scrubbing it so clean?" Wesley shouted. "Are you going to live in there?"

"Maybe yes. Maybe no," chuckled Mr. Gorizia.

"You would have more room in there than you have now behind your old store!" shouted Fred, watching to see if the girls in front of him laughed.

"I'll tell you boys," said Mr. Gorizia, as he looked over the side of the truck. "I am going to haul pretty special load. Pretty special load."

"Pretty special load of what?" asked Wesley.

"Probably pretty special load of bananas at five cents a pound!" shouted Fred. That surely should make the girls laugh, he thought.

"Just pretty special load. No, Tony?" he smiled as Tony came to the side of the truck.

"No, Tony? Yes, Tony?" the boys mocked him down the street.

Tony turned his flushed face away from them, picked up the broom, and helped his father clean and polish the truck inside and out.

This happened after school on Friday. Little wonder why there was an awkward silence among the group nine o'clock the next morning.

"Imagine this!" Fred said softly to Wesley when they were all seated in the truck and little Mr. Gorizia was gaily shouting, "Special load, sure enough! Here we go!"

"This is Saturday, his busiest day," Arthur said soberly.

"That's just what I was thinking. If we had only known Tony's father was taking us—"

"Yes, I know," Fred moved uncomfortably on the bench. "It's a wonder he would even drive us to the corner, after the way we acted yesterday."

"I don't know why we always try to act smart when we pass his fruit store," Arthur admitted. "My mother says Mr. Gorizia is one of the most honest men she has ever seen."

"That's what my mother says," Philip joined in from the opposite bench. "She would not buy fruit or vegetables anywhere else."

Similar whispers were going up and down the long benches. No one had been especially kind to Tony, although he had moved into the neighborhood almost two years ago. Some felt too good to associate with him because he was Italian and his parents spoke broken English which sounded funny to them. Some students had been too busy with their own circle of friends to bother about him. Some just did not think. Others did not care.

"Where is Tony?" some one suddenly asked. He was not in the truck. "Maybe he is sitting up in the front with his dad," some one else suggested.

Then the truck moved to the side of the road and stopped. They had just crossed the railroad tracks which marked the city limits. Mr. Gorizia jumped from the driver's seat. He took several steps backward in order to get a better look at the truck full of girls and boys.

"Everything O. K., Special Load?" he cried gaily.

"Everything's O. K.!" every one shouted at once.

Fred stood up. "Where's Tony?" he called.

"Tony? He here. With me."

"We want him to ride with us!" shouted Fred. Immediately, the whole group chimed in with similar remarks. For a moment, little Mr. Gorizia stood speechless. Then he smiled, but it was a different kind of smile than his usual one. It seemed—well, it seemed to come from the very bottom of his heart. It made his eyes glow with a happy light and his voice sound softer.

"You want *my* Tony?" he said in an awed tone. "You want him *there*, with *you?*"

Now Miss Matthews stood up.

"Yes, Mr. Gorizia," she said. "We want Tony here with us. After all, he is one of us, you know." She had been wanting to say those words in front of the class for a whole year. But she knew that unless she said them at the right time, things would be even more unpleasant for Tony. Surely, this moment was the one for which she had been waiting. When Tony hesitantly stepped from his side of the driver's cab to be greeted with cheers from the group, led by Fred and Wesley, Miss Matthews knew she had not been mistaken.

Prayer Hymn: "Open My Eyes That I May See."

Prayer (by the teacher).

Offertory Service:

(Play softly "Beautiful Words of Jesus" throughout the entire offertory service.)

Jesus said, "Go ye therefore, and teach all nations, baptizing them in the name of the Father, and of the Son, and of the Holy Ghost."

When Jesus said, "All nations," He included every part of this great world. He included every race and every nationality. We can not all go to foreign lands, but we can all do our part right here at home to carry out Christ's Great Commission. By sharing through the Bible school and church, we are helping carry on all phases of the work, including missionary work abroad. We are also showing that we truly believe all men are children of God and all men are brothers in Christ when we share in the work by bringing our gifts.

(Conclude with a brief prayer of thanks by one of the students.)

Adult Leader:

Our theme is "Overcoming Prejudices." First of all, what are prejudices? Why should they be overcome? And how can we overcome them?

When we overlook all the good qualities in a person, and dislike him because of his color or his race or because he came from a certain foreign country, we have a prejudice against him. Or, in other words, we are not willing to treat him fairly because we do not like him.

As we learn through our object lesson, God made all people, not only those with white skins or those who live in America. God made the Chinese, Japanese, and Arabs, in the Near and Far East. He made the Eskimos of the Northlands, the Negroes and the Indians in our own country. We can only show our love for Christ by loving and helping others. That means every one, everywhere, no matter who they are or what the color of their skin might be.

(Display the poster showing a wigwam representing all races other than the white in our own country, and the Chinese rice bowl representing all peoples of foreign lands; patterns are given in *Patterns for 52 Visual Lessons*. Let the students make wigwams.)

Benediction.

SERVICE NO. 18—MAY

Growing in Stature Through—

GENTLENESS

Be gentle unto all men.—2 Timothy 2:24b.

Prelude: Use "Lead Me Gently Home, Father," as a solo or a duet.

Call to Worship:

    Hear our prayers, O gentle Saviour;
      Hear our hymns of praise.
    Take our hands, O gentle Saviour;
      Lead us in Thy ways.

Hymn of Praise: "The Touch of His Hand on Mine."

Story: A LITTLE DOG SPEAKS.

Prince was a prince of a dog. We all loved him. The day he was run over by a car down the road I stayed behind the barn, my head buried in my paws. Nickie grieved, too, but Nickie is only a pup. He hadn't known Prince as long as I had. I waited two days before I told either of the horses or any of the cows about Prince. I did not want to speak about it. Just thinking about Prince lying helpless on the road brought such a big lump to my throat I could not speak.

I was with Prince when it happened. When I tell you he was one of the best hunting dogs that ever lived, you no doubt will say, "Why, then, did he get run over? Aren't hunting dogs supposed to be alert and quick?" Yes, they are. And Prince surely was both. But he had stepped on a thorn a few minutes before. The road was clear when we started across. We had purposely waited. Just as Prince was limping painfully across the road a car came tearing down the highway at a terrific speed.

"Hurry, Prince! Hurry!" I barked excitedly. But the injured Prince did not have a chance. I still believe if the driver would have stopped and taken Prince to the doctor, or even just told Jeffry about it right away, Prince could have been saved.

For a moment I stood paralyzed with fear. What should I do? Leave Prince lying there on the road, right in the path of other cars, while I went for Jeffry? Or should I stay with him and hope that some one would soon come along who knew us? I bent over Prince. "Tell Jeffry," he whimpered in pain. "Tell Jeffry." I never ran so fast in my life.

GENTLENESS

Jeffry was in the kitchen eating breakfast. I scratched on the screen door and whined.

"There's that good-for-nothing dog of yours," he said to Freddie. "Make him stop that infernal whining."

That was the first (and the last) time I disobeyed Freddie. But no matter what he said to me, I kept whining and scratching on the door. Jeffry had never liked me. I knew it. He often kicked me, and once he threw a piece of wood at me when he saw me with Prince. I knew why he didn't like me. I was just a common, ordinary dog, while Prince was a thoroughbred. Jeffry did not want Prince to associate with anything but a thoroughbred like himself. But Prince and I were real friends. He was too devoted to Jeffry to ever make him angry, so he decided we should only chum together away from the farm. When Jeffry was about, I was to stay far away from Prince. "It would be best for you, too, Dusty," Prince had said. "It hurts me every time I see Jeffry abuse you the way he does."

I kept whining louder and louder, and scratching frantically. I was growing desperate, thinking of Prince alone out there on the road.

"What's the matter this morning, Dusty?" young Freddie said, coming to the door. "You know you are not allowed indoors." He opened the screen door to come out, but with one quick move I was across the kitchen, tugging at the leg of Jeffry's trousers.

"What's the matter with this crazy dog?" Jeffry scowled, kicking me away from him. By that time I was wild with excitement. "You must come at once!" I barked. "It's Prince! It's Prince down on the road!" I barked so furiously and circled his chair so wildly I was afraid they would think I had gone mad.

"He is trying to tell you something," Mrs. Martin said.

Mr. Martin hurriedly pushed back his chair and stood up. "Let's go with him, son," he said. "See where he leads us."

With one great leap I was across the kitchen. I pushed the door open without any help and went racing down the drive. I kept looking back over my shoulder to be sure they were coming. As soon as we reached the highway, Jeffry saw for himself. He reached Prince quicker than it takes me to tell. But Prince was dead.

The only consolation I could find in the accident was the thought that maybe Jeffry would love me as he loved Prince. No. Not really love me as much. I could not expect that. But maybe he would let me follow him around the farm and be with him all day as Prince had always been. If anything, Jeffry hated me more. Every time I came near him, he would abuse me. Once he threw his rake at me and said, "Why couldn't it have been you!" I hung my head, and with my tail hanging down between my legs I went to the barn to talk it over with Daisy, the kind Jersey cow.

Soon after that we had a long rainy season. The creek had almost as much water in it as the river. It was much too deep for Nickie or me to wade across, and many places were so deep we were almost afraid to swim across.

I always waited for Freddie at the end of the lane and ran to meet him as soon as he came into sight. He had taught me to carry his books, which he tied together with a leather strap. That was the high spot of my life. I knew what time school was dismissed without any one's telling me.

"I feel nervous about Freddie today," I told Nickie. "I wish he were safely home from school."

"Freddie is just a little fellow," Nickie said, "but he can take care of himself."

"I know he can," I said. "But just the same I feel nervous." I started out for the lane earlier than usual. Then I turned back and found Nickie playing with his shadow near the side porch. "I wish you would come along with me, Nickie," I said. "I feel so uneasy."

"O. K.," he said. "If it will make you feel better, I'll be glad to come along."

We did not wait at the end of the lane that day. We kept walking toward the creek. Freddie had to cross it. There was a narrow footbridge down a ways. We were still a little distance from it when I saw Freddie. He started across the bridge, then stopped. A large tree had fallen across the creek near the bridge. He eyed it and I hurried. He was in the middle of the fallen tree before I reached the creek bank. I was afraid to bark or even make the slightest noise, for Freddie was having a hard time keeping his balance. He was only six, and small for his age. Then I saw his foot slip. I sprang forward, but I was too late to catch him as he fell into the water. However, I was quick enough to grab him by the collar of his jacket. I held it fast between my sharp teeth. I knew the water was very deep and that little Freddie could not swim. I dug my claws deeper into the tree trunk and tightened my grip on his collar.

Poor little Nickie. He came panting to my side, shivering with terror. "Nickie," I said between my clenched teeth. "You must run home as fast as you can and get help." I wanted to tell him to find Jeffry and whine and pull on his trouser leg as I had done when Prince was run over. But Nickie was gone like a flash. He is only a pup, but he surely ran fast.

Then it seemed as if hours passed. My legs were getting stiff and cramped and numb. My jaws ached. I had to keep my whole body rigid and tense. I dared not move a single muscle for fear of losing my balance or my grip on Freddie's collar. Then I closed my eyes. When I opened them I saw Jeffry and his father racing toward us. What a relief that was!

Mr. Martin carried little Freddie home, holding him tightly in his strong arms. Jeffry bent over me. If only he pats me gently just once, I thought. Just once! Instead, he picked me up and held me close to him.

"Dusty," he said softly, "you are a thoroughbred—a true thoroughbred. We're going to be pals hereafter. No one but a real thoroughbred could have done what you did today."

And now I'm the happiest dog in the world. No one knows better than I do, the difference a little kindness makes!

Thoughts on the Theme: (*An object lesson by one of the students.*)

(Provide the student with two brushes—one with very soft bristles, such as a baby's hairbrush; one with extremely stiff bristles, such as a painter's wire brush or a suede-shoe brush.)

The bristles in this brush are so soft it would be hard for us to brush in any way with it but gently. As I rub the bristles over my hand, they feel soft and pleasant and soothing. The bristles in this brush are just the opposite. They are stiff and coarse. It really hurts my hand when I rub it over these bristles.

People are just like these two brushes. Some are gentle all the time. They are like this brush. They go about being pleasant and kind. They touch everything in a gentle, soothing, loving way. They are not only kind and gentle to the members of their family and their friends, but they are kind and gentle to animals as well.

Some people are always unkind and harsh. Their actions are rough and coarse. They are not only discourteous and rude to every one they meet, but they are even cruel to helpless animals.

If we wanted to make this brush as soft as this one, we would first have to pull out all of these coarse, stiff bristles and throw them away. Then we would have to fill the holes with soft bristles. That is just what a person must do who acts rough and coarse all the time. He must pull out all his bad habits and throw them away. Then he must fill his life with kindness. When every bad habit has been replaced by a kind, loving one, he will find he is always gentle and thoughtful to those about him, and to animals as well.

Prayer Hymn: First verse of "More Love to Thee."

Prayer (by the teacher).

Offertory Service:

(Play "Jesus Meek and Gentle" while the Scripture is read and while the offering is taken.)

Bring ye all the tithes into the storehouse, that there may be meat in mine house, and prove me now herewith, saith the Lord of hosts, if I will not open you the windows of heaven, and pour you out a blessing, that there shall not be room enough to receive it (Malachi 3:10).

Adult Leader:

(Use the poster described in *Patterns for 52 Visual Lessons* as you develop the following thoughts:)

In his letter to the Galatians, Paul wrote, "The fruit of the Spirit is love, joy, peace, longsuffering, gentleness, goodness, faith" (Galatians 5:22).

When we think of fruit, we think of a tree, for most of the fruit we eat grows on trees. There are several things necessary in order to have a tree yield good fruit. First, the tree must be strong. It must be healthy. It must have a sturdy trunk securely embedded in the ground so that strong winds will not uproot it. Then the ground in which it is planted must be good ground.

Paul speaks of the "fruit of the Spirit." The spirit, then, is like the tree trunk. As the fruit of a tree depends upon the condition of the trunk and how firmly the trunk is planted in rich soil, so the fruits of our spirit—love, joy, peace, longsuffering, gentleness, goodness, faith—depend upon the condition of our soul and how firmly we believe in God's Word.

Benediction.

SERVICE NO. 19—MAY

Growing in Stature Through—

PRAYER

Confess your faults one to another, and pray one for another, that ye may be healed. The effectual fervent prayer of a righteous man availeth much.—James 5:16.

Prelude: Use "My Prayer" as a solo by one of the students.

Call to Worship:

> The Lord is righteous in all his ways, and holy in all his works.
> The Lord is nigh unto all them that call upon him, to all that call upon him in truth.
> He will fulfil the desire of them that fear him: he also will hear their cry, and will save them (Psalm 145:17-19).

Hymn of Praise: "Did You Think to Pray?"

Thoughts on the Theme: (An object lesson by one of the students.)

(Provide the student with a box of radio parts.)

Once the parts in this box were a radio that had a soft, lovely tone. But one day something went wrong. It was not very serious at first, for the radio still played. But the tone was not clear. The man who owned the radio thought he knew all about repairing it. The book of instructions that had been sent with the radio had been put aside. But the man was positive he knew all about repairing the radio without reading the instructions. The more he tinkered the worse the tone sounded. He soon became nervous and fussy. Finally, the radio would not play at all. That made him irritable and cross. He lost his temper and upset every one in the house. Then he decided to take the whole thing apart. He ended with this sorry mess. Now he realizes that he does not know everything about a radio, and that the only way his will play once more is to take it to an expert radio mechanic.

Many people are like this man. They are happy as long as everything runs smoothly. But when any trouble comes along, they think they can take care of it all by themselves. They think they know all the answers. So they try this and they try that, but everything fails. They find they are getting deeper and deeper into trouble. A Book of Instructions has been given to them, but like the man, they have put it aside and have forgotten it. So they become unhappy. They lose their temper. They say and do things which hurt others. There is only one way for them to put their lives back in tune, and that is to take their burdens to God in prayer. As an expert mechanic can take this pile of broken parts and rebuild a radio that will again play beautiful music, so God can take a broken, useless life and make it righteous and happy again. But we must first ask Him to help us. The only way we can talk to God is through prayer. And then we must read and follow His Book of Instructions—our Bible.

Story: THE MYSTERY OF OOLLA-WAKEE.

Shallee-Wan is a secluded village deep in the heart of the African jungles. About a century ago it was located on the rugged west coast. The natives were peace-loving and spent much of their time fishing. But one day white men came into their village, bringing much sorrow. They forced many young men and boys aboard their ship and carried them to a faraway land as slaves. Fearing the white men would return, the natives moved Shallee-Wan inland, away from the pleasant coastal waters. Each time word came to them that white men were anywhere near, they packed in haste and moved deeper and deeper into the jungles. Only a few of the very aged natives remembered the slave traders' visit. They had been boys too young to be carried away. But the fear of the white man had grown with each generation.

They were no longer the peace-loving Shallee-Wans. Each time they moved to a new location they met unfriendly tribes who claimed the land on which they settled. As time passed by, they, too, became a warring tribe. For several years there had been constant warfare between them and the Oolla-Wakees. Then suddenly the neighboring tribe withdrew and became silent. This aroused suspicion in Oke-Meteeka, so he sent scouts to spy on the enemy. Now the young chieftain sat silently, listening to their report.

"Everything seems so strange in Oolla-Wakee," said the first scout. "I can not tell Oke-Meteeka what it is. The people—they seem so different. I know not why."

"They are kind, Oke-Meteeka," added the second. "They are kind to each other. They seem happy. They even smile. It is all so strange."

"Did you see anything else?" inquired Oke-Meteeka.

"Yes, and that is even stranger," replied the first scout. "There is a new house in the village—the biggest one I have ever seen. People go in and out all day. Many go even at night. Some go in looking tired. Some look sad. Some look troubled. But they always come out smiling and happy."

Oke-Meteeka sat erect. "Tell me more!" he ordered.

"We saw no more," the second scout said sadly, shaking his head.

Oke-Meteeka could not sleep that night. He walked restlessly in the moonlight outside his straw hut. That is what his people needed— to be kind to each other, to smile, to be happy. His people had grown bitter and full of hate. His father before him had tried to lead them to happiness, but had failed. The painted medicine men had tried, but they had failed. Now he must try. There must be some secret about it. Some magic. That was it! There was some magic to happiness! And the Oolla-Wakees had found that magic. He must find it, too. He must make his people happy. He awakened the two scouts, exclaiming:

"Arise! Make ready! We shall depart at sunrise! We shall go to Oolla-Wakee and learn their magic!"

For four hours Oke-Meteeka and the two scouts laid motionless on a slight bluff overlooking Oolla-Wakee. It was all true, just as the scouts had said. Men and women went in and out of the big house all day. They always came out smiling and looking happy. Now even children were going in. The Oke-Meteeka sprang to his feet, his eyes wide with bewildered amazement. A white man had come out of the house! Now another! White men! He turned in fear and panic, his scouts close at his heels. The white men had come again! They must pack at once and move deeper into the jungle. After several fleeting steps he suddenly stopped. Something was wrong. If the white men were hurting the Oolla-Wakees, why were they so happy? Why were the children holding the white men by the hand? He crept back stealthily to his former position behind a clump of underbrush to watch more closely. After a while he stood up.

"Wait here," he told his scouts. "Oke-Meteeka will go and find the mystery. The white men are not harming the Oolla-Wakees. They seem kind. Watch here and come if I call."

Oke-Meteeka made his way cautiously between the rows of grass houses to the new big one built in a large clearing. He was very surprised to be recognized by several men, and then spoken to kindly. He grew tense when the chieftain of Oolla-Wakees suddenly stepped from his straw hut and held out his hand. "Greetings to you, my brother," he said. "I know why you come. You come to see white teachers. They do much for Oolla-Wakee. They will do much for Shallee-Wan, too."

"I have come to learn their magic," Oke-Meteeka said, "so I can take it back and give it to my people."

"Magic?" said Mo-Shobee, in surprise. "Ah, yes, it is a magic. The white teachers taught us about Jesus. Then they taught us to pray. And prayer is like magic. We pray when we are sick. We pray when we are sad. We pray when we are in trouble. We pray when we are afraid. And always God hears and makes us feel happy again. Come, Oke-Meteeka, I will take you to the white teachers."

It was the first time Oke-Meteeka looked into a white man's face. "His eyes are kind," he thought. "He will not harm my people."

Then in his native tongue he said to the missionary, "White teacher, teach me to pray."

Prayer Hymn: The first two verses of "Loving Father, God, Jehovah."

Prayer (by the teacher).

Offertory Service:

Jesus said, "Come unto me, all ye that labour and are heavy laden, and I will give you rest" (Matthew 11:28). He did not say "Come" only to the rich, or only to the powerful, or only to the famous. He said, "Come, all that labour and are heavy laden." That means you and it means me. It means our families and our friends. It means every one in this church. It means every one in this city. It means every one in the whole world. Jesus invites all of us to bring all our troubles, our fears, our wants, our hopes, our needs, to Him. Then, if we do, He promises to take them all from us and give us rest, which means peace, joy, and happiness.

When Jesus gives so much to us, how can we withhold our gifts from Him?

(Play "Willing Am I" while the offering is taken and during the short dedicatory prayer by one of the students.)

Adult Leader:

(Display the poster suggested in *Patterns for 52 Visual Lessons* and refer to it while you develop the following thoughts:)

Somehow we always appreciate the things we work for more than the things which are simply given to us without any effort on our part. That is why God, in His infinite wisdom, planned that we must do our part to have our prayers answered. You could pray night after night, that when you awakened in the morning you would find a beautiful red bicycle parked beneath your window, ready for your use. And morning after morning, you would awaken to find no bicycle. But if you wanted a bicycle and prayed that God would give you wisdom and strength to make the most of opportunities you might have to earn a bicycle, you would be praying as Jesus taught us to pray. Ask, seek, and knock, He said, "and it shall be opened unto you" (Matthew 7:7).

Ask. That means using our lips to pray. That means asking with a faithful, sincere heart. *Seek.* That means keeping our eyes open so we see the opportunities God sends to us as answers to our prayers. *Knock.* That means using our abilities, courage, wisdom, and determination to do our best and make the most of the opportunities God gives to us. *And it shall be opened unto you.* If we pray believing, if we keep our eyes open to the blessings God sends us, if we try earnestly to do our very best in every way each day, Jesus promises that our prayers will be answered.

(Have the pupils make "open door" folders as described in the book mentioned above.)

Benediction.

SERVICE NO. 20—MAY

Growing in Stature Through—

SPREADING HAPPINESS

He that hath mercy on the poor, happy is he.—Proverbs 14:21b.

Prelude: Have a group of students sing the verse of "He Keeps Me Singing," and a student duet sing the chorus.

Call to Worship:

For, lo, the winter is past, the rain is over and gone;
The flowers appear on the earth; and the time of the singing of birds is come (Song of Solomon 2:11, 12).
How great is our Father's love for us, His children here on earth!

Hymn of Praise: "I Love to Tell the Story."

Thoughts on the Theme: (*An object lesson by one of the students.*)

(Provide the student with a compass and a piece of white paper mounted on a piece of stiff cardboard. If possible, have the cardboard supported on an easel back, so the class can easily see the piece of white paper.)

As all of you know, a compass is used for drawing a circle. We can draw very small circles, or we can draw large circles, depending upon how wide we open the compass, how large the compass is, and the size of the paper we use. We can also make a very faint, uncertain circle by pressing very lightly, or we can make a heavy, even, permanent line by pressing harder as we move the compass around.

We are like this compass. The piece of paper is like the world in which we live. And the amount of happiness we bring to others is like the circles we draw with the compass on the paper. If we keep to ourselves, think only of ourselves, and do very little to help others, it is like drawing a very small circle on a very small piece of paper. The more happiness we spread, the bigger the circle becomes. And the bigger the circle becomes, the larger piece of paper we need. In other words, the more happiness we spread, the more friends we make, and the bigger our world becomes.

When we spread happiness half-heartedly, or for any reason other than love, it is like drawing a faint circle, for such kindnesses are not genuine and will not last long. But when we spread happiness out of love, it is like making a definite, permanent line that will not be easily erased.

To use a compass, we first put the pointed end at a certain place on the paper which later becomes the very center of the circle. Spreading happiness must begin in our homes, for our homes are the very centers of our lives.

Story: THE SUNSHINE MAN.

There we were, the six of us fellows, lined along the east side of Murdock's Lake, each holding fast to his favorite bamboo fishing pole, when a long, thin shadow suddenly fell between Sid and me. There was no mistaking that long, thin shadow. It was Mr. Murdock himself. I recognized him instantly from the description I had heard of him, and jerked my pole out of the water so quickly I almost lost the prize catch of the morning, a catfish bigger than any I had ever seen, let alone caught. There I stood as if I had suddenly turned to stone, the catfish dangling from my pole in midair. I did not have the courage to look around me, but everything had suddenly become so quiet, I knew the other fellows had also seen the shadow. Then I heard Mr. Murdock say, "That's a beautiful catch, son. Better pull it in or it will get away from you." I was slow to react, let me tell you! Finally, I did manage to land the fish, but that only added to my embarrassment, for there were two good-sized bass which I had already caught.

It had been a wonderful morning for fishing. None of us fellows had ever caught so many fish before. Without raising my head, I shifted my eyes to the right. What I saw made my cheeks turn a deeper red and my head spin like a top. Near Sid were three fish. Between Earl's bare feet were two fish. I glanced to the left of me and saw nothing but bare feet and fish. Then Mr. Murdock spoke again.

"What is your name, son?"

Without looking up, I knew he was talking to me.

"Peter," I said. "Peter Drake."

"You are quite a fisherman, Peter. Do you always have such luck?"

"No, sir," I said without much feeling. Somehow I did not expect him to believe me. "We have never been so lucky before!"

"Then why are you all looking so gloomy?" Mr. Murdock asked, glancing at each of us in turn. "Surely such a catch should make any Saturday morning a happy one."

"You have caught us fishing in your lake," I stammered, and looked at Carl. He always knew just what to say. As I expected him to do, Carl stepped forward, squared his shoulders, looked straight into Mr. Murdock's eyes, and said:

"We have been coming out here about once a month to fish in your lake. There is a low place in the stone wall near the big sycamore tree where we always crawl over. I suppose it will sound funny, but this is the first time we have caught so many fish. I guess there isn't anything else to say, Mr. Murdock. We know we should not fish here in your lake."

"Why not?" asked Mr. Murdock. His voice sounded—well, sort of gentle, but at the same time it was firm and clear.

"Because you do not allow any one to fish in your lake," Earl quickly replied.

"Who told you I do not allow any one to fish in my lake?"

"Why, every one in town," Carl said in surprise. "That is, every one in town *knows* you do not allow any fishing in your lake."

"What else does every one in town know about me?" Mr. Murdock asked, trying hard to hide a smile.

We all paused awkwardly. "Come, now," Mr. Murdock smiled as he looked from one to the other. "Tell me what else people say about me."

Nobody spoke. Then finally I began nervously, "Well, sir, people say you are—odd. They never see you about. That is, they never see you about during the day, but they see you prowling about during the night. Some people say they have not seen you for many years. And every one notices just one dim light burning in your big old mansion on top of the hill overlooking the lake. They say—" I stopped abruptly and my cheeks turned deep red. Even though I was just twelve years old, I knew there must be some mistake. The things I had heard about Mr. Murdock could not possibly apply to this kind-looking gentleman who stood smiling down at us. Mr. Murdock patted my shoulder and said, "Sit down. All of you. I want to tell you why I am never around here during the day. You see, I do not live here. I have not lived here for more than ten years. Have you boys ever heard of Bobtail Heights?"

We all assured him we knew Bobtail Heights was the Negro section of a near-by town. When Mr. Murdock said, "Well, boys, that is where I really live," our eyes and mouths popped open wide. And then he told us this story:

His father had been a doctor—and a good one, too. Because he came from a very wealthy family, it always bothered him when he saw any one in need. One day, he happened to be riding through Bobtail Heights when he noticed a crowd gathered around some object on a street corner. Feeling that some one might possibly be hurt and need help, Dr. Murdock jumped from his carriage, his black

SPREADING HAPPINESS 103

medical bag in hand. It was little Sammy, who had been run over by a large black carriage. The driver had not stopped. When Dr. Murdock said, "We must get him to a hospital at once," every one looked at him in great surprise. Then one old man said sadly, "Only white folk have hospitals. We ain't got no hospitals, sir. We ain't got no money." Dr. Murdock took little Sammy to his own home—the big old mansion overlooking the lake—and nursed him until he was well. After that, he went to Bobtail Heights two days every week and moved from house to house, taking care of the sick and cheering every one as he went along. One day a little old lady turned her dark face up to his and said:

"Do you know what we call you, Dr. Murdock? The sunshine man. For sunshine brings happiness everywhere it goes. And that's just what you do for us here in Bobtail Heights."

"Ten years ago my father died," Mr. Murdock said in his gentle way. "Since then I have been carrying on his work. The only difference is that I do not help the people at Bobtail Heights twice a week. I help them every day."

All of us sat as if petrified, looking up into the face of Dr. Murdock. Finally, I said, "That's why people never see you around town. You are never here."

Dr. Murdock smiled and nodded. "I come here one Saturday a month," he explained, "but I always arrive very early in the morning and leave again after dark."

"But the light in the window?" Sid questioned.

"And the person who walks around outdoors at night?" Carl asked.

"Oh, that's Sammy, the little boy who was run over the first day my father drove through Bobtail Heights. He is an old man now, but he still wants to carry on his work as gardener and caretaker of the old house up on the hill."

* * * *

I paused and looked across my desk at the young newspaper reporter who had been sent out to interview one (or all three) of us doctors who built the Sunshine Clinic in Bobtail Heights.

"Well," I said smilingly, "you wanted to know why we three doctors built this small hospital and why we named it the Sunshine Clinic. Sid, Carl, nor I would have become doctors had it not been for Dr. Murdock. We built this clinic in honor of the work started here by his father, and we carry on this work among the needy in honor of our dear friend, Dr. Murdock, who kept alive the sunshine started by the sunshine man."

Prayer Hymn: "I Gave My Life for Thee."

Prayer (by the teacher).

Offertory Service:

>Do you want to help spread gladness?
>   Do you want to spread the story
>Of the loving Christ, our Saviour,
>   Who arose in all His glory?
>Come, then, sing with hearts rejoicing!
>   Bring your gifts to show your love
>For God, our kind and loving Father,
>   Who sends blessings from above.

(Sing "Something for Jesus" while the offering is taken. Close with a short prayer of thanks by one of the students.)

Adult Leader:

(Display the poster described in *Patterns for 52 Visual Lessons* and refer to it as you develop the following thoughts:)

In order to have a garden we must decide, first of all, what we want to grow. Then we must plant the right seeds. We can not expect the right kinds of flowers or vegetables to grow unless we plant the right kinds of seeds. After the seeds are planted, we must water them. If we neglect to do so, the seeds will not grow.

Our lives are much like gardens. They are happy or unhappy, useful or useless, depending upon the kind of seeds we sow. If we plant happiness in our lives, love will be sure to grow *if* we water it carefully with co-operation, kindness, consideraton of others, willingness to help, friendliness, cheery words, and smiles. (If time permits, have pupils discuss these qualities, and add others to the list.)

After we plant a garden, we stick little signs in the ground so that we can know where we planted the seeds. Where shall we plant our seeds of happiness so love can grow? Yes, at home, at school, and at play. In fact, everywhere we go.

(Have the students make individual sprinkling can "Happy Birthday" folders; patterns are given in the book named above.)

Benediction.

SERVICE NO. 21—JUNE

Growing in Stature Through—

LOYALTY TO FRIENDS

Greater love hath no man than this, that a man lay down his life for his friends.—John 15:13.

Prelude: Have a group of students sing, "There Is No Friend Like Jesus."

Call to Woship:

As you join in worshiping the Lord;
> Let your heart therefore be perfect with the Lord our God, to walk in his statutes, and to keep his commandments, as at this day (1 Kings 8:61).

Hymn of Praise: "What a Friend."

Thoughts on the Theme: (An object lesson by one of the students.)

(Provide the student with two pieces of cloth and two small bowls of water. Use one piece of cloth dyed with fast colors and one with colors that fade. If no material can be found with colors that fade, dye a small piece, but do not rinse it thoroughly, so that much of the color will come out when put into the bowl of water.)

These two pieces of material are alike in many ways. First, they are both made of cotton. The weave is the same. That tells us they were both woven on the same kind of loom. They are the same size. They feel exactly the same. But there is one important way in which they are very different.

When I put this piece into this bowl of water, the water remains clear, and the color in the material remains the same. But when I put this piece of material into this bowl of water, it immediately begins to fade. See how discolored the water is already? The longer I leave the cloth in the water, the more the color will fade.

Our theme this morning is "Loyalty to Friends," or being a true friend, for loyalty means being true. These two pieces of cloth illustrate for us the difference between true friends and false friends. A true friend is steadfast and unchanging. A true friend is like this piece of material whose colors have remained the same. A false friend is like the other piece. He appears to be true until he is put to the test. Then, like this material that faded, he proves he is false. When I put this piece of material into the bowl, the water was clear and clean. Now it is discolored—it is no longer clear, it is no longer useful. That is the way a false friend spoils a friendship. Loyalty keeps a friendship clear and clean over a long period, just as this piece of cloth made of true colors will keep this water, no matter how long it remains in the bowl.

Story: WANTED: A TRUE FRIEND.

Really, you could have heard a pin drop. That is how quietly the twenty girls sat in the cooking room of Bradford Junior High. Miss Benson stood before the group with a stern, grave look upon her usually smiling face. The girls had never seen her look so serious. Her eyes kept moving from girl to girl. Always they returned to Elaine, who sat erect and motionless. Finally, after what seemed to the girls like hours, Miss Benson spoke in a strange-sounding, cold voice:

"This is the first time anything like this has happened in one of my classes. I hardly know what to say or do. Maxine's ring disappeared from the tray on the top of my desk. No one but you twenty girls were in this room with me. That is, no one other than the five visiting students from the university. I know none of them took the ring. In the first place, I know them all personally, and am, therefore, positive none of them would do such a thing. In the second place, they all merely passed the desk hurriedly. None of them stopped near the front of the desk long enough to remove anything from it. So one of you girls must have taken the ring. This makes me most unhappy. I have always felt I could trust all of you completely. I shall give you five more minutes. If the girl who has taken the ring comes forward now and confesses and returns the ring to Maxine, nothing more will be said about this unhappy affair. Otherwise, I shall have to take steps to find the guilty person."

Elaine sat as if carved from stone. Her hands were cold. Her face was pale. She could tell by the way Miss Benson was looking at her—half accusingly, half pleadingly—that she was thought the guilty one. But Elaine had not taken the ring. She had not even touched the ring. In fact, she had never touched a single thing on Miss Benson's desk.

It was a rule that all the girls had to remove their rings, bracelets, and watches upon entering the cooking room. They were always placed in the little metal tray on the top of Miss Benson's desk until the cooking lesson was over. As Miss Benson had said, no one other than the five visiting students had been in the room with them. These five students came once a month to listen to Miss Benson teach and to watch the girls cook. They were preparing to teach cooking, and these visits were part of their university training. Elaine had seen the five young women pass Miss Benson's desk. They had passed too hurriedly to even notice the rings, let alone take one from the tray. Elaine knew that of all those in the room that afternoon, she had the best opportunity to take the ring. Her cooking unit was directly in front of Miss Benson's desk. She could easily open her unit drawer with one hand and reach anything on the top of Miss Benson's desk with the other. No one else had been near the desk that period.

"This is your last chance, girls," Miss Benson was saying in a strained voice. She paused and looked pleadingly at Elaine. No one stirred. Then Miss Benson said wearily, "You may all be dismissed but Elaine. Elaine, I would like to see you alone."

Miss Benson did everything in a quiet, gentle way. It was plain to be seen how unhappy she was to question Elaine. But to all her questions and pleadings Elaine would only say, "I did not take Maxine's ring, Miss Benson. I did not even touch it."

The next morning Elaine found herself an outcast. The few girls who replied to her "good morning" did so coolly, and then turned away abruptly. Even her own particular chums hurried away from her while passing to the various classes. As the morning went by, the lump in her throat grew bigger. When the noon lunch bell finally rang, Elaine was ready to hurry off by herself and cry. Then she felt a friendly arm across her shoulders.

"Come, eat lunch with me," Sharon said with a smile so warm and so friendly Elaine's eyes filled with tears. That began a lasting friendship between the two girls. Sharon was the most popular girl in the class, but she deserted all other friends during the school hours. She walked to and from school with Elaine, ate lunch with her, and was with her every possible moment during the day.

A month passed by. The five young women from the university again visited the cooking class. They stood with Miss Benson in a corner, chatting quietly as the girls made their first recipe of bran muffins.

"I enjoy watching the girls work," Dorthea Grayson was saying. "Each one does the same thing in a different way."

"I find the girl nearest to Miss Benson's desk the most interesting," Natlie Henderson said.

"So do I," agreed Hazel Rutland. "She does everything in such a neat, efficient way. She must be a good student."

"Yes, she is," Miss Benson said with a frown. "I—I—I have been greatly disturbed about her recently. A most unfortunate thing happened a while ago. In fact, exactly a month ago today. Shortly after you girls left the room last month, we discovered a ring was missing from my desk."

"A ring!" cried Marilyn McCall.

"What kind of ring was it?" asked Ruby Hudson, excitedly.

"Why, I really do not know exactly," Miss Benson answered with a puzzled frown.

"Please call the girl who lost the ring," Marilyn said as she opened her bag and drew out her small coin purse.

Miss Benson beckoned Maxine to them.

"It was a yellow-gold ring," Maxine described, in answer to Miss Benson's question. "It had a red stone."

"How was the stone fastened to the ring?" Marilyn asked.

"With prongs," Maxine explained. "One of the prongs was loose. In fact, that is why I wore the ring to school that day. I was supposed to drop it off at the jeweler's on my way home."

Marilyn eagerly opened her coin purse and pulled out the ring.

"How stupid of us not to have asked Miss Benson about it immediately!" exclaimed Grace Morgan.

After hearing Marilyn's story, Miss Benson requested her to tell it to all the girls in the class. They sat upon their round kitchen stools and listened attentively.

"When we visited the class last month, I was wearing a dress with a stole which is edged with soft wool fringe," Marilyn began. "I was warm when I entered the building, so I took off the stole and carried it over my arm the rest of the afternoon. When we left here, we rode the bus downtown. Then we had a bite to eat in a little sandwich shop. I then left the other girls and went to the library. After spending an hour in several different departments, I took a bus home. After dinner that evening I went to a meeting and wore the stole. It was not until I was home again, folding the stole to put it away, that I discovered the ring. I called the four other girls immediately. They were as amazed as I, and none of them had the slightest idea when or how the ring became fastened to the wool fringe. We all watched the lost-and-found column in the papers the next week. Then I went to the sandwich shop and the library and left word that I had the ring if the owner was found. It did not occur to any of us that I picked up the ring here. Apparently, when I passed Miss Benson's desk the stole over my arm brushed the tray and the loose prong caught in the soft wool fringe."

Of course, every one was sorry that Elaine had been wrongly suspected. But Elaine shook her head and said, "I am not sorry it happened. For I have never had such a wonderful friend as Sharon.

But more than that, this experience taught me how much loyalty to a friend means. Really, girls, I am glad it happened—glad it happened to me."

Prayer Hymn: Sing softly "I Must Tell Jesus."

Prayer (by the teacher).

Offertory Service:

At the opening of this service we sang, "What a Friend We Have in Jesus." When we think what a wonderful friend He really is to all of us at all times, we realize more fully what a wonderful gift God gave to the world when He sent His Son. "Thanks be to God for his unspeakable gift" (2 Corinthians 9:15). How can we do otherwise than give our best to Him?

(Play softly "What a Friend" while the offering is taken. Conclude with a short dedicatory prayer by one of the students.)

Adult Leader:

(Display the poster described in *Patterns for 52 Visual Lessons* and use it as you develop the following thoughts:)

When you look into the mirror, what do you see? Do you merely see the color of your hair? The color of your eyes? The shape of your face? The kind of expression you happen to be wearing? Or do you sometimes try to see yourself as others see you?

It is a good thing for all of us to take time once in a while to examine ourselves critically and look for our own shortcomings and faults. It is a good thing for us to ask ourselves questions like these: What kind of friend am I? Am I patient? Am I steadfast? Do I control my temper? Am I honestly trying to be a better Christian every day?

The very next time you are near a mirror,

> Stop and look yourself in the eye,
> And ask, "What kind of friend am I?
> Am I sincere and loyal and true?"
> Now really—what kind of friend are *you?*

Benediction.

SERVICE NO. 22—JUNE

Growing in Stature Through—

MEEKNESS

Blessed are the meek: for they shall inherit the earth.—Matthew 5:5.

Prelude: "Jesus, Meek and Gentle" sung as a solo.

Call to Worship:

    Leader: Who shall seek the Lord?

    Students: *Seek ye the Lord, all ye meek of the earth, which have wrought his judgment; seek righteousness, seek meekness* (Zephaniah 2:3).

Hymn of Praise: "More Like the Master."

Introduction by One of the Teachers:

Jesus said, "Blessed are the meek: for they shall inherit the earth." If meekness were not so important—or if it were not important for us to develop meekness in our everyday life—surely Jesus would not have mentioned it so definitely.

Meekness includes three important things: (1) Being mild of temper or controlling temper; (2) being patient at all times; (3) being long-suffering or showing love for others even in the face of wrongs done to us.

Today we shall think about the first of these three—controlling temper.

Thoughts on the Theme: (*An object lesson by one of the students.*)

(Supply the student with a rubber band.)

Here is a rubber band. First of all, it was made to use. Next, it was made in such a way that it can be stretched just a little, quite a bit, or until it breaks. Sometimes when it breaks it hurts or stings the person who may be holding it. Sometimes when it breaks it flies out of control and hurts any one who happens to be standing near by. Our tempers are just like rubber bands. First of all, they were made to use. That is, God gave to each of us minds of our own. If we had no minds of our own, or if we did not use them, we would be like dolls—without the ability to think. We would be perfectly willing to do anything any one told us to do, whether it was right or wrong.

When we stretched the rubber band just a little, it did not break.

No one was hurt. And it went right back into shape, ready to be used again. When we stretched the rubber band too far, it broke. Perhaps we just hurt or stung our own fingers. Perhaps the rubber band flew out of our hands as it broke and hurt some one near by. When we lose our tempers we not only hurt ourselves, but we often hurt those about us. When a rubber band is once broken, we can only repair it by tying both ends together with a knot. Of course, this knot will always be seen, and the more we break the rubber band the more knots appear. Every time we lose our temper, it is like tying a knot on our heart. Perhaps we feel that we can hide those knots from others, but nothing can be hidden from the eyes of God.

Story: THE PORCELAIN VASE.

There was a tense moment when Theodore looked wildly around the room for a handy object. Then there were several loud crashes—the vase he hurled across the room struck the lamp, which fell against the wall with enough force to jar the mirror from its hook and send it smashing on the floor. Instantly a strange quietness settled upon the whole house. It seemed that even the clock stopped ticking. Then suddenly, without the slightest sound, Mother's quiet form appeared in the doorway. Without a word she looked across the living room to the smashed vase, the overturned lamp, and the broken mirror. As Mother's eyes lingered on the scattered pieces of the fine porcelain scattered on the rug, Theodore suddenly realized what he had done. He had broken the porcelain vase! The lamp shade could probably be straightened and the mirror could be replaced, but the porcelain vase—there would never be another one just like it.

His great-great-grandmother had brought that vase from England when, as a young girl, she had crossed the ocean to find a new home in a new world. Her parents had told her there would be only room for clothing. Everything else had to be left behind. But Great-great-grandmother Candis had managed to conceal the porcelain vase in the small bag allotted for her belongings. Years later, as a pioneer mother, she packed the porcelain vase again. This time it did not cross an ocean in a sailboat, but it crossed the rugged Allegheny Mountains in a jostling covered wagon. It remained in the log cabin in the Hocking River Valley until Theodore's great-grandmother, Lucinda, carefully packed it in one of the sturdy flour barrels. Again it was placed in a covered wagon. This time it took a long trip westward—across the Mississippi. It was one of the few pieces Theodore's grandmother had saved when a violent tornado destroyed their prairie home. Because of its history, his mother was especially fond of that porcelain vase.

Now it lay on the living-room rug, a hopeless pile of jagged pieces.

After what seemed to Theodore an hour, he finally had the courage to look at his mother's quiet face.

"If only Mother would say something," he thought. "If only she would scold me or punish me." Finally, he managed to stammer, "I—I—I am sorry, Mother. I—I—I am very, very sorry."

"When you lost your temper and broke the garage window, you said you were sorry. When you lost your temper and hit your younger sister with your book, you said you were sorry. When you lost your temper and spoke disrespectfully to your teacher at school, you said you were sorry. Yesterday morning you lost your temper at breakfast and upset your glass of milk. You said you were sorry. Now, because I said you could not play baseball until you studied the spelling words you missed at school today, you have broken my beautiful porcelain vase.

"You always *say* you are sorry, but you never *act* as if you are sorry! I am afraid I can not believe you until you prove that you are truly sorry by trying to overcome your terrible temper.

"Pick up every piece of the porcelain vase. Carry them to your room. You may not play baseball again until you have glued these pieces together. And if I were you," Mother added, as she noticed Theodore's cheeks growing crimson, as they always did just before he lost his temper, "I would think twice before I broke anything else. From now on, you shall have to repair everything you break as a result of losing your temper before you may play with the baseball team again."

Left alone, Theodore hurriedly gathered together all the pieces and carried them to his room. He would glue the vase together in a hurry, he told himself. He simply had to get to the playground as soon as possible. The team would be waiting for him. But after an hour of steady work, he became cross and impatient. It would take forever to get all those pieces glued together. It was just like gluing the pieces of a complicated jigsaw puzzle together. Why did Mother want the old vase anyway? He would save all the money he earned running Mrs. Markham's errands and buy Mother a bigger and prettier one. But Mother shook her head when he made such a suggestion.

"No," she said. "You may not play baseball until you have glued together my porcelain vase."

The next two weeks were unhappy ones for Theodore. He started by working for an hour each day, fitting the pieces together. But it was such slow work he soon became impatient. He could hear the voices of the other players as they practiced in the vacant lot across the street. He wondered who was taking his place. Finally, he became so angry with himself for having broken the vase, with his mother for insisting that he glue it together again, and with the team for playing without him, that he lost his temper. With one big sweep of his right hand and arm he sent the broken pieces flying across his room. That happened three times, but it only meant that he had to begin all over again. Then he began to realize that if he spent two afternoons piecing the vase together and then in a fit of temper threw them all on the floor, he would never get finished. Soon he found he was able to sit in his room and work for a whole hour without becoming impatient even once. Then he began to make real progress. The pieces glued together were beginning to look like the porcelain vase. And then—after weeks of steady work and no baseball—Theodore glued the last piece in place. He could hardly wait until the next day when the glue would be dry and the vase could be taken downstairs.

Mother looked up from her book as Theodore entered the living room. She smiled at him as he carefully placed the patched vase in her lap.

"Put it in its place on the top of the bookcase," she said. "Then I can enjoy looking at it once more."

Theodore proudly crossed the room, and, handling the vase very carefully, he placed it on the bookcase. He stepped back to get a better look. Then suddenly his eyes widened and his lips trembled.

"Oh, Mother!" he cried. "It isn't pretty any more. I can see every place I glued it. It just looks like an ugly, cracked old vase!"

"To me the vase is more beautiful than ever," Mother said. "Every time I look at it I shall not see the cracks and the glued pieces. I shall see your changed disposition. When you smashed the vase you were an impatient, ill-tempered boy who always wanted his own way about everything. As you glued the pieces together you developed patience and obedience. But most of all, you learned how to control your temper. That is why I say, to me the vase is more beautiful than ever."

Prayer Hymn: " 'Tis the Blessed Hour of Prayer."

Prayer (by the teacher).

Offertory Service:

Jesus said, "Lay not up for yourselves treasures upon earth, where moth and rust doth corrupt, and where thieves break through and steal: but lay up for yourselves treasures in heaven, where neither moth nor rust doth corrupt, and where thieves do not break through nor steal" (Matthew 6:19, 20).

The only way we can lay up for ourselves treasures in heaven is through obedience to God's Word. That means showing our love for Jesus through kindnesses done to others and through sharing so that God's kingdom on earth will continue to grow.

(Play "His Love for Me" while the offering is taken. Conclude with a dedicatory prayer by one of the students.)

Adult Leader:

As we said at the beginning of this service, meekness means three different things—being mild-tempered or controlling temper; being patient under injuries or in the face of wrongs done to us; being longsuffering or showing love at all times. Today we are studying the first meaning, meekness. We shall study the other two parts the next two weeks.

We can not be meek and at the same time have a violent or bad temper. In both the Old and the New Testaments we find the promise that the meek shall inherit the earth. (Have one student read Psalm 37:11 and another one read Matthew 5:5.)

Draw the following puzzle on the blackboard. If none is available, use a piece of poster paper. When the proper letters are filled in the squares (up and down), the letters in the heavy box (across) will spell MEEKNESS. Make a game of it. Ask the question and give the Biblical reference. The first one with the correct answer scores one for his side. Write the letters in the proper squares before asking the next question.

1. Which man was very meek? Numbers 12:3. (Moses.)
2. What shall the meek do and be satisfied? Psalm 22:26. (Eat.)
3. What shall the meek inherit? Psalm 37:11. (Earth.)
4. As the elect of God, we are to put on bowels of mercies, ..., humbleness of mind, meekness, longsuffering. Colossians 3:12. (Kindness.)
5. We are to show meekness unto all men and to speak evil of .... man. Titus 3:2. (No.)
6. With what shall God reprove the meek of the earth? Isaiah 11:4. (Equity.)
7. God arose to judgment, to .... all the meek of the earth. Psalm 76:9. (Save.)
8. With what will God beautify the meek? Psalm 149:4. (Salvation.)

(Have the students make the folder described in *Patterns for 52 Visual Lessons.*)

Benediction.

SERVICE No. 23—JUNE

Growing in Stature Through—

PATIENCE

In your patience possess ye your souls.—Luke 21:19.

Prelude: "Holy, Holy, Holy."

Call to Worship:

> O come, let us worship and bow down: let us kneel before the Lord our maker (Psalm 95:8).
> For the Lord is great, and greatly to be praised (Psalm 96:4).

Hymn of Praise: "In the Garden."

Thoughts on the Theme: (*An object lesson by one of the students.*)

(Provide the student with a piece of chalk and a blackboard. A portable blackboard on an easel will do.)

BIBLE ARITHMETIC

All of us understand simple problems in addition. For instance, if we put down a column of figures like this:

$$\begin{array}{r} 248 \\ 10 \\ 2{,}100 \\ 9 \\ 500 \\ \hline 2{,}867 \end{array}$$

and added them together correctly, we would find the answer is 2,867. But if we made just one mistake in our addition, then we would not have the correct or true answer.

Now let us work a problem in Bible arithmetic. Let us turn to 2 Peter 1:5-7 for the points to be added. (Read aloud these verses.) We are to add virtue to our faith. Faith, then, is our first point; virtue, our second. To virtue we are to add knowledge; to knowledge, temperance; to temperance, patience; to patience, godliness; to godliness, brotherly kindness; and to brotherly kindness, charity. (List each point as mentioned.)

115

FAITH
VIRTUE
KNOWLEDGE
TEMPERANCE
PATIENCE
GODLINESS
KINDNESS
CHARITY

A CHRISTIAN LIFE

If we start out with faith and add each of these things to our faith, we shall truly lead a Christian life. But, like the problem we just worked with numerals, if we fail to add any one of these to our life, we will not arrive at the correct answer. Or, in other words, we will not lead a truly Christian life.

It is easy for all of us to understand $2 + 2 = 4$.

Now let us work that out in Bible arithmetic.

A Christian life = living for Jesus.

Living for Jesus = receiving His promises.

In his letter to the Hebrews, Paul wrote, "For ye have need of patience, that, after ye have done the will of God, ye might receive the promise" (Hebrews 10:36). When we live a Christian life we are doing the will of God. Then we are told all we need is the patience to wait for God to send His promises to us.

Story: THE LITTLE BIRD WHO WOULD NOT GIVE UP.

It had been a birthday present from Aunt Clara and Uncle Ted. The day it arrived, Gerald was the happiest boy on the street. All the makings of a model airplane! And such a big one, too! When he would finish building it, he would invite all the other fellows in to look at it. It would easily be twice as big as Marty's. And even the one Joe just finished building would not compare with this one.

He hurried home from school the next day, eager to begin the assembling. He was too impatient to start putting it together to unpack the many pieces carefully. Instead, he poked and jabbed around in the box, trying to find the proper parts. It was slow work, for there were so many pieces, each a different shape and size. Finally, he decided it was too big a job. He wanted to build it all right, but it would take him too long. He would rather go bicycling instead.

He was about to open the garage door to get out his bike when a little bird caught his eye. The bird was trying to drag a piece of straw more than twice his size. He would jerk his head vigorously to move the straw a fraction of an inch. Then he would take a few staggering steps backward. Again and again he jerked his head, and again and again he staggered backward, each time gaining a few small paces. Then Gerald spied the beginning of a nest in the lower branches of a small tree. He quietly sank into the grassy lawn near the side of the garage to watch the little bird. Just then the end of the straw which had been dragging on the ground became caught under a stone.

"Now he will have to give up," Gerald thought. "He will never be able to pull the straw loose."

But the little bird did pull the straw loose, although he fell backward to the ground several times before he succeeded. Each time he scrambled to his feet with more determination than before. After several unsuccessful attempts, he finally succeeded in carrying the straw the short distance from the ground to the lower limb. At last it was safely woven into the nest.

"Now he will probably rest," Gerald thought. Instead, the little bird flew directly to a chicken feather which he must have seen while pulling the straw. He held it securely between his bill and again started toward the nest.

Gerald was so intent in watching the little bird that he did not notice a stray cat sneaking slyly toward the nest. With one nimble leap the cat sprang toward the bird, only to find the bird too quick for him. Leaving the feather behind, the bird flew to a top branch of a near-by tree. Just then a very large neighboring dog spied the cat, that was now sitting quietly watching the bird. The next moment the dog barked and the cat hissed. She stood with arched back as the dog circled around her, barking and snapping. Then the cat sprang at the dog, but missed him. As the dog leaped aside, his bushy tail swept across the lower branch and scattered the half-built nest on the ground under the tree. The cat suddenly disappeared, and after a few low, gruff growls, the dog continued calmly on his way.

"Oh, the poor little bird!" cried Gerald. "After all his hard work, his nest is ruined! Whatever will he do now?"

When the dog was at a safe distance the little bird came fluttering down. He walked up and down under the young tree, chirping mournfully. Then, without wasting more time, he started toward the large piece of straw and patiently began his long, hard pull once more. Piece by piece was carried back to rebuild the nest.

As Gerald pedaled down the street he kept thinking about the little bird. "He just would not give up," he thought. "No matter what happened, he tried again." Gerald intended to turn right at the corner. Instead, he turned around and started toward home. "If that little bird can do it, so can I," he thought. "He just would not give up, and neither will I."

Mother had to call Gerald twice for dinner that night. When she asked what was so interesting in his room, Gerald replied, "My airplane."

"But I thought you said you could not put it together," she said, looking very pleased.

"I couldn't," Gerald answered, "until I took a lesson from a little bird who would not give up."

Prayer Hymn: "I Must Tell Jesus." Sing first verse softly as the prayer hymn, and the second verse as the prayer response.

Prayer (by the teacher).

Offertory Service:

The earth is the Lord's, and the fulness thereof; the world, and they that dwell therein (Psalm 24:1).

When we bring our offerings to God, we are merely returning to Him that which He already owns, but has permitted us to use and enjoy. Let us bring these gifts to God now.

(Play "Holy Is the Lord" while the offering is taken. Conclude with a dedicatory prayer by one of the students.)

Adult Leader:

In a great many schools today the students participate each year in a track meet. Often a special athletic field is planned, not only where track meets may be held, but where students may practice the various sports. The reason we practice anything—including high jumping, broad jumping, pole vaulting, and racing—is to become more perfect. Or, in other words, to overcome any difficulties which keep us from being the very best.

At some athletic events there are obstacle races. A number of various objects are placed in the path of the runners. In order to win such a race, the runners must be trained to overcome these obstacles.

In his letter to the Hebrews, Paul gave advice concerning running a race. He said, "Let us lay aside every weight, and the sin which doth so easily beset us, and let us run with patience the race that is set before us" (Hebrews 12:1). Let us think about some of the weights which keep us from becoming good Christians. (Refer to the poster described in *Patterns for 52 Visual Lessons*. Encourage students to name other undesirable traits which act as obstacles to righteousness.)

Benediction.

SERVICE NO. 24—JUNE

Growing in Stature Through—

LOVE

And now abideth faith, hope, and love,* these three; but the greatest of these is love.—1 Corinthians 13:13.

Prelude: "He Is Love" played softly.

Call to Worship:
>If you love the Lord with all your heart,
>*The Lord shall preserve thee from all evil: he shall preserve thy soul. The Lord shall preserve thy going out and thy coming in from this time forth, and even for evermore* (Psalm 121:7, 8).
>Come and let us worship Him.

Hymn of Praise: "Love Divine."

Thoughts on the Theme: (*An object lesson by one of the students.*)

>(Provide the student with two spoons—a sterling-silver one kept beautiful through constant use, and a plated one badly tarnished.)

One of these spoons is sterling silver, the other one is not. All of you, I am sure, can tell which is the real silver and which is the imitation silver. Yes, this is the real-silver spoon. However, if we would put this sterling-silver spoon away and did not use it for a long time, it would lose its shine and loveliness. Soon it would become dull and tarnished, too. The reason this spoon remains shining is because it is used all the time.

This silver-plated spoon was once shining, too. Strangely enough, it lost its beauty and shine through use. Now, as you see, it is so tarnished and discolored no one cares to use it. The reason this spoon lost its beauty through use is that it was not made of pure or genuine silver. When it was new, perhaps some people mistook it for sterling silver.

The love we give to God is much like these two spoons. When we pretend we love God by coming to Bible school and church, but do not follow His Word throughout the week, we are like this silver-plated spoon. We can fool people at first by pretending our love for God is real and genuine. But soon people will see that we do not follow Jesus outside the church. They will realize that our love is not true and genuine. The selfish and unkind things we do and the

---
* For this word, use the reading of the American Standard Version "love," rather than "charity" of the Authorized Version.

untruths we say will make our love for God look as tarnished as this discolored spoon. Just as no one wants to use this spoon, so no one will want to be with us.

When we show our love for God through loving kindnesses done to those about us each day, we are like this sterling-silver spoon. The more we do for others the more beautiful our love for God will grow. And the more our love for God grows the more we shall want to do for others. So, you see, the more we use our love—or the greater love we show for others—the more sincere and genuine will be our love for God.

Story: THE POTTED RED GERANIUM.

To the little potted red geranium, the world had been filled with happiness and beauty until she was taken from the greenhouse and placed on the display counter in the florist's shop. Her four blossoms were such a cheerful, bright red, and her many shapely leaves were so green and fresh-looking, the florist placed her upon a raised display standard in the very center of the counter. A few moments later the little geranium received her first great disappointment.

Two smartly dressed young women entered the shop and stood directly in front of the counter.

"Frankly, I don't feel like sending her even a dandelion," the first one said. "What has she ever done for us?"

"I know," the second one replied. "I feel the same way. But we are expected to send her something. After all, she is our boss."

The little red geranium sat as if petrified. Up until this very moment she had thought the whole world was filled with nothing but love. The workers in the greenhouse had all been so kind and thoughtful, it was a severe shock to the little flower to suddenly realize that all people did not love each other and that every deed was not done out of love. The four beautiful blossoms blushed a deeper red at the remarks they had overheard. They were still whispering their surprise and disappointment when an important-looking businessman rushed in.

"Can you get out a rush order for me, Tom?" he exclaimed hurriedly. "A new bakery is opening on Main Street today. I wasn't going to send them any flowers because I didn't think I would ever get an order out of them. But they just phoned one in. So can you send them a basket of flowers with a card saying I wish them success? No, you had better use my business card to be sure they know I sent it. Business is business, you know."

This was too much for the red geranium. Her four blossoms began to droop and her leaves felt limp and weak. Was the whole world filled with selfish people? Didn't any one do anything out of love? Her blossoms half closed in shame.

A middle-aged woman was the next customer. She handed the florist a slip of paper with three calling cards attached.

"Will you please send a little plant to each of these three women?" she asked. "Nothing expensive. I am running for president of our club, and I want to keep my name before the important leaders."

Upon hearing this, the four blossoms closed tightly and the leaves hung as if lifeless from the slender stems.

"Oh! Oh!" sobbed the little red geranium. "And to think I was so happy when I left the greenhouse this morning. I was so sure I would at last be a part of this beautiful world! Now I find it all so different. What if I had been sent to the young women's boss? I would have withered from shame to think I was sent without love. Or what if I had been sent to the bakery only because the man wanted more orders? Or what if I had been sent to one of the three women just because the other one wants to be president of her club? Oh, I am so unhappy. I shall not open my beautiful blooms again until I find true love once more."

So the little red geranium grew more limp and more wilted as the morning went by. The young man who wanted flowers sent to an aunt he did not like just because she was rich and he hoped she would will him some of her money, made the little plant feel worse. So did the woman who wanted a flower sent to a sick neighbor, not because she loved the neighbor, but because she was afraid people would talk about her if she did not. By noon the potted geranium looked so wilted the florist was greatly concerned.

"Whatever has happened?" he wondered. "It was such a beautiful flower this morning!" He gave it a drink of cool water and paused beside it between every customer that afternoon. But every time he looked at the little geranium it seemed more lifeless. Then four children entered the florist's shop, speaking in quiet voices. When they held out a quarter and said they wanted to buy a plant, the florist shook his head slowly.

"I have no plants for a quarter," he told them gently. "You see, all of these plants cost much more. Go home and get more money, then I shall be glad to sell you any one you like."

"This is all we have," the little girl with bangs said sadly, "and we wanted to buy a flower for our teacher."

"She is sick," said the little girl wearing glasses, "and we miss her very much."

"She is so kind to all of us," said the freckled-face little girl. "Every one loves her."

"Haven't you a little flower we could have for a quarter?" asked the little red-haired girl. "One tiny little flower no one else will want? Just one?"

The florist slowly shook his head. Then he said, "Wait. Maybe I have one. How about this little red geranium? It was the most beautiful flower that came from the greenhouse this morning, but it looks a little wilted now."

The four little girls eagerly gathered around the little plant.

"What beautiful red blossoms!" said the one.

"And look how many leaves it has!" said another.

"Maybe it just needs sunshine. If we take very good care of it over the week end, surely it will be beautiful by Monday. Then we can take it to Miss Morgan after school."

"We could put it out in the sunshine every day," the little freckled-faced girl said, "and bring it in every night to be sure nothing happened to it."

"And we could water it carefully," added the little girl wearing glasses.

The little geranium was so happy she could hardly keep her blossoms closed. At last! At last she would be able to help make this world a beautiful place! It was hard to keep from lifting her blossoms and smiling beautifully once more. She wanted to straighten her stems and stretch her leaves upward again. She waited, trembling, while the florist placed the quarter in the cash register and handed her to the four little girls.

The little girls hovered over her so lovingly, she could not wait another moment. Just as the little girls opened the door, she raised her four crimson blooms and smiled into their happy faces.

The little girls screamed in delight. Their wishes had come true, sure enough! No one could ever have imagined any prettier geranium than this one!

"Look! Look!" they cried. "The blossoms have opened. It is beautiful!"

"Well, I declare!" the florist exclaimed in great surprise. "I never saw anything like this before. I guess all it needed was a little fresh air."

But the little potted red geranium knew better. It was not a little fresh air she needed. It was a great deal of love.

Prayer Hymn: Have the first verse of "I Must Tell Jesus" sung softly as a solo before the prayer. Sing the second verse in unison as a prayer response.

Prayer (by the teacher).

Offertory Service:

Leader: *What shall I render unto the Lord for all his benefits toward me?* (Psalm 116:12).

Group: *Vow, and pay unto the Lord your God: let all that be round about him bring presents unto him that ought to be feared* (Psalm 76:11).

(After the offering is taken have sentence prayers of thanks by the students.)

Adult Leader:

(Use the fan poster described in *Patterns for 52 Visual Lessons,* as you develop the following thoughts.)

This is the time of year when we think of all kinds of fans to help keep us cool. Some fans are the spreading kind made of several parts which open. These fans are not very effective if we try to use them closed. If we open them just a little, they create more breeze when we move them back and forth than the closed fan created, but they are still not as effective as if we opened them all the way. The wider we open a fan the more useful it becomes, for the larger the space it cools.

Love works the same way. The more love we give the more lives we touch, and the more happiness we create. We can not get the full benefit of a fan until we have opened it as wide as possible. We can not do our whole part in building God's kingdom on earth unless we open our hearts wide and show our love for Christ through our deeds of love to every one we meet each day. (Have the students make the booklet described in the book mentioned above.)

Benediction.

SERVICE NO. 25—JULY

Growing in Stature Through—

TRUSTWORTHINESS

I therefore . . . beseech you that ye walk worthy of the vocation wherewith ye are called.—Ephesians 4:1.

Prelude: "I'm Trusting My All in His Hands."

Call to Worship:

    Leader: How long shall the Word of God remain? How long shall the Word of God endure?

    Students: *The grass withereth, the flower fadeth: but the word of our God shall stand for ever* (Isaiah 40:8).

Hymn of Praise: "Where He Leads Me."

Thoughts on the Theme: (*An object lesson by one of the students.*)

    (Provide the student with two electric toasters—one automatic, the other nonautomatic.)

To toast bread in this toaster you must place a piece inside. Then you must watch it closely. If you walk away or turn your back for a moment, the bread will burn. That means the toast is wasted and there is an unpleasant odor of burned bread in the kitchen.

But this automatic toaster is different. You put your bread into these slots, turn on the electric current, and forget all about it. The toaster goes right ahead and toasts the bread. When the bread is ready, the toaster automatically shuts off and pushes the toast out at the top, ready for use. No one needs to watch this toaster to see that it does the job right.

Some people are like this first toaster. When they are given jobs to do, some one must stand over them and watch them carefully or they will not do the work right. They can not be trusted to perform properly when left alone even for a minute.

Some people are like the automatic toaster. When they are given a job to do, they go right ahead on their own and work quietly and thoroughly. No one needs to watch over them. They do their work quickly and well.

People who are like *this* toaster are unreliable. They can not be trusted. But people who are like *this* toaster are reliable and dependable. They prove themselves worthy of trust. Therefore, we call them *trustworthy.*

If your toaster, even the automatic one, suddenly will not work, you lose your confidence in it. You have it repaired, but you never again are quite as confident that it will do its job. Covet that word *trustworthy* for yourself.

Story: GRANDFATHER LOREY'S WILL.

Grandfather Lorey rocked gently in his big wicker rocking chair in the shade of the sycamore tree. Jim and Dave sat on the grass near by. He had been talking to his grandsons for a long time. Finally he said:

"Well, boys, do you understand my orders? You are both to spend two hours every day dusting the books in my library in town."

"Yes, Grandfather," the two young men answered in unison.

"I can trust you both, then, to follow out my orders?"

"Yes, Grandfather," they said again.

Grandfather Lorey often requested his two grandsons to spend the week end with him at his country home. He would sit with the two in the shade of a tree and talk to them about honesty, responsibility, and the importance of always being fair.

"You are no longer boys," he would say. "You are young men— young men who are ready to start out in life. It is important for you to start out on the right road. You must prove yourselves to be trustworthy at all times."

Grandfather Lorey was an old man—almost eighty-five—but his mind was sharp and keen. He had sold his business and retired to his country home. The big house in town with wide stairways and rambling rooms had been closed for several years. The first floor of the entire east wing was a huge library, for Grandfather Lorey was a lover of books. These were the books Jim and Dave had promised to dust.

"This is the craziest thing I ever heard of," Jim declared as he and Dave entered the quiet, deserted town house. "Why in the world does he want his books dusted?"

"Nothing matters to us but that we promised Grandfather we would," Dave replied, leading the way down the wide hall to the library.

"Sometimes I wonder about Grandfather. It will take us a year to dust every book in his library!" Jim groaned.

"It does not make any difference how long it takes. We said we would spend two hours each day dusting. That is all that matters to me."

Jim dusted listlessly about a half hour. Then he tossed his cloth onto the large mahogany desk and said:

"That's enough for me. Wake me up when the two hours are over."

With that he stretched out on the leather couch between the tall windows and dozed off to sleep. Dave went right on dusting.

"You are foolish, Dave," Jim said the next day. "Grandfather Lorey has not left his country house for the past five years. He will never know if we dusted these fool books or not. This is just a silly whim of his."

"It makes no difference," Dave insisted. "We promised we would carry out his orders."

Weeks passed by. Jim had formed the habit of arriving late and then stretching out on the leather couch to spend the remaining time reading or napping. Months passed by, and Grandfather Lorey became ill. When Jim was told the doctor ordered Grandfather to remain in bed, he stopped going to the library altogether. Now that Grandfather had to remain in bed, there was no chance of his deciding to drop in and surprise them one afternoon.

"You are foolish to keep going there and dusting those old books," he told Dave. "It is just a waste of time. Besides, Grandfather has forgotten all about our making that silly promise."

But Dave shook his head.

"It does not make any difference to me if Grandfather remembers or not," he said. "We promised we would spend two hours a day dusting his books for him. I shall keep my promise to the end."

Two days later, Grandfather Lorey quietly passed away at his country home.

Then Jim and Dave each received a letter from Mr. Willett. Grandfather Lorey's will was to be read, the attorney had written, and it was requested that both Jim and Dave be present.

"We are the only real heirs to Grandfather's fortune," Jim told Dave on the way to the attorney's office. "I am sure Grandfather divided everything between the two of us. I have already made plans for spending my share."

"Now that we are all here we shall begin," Mr. Willett said, clearing his throat. Then he proceeded to read Grandfather Lorey's will. He read the generous amounts Grandfather had willed to the church, the children's home, the hospital, and the university. Then he read how much Grandfather had bequeathed to the various faithful workers both in his business and at home. Then he read:

"To my grandson, David Harris, I leave my country house, my town house, and the balance of my stocks, bonds, and cash."

Jim gasped aloud in amazement. He jumped to his feet, but

Mr. Willett cleared his throat and continued reading, in his calm way:
"To my grandson, James Lorey, I leave the leather couch in the library of the town house. This will assure him I have not been fooled these many months."

Prayer Hymn: "'Tis the Blessed Hour of Prayer."

Prayer (by the teacher).

Offertory Service:

(Play softly "Give of Your Best to the Master" while the following poem is read by one of the students and while the offering is taken:)

> Christ blessed the little children as He took them on His knee.
> He showed great lovingkindness on the shores of Galilee.
> He gently held a withered hand and gave it strength once more.
> He suffered on a cross of shame; our sins for us He bore.
> This gentle, loving Christ who gave His all that we might live,
> Deserves the very best of all that we may have to give.

(Conclude with a short dedicatory prayer by one of the students.)

Adult Leader:

(Use the poster described in *Patterns for 52 Visual Lessons* as you develop the following thoughts:)

A violin is made to play beautiful music, but there are certain things necessary. The violin must be in tune and it must have four good strings. If even one of the strings is broken, it will ruin a tune.

Our lives are much like violins. God created us to live beautiful lives. Just as music is written on a page so we can know which notes to play, so God has given to us the Bible so we might learn how to live Christian lives.

Living up to obligations and keeping promises make us worthy of trust—or, to say it another way, make us trustworthy. Promises are like the strings on a violin. When we prove ourselves trustworthy by living up to our promises, we are like a violin with four good strings. A broken promise is like a broken string. Just as broken strings ruin a tune, so broken promises ruin a life.

(Have the students make the violin described in the book mentioned above.)

Benediction.

SERVICE NO. 26—JULY

Growing in Stature Through—

SELF-CONTROL

For a bishop must be blameless, as the steward of God; not selfwilled, not soon angry.—Titus 1:7.

Prelude: "Whispering Hope" sung as a duet.

Call to Worship: (Read in unison by students and teachers.)

> Give thanks unto the Lord, call upon his name, make known his deeds among the people.
> Sing unto him, sing psalms unto him, talk ye of all his wondrous works.
> Glory ye in his holy name: let the heart of them rejoice that seek the Lord (1 Chronicles 16:8-10).

Hymn of Praise: "My Saviour's Love."

Thoughts on the Theme: (*An object lesson by one of the students.*)

(Provide the student with a pair of scissors.)

Scissors are a handy tool. We use them for cutting all kinds of materials. Dressmakers, tailors, and milliners would find it difficult to get along without them for just one day. Even around our own homes we would be handicapped without scissors, for they are useful in many ways. But if we look at a pair of scissors closely, we soon discover how dangerous they can be if they are not properly used. The blades are pointed and sharp. A careless person, or one with no self-control, could do a great deal of damage with them. Yet they were made to be useful.

As long as the scissors lie here on the table, they are perfectly useless. They will remain useless until some one who has learned how to use them picks them up and puts them to proper use.

When we fail to use self-control, we are just like the person who does not know how to use a pair of scissors correctly. We hurt others with sharp words and unkind acts. We are thoughtless and misuse the talents and abilities God has given to us. When we do not try to use our talents and abilities, we are like the scissors lying idle on the table. To become useful tools in God's kingdom we must learn how to develop our talents and abilities through the use of self-control. Since temperance is another word for self-control, we could say that we can only become useful tools in the kingdom of God by developing our talents and abilities through the means of learning how to be temperate in every phase of our lives.

SELF-CONTROL

There are many ways of showing intemperance. Some ways we may have overlooked, but let's listen now to Sally.

Playlet: LET'S LISTEN TO SALLY.

(*This playlet can be read by the teacher in place of the story, or the parts can be read by the various students.*)

SCENE: The living room of the Clayton family.

CHARACTERS: Mr. and Mrs. Clayton.
  Mary Lou } 13-year-old twins
  Mary Ann }
  Dick—15 years old
  Larry—17 years old
  Sally Miner—14-year-old friend

(*As the scene opens,* MARY LOU *is reading,* DICK *is entering the room drinking a bottle of Coca-Cola;* LARRY *is seated at a table writing, and* MARY ANN *is looking over his shoulder, eating chocolates.*)

LARRY—I can't think of any one else, can you? It seems we have invited every one.

MARY ANN—How about Bill Higgins?

LARRY—He's here (*pointing with pencil to list on the table*).

DICK (*placing empty coke bottle beside two empty ones on the table*)— How many have you invited so far?

LARRY—Fifteen, not counting ourselves.

MARY LOU—Mother said we could invite twenty, ourselves included. So we can invite one more.

DICK (*pausing at door*)—Can you think of any one else?

LARRY—No. How about you, Mary Ann? Can you think of any one else to invite? (*Pause.* MARY ANN *continues reading. Enter* DICK *with a fresh bottle of coke.*)

LARRY—Mary Ann!

 (*No response.* MARY ANN *continues to read, completely unconscious of others.* LARRY *jumps to his feet and bangs his fist on the table.*)

LARRY—MARY ANN! CAN YOU?

 (MARY ANN *gives startled jerk. Knocks book to the floor.*)

MARY ANN (*hurriedly and vaguely*)—Oh, yes! Yes! That's fine!

 (MARY LOU *giggles and reaches for another chocolate.* DICK *continues to drink his coke.*)

LARRY (*shouting*)—What is fine? I ask you, Mary Ann, what is so fine? You haven't been listening! You've been sitting here reading! Read! Read! Read! All you do is read! This is your wiener roast as much as it is ours! I think you could at least help us plan it!

DICK—Take it easy, Larry. Take it easy.

(*Enter* SALLY MINER, *unnoticed.*)

LARRY (*still shouting*)—But it isn't right, Dick! Mary Ann always gets away with it. Every time there is something to be done, you can never find her. A half hour later she turns up in some corner reading. She never does her share of anything.

MARY ANN (*finding her place in the book*)—All right. All right. What would you like me to do? We can't all sit around writing down who should be invited. That would be silly. One list is enough.

LARRY—You could at least help us decide on one more guest. We have nineteen, counting ourselves. Mother said we could invite twenty. We have invited every one we can think of.

MARY ANN—Well, then, how about Sally Miner? Have you included her?

MARY LOU—Of course not. We wouldn't invite her.

DICK—Because of her father?

LARRY—Certainly. You know all the things being said about her father. We couldn't invite her.

MARY LOU—The last time we girls were invited to the Smith home, Sally's father spoiled everything. He came there right from the tavern, where he practically lives, and acted simply *terrible*. No one ever invites Sally any more.

DICK—Well, it isn't Sally's fault. Why should she be left out of everything because her father drinks all the time? Put her name on the list. Let's invite her.

LARRY—We certainly shall *not* invite her! What will the neighbors think?

MARY ANN (*without looking up from her book*)—Put her down anyway. Maybe she won't come.

LARRY (*raising his voice*)—I'll *not* put her name down! And I'll not be here that evening if she is here! You know very well her father has no self-control. People will think we are like that, too. If Sally comes here, I'll spend the night with Uncle Jim.

SALLY—You need not worry, Larry. I will not come to your wiener roast.

(*All turn toward her in surprise.*)

SALLY—I did not mean to listen, but when I rang the bell, your mother came to the door. She said you were all in here. I could not help hearing what you said. Self-control! What do you know about such things, Larry Clayton! And the rest of you, too, for that matter! (*Enter* MR. AND MRS. CLAYTON. *They remain standing near doorway, unobserved, and show both surprise and interest.*) You think intemperance and self-control apply only to the habit of drinking! Well, they do not. They only begin there. None of you has much room to talk. You, Mary Lou, are never without a bag of chocolates in one of your pockets. Even while we pass from one class to another at school, you munch your chocolates. Your fingers are never without a chocolate smudge on them. How much self-control have you? And you, Mary Ann. You are practically failing in at least three subjects this semester because you place reading before studying. You are never without a library book or a magazine. Even today you were punished in study hall because you were caught reading instead of using that hour for study, as you should. How much self-control have you? And you, Dick. I see you every day at noon drink two cokes. And you stop on the way home from school for another one. I dare say you have had all three of those bottles since dinner. How much self-control have you? And you, Larry. You think one must overindulge in drink in order to be intemperate! How about overindulging in temper? You fly into a tantrum over the slightest thing. How much self-control have you? You say you do not want to be seen with me for fear people will think you are like my father. Perhaps I should not be seen with you for fear people will think I have no more self-control than any of you. You need not worry. I shall not come to your wiener roast, now that I know how you feel about me.

(*Exit* SALLY, *sobbing.*)

MARY ANN—Well, I never!

DICK (*whistles*)—Phew!

MARY LOU—Can you imagine that!

LARRY—Of all the nerve! Telling us *we* have no self-control! You wait until I see her tomorrow! What I'll tell her! Why—"

MR. CLAYTON—Larry, that will do. Sit down, son, and hold your temper. If I were you four, I would listen to Sally and give her words a little consideration.

MRS. CLAYTON—A great deal of consideration, I would say. Your father and I have been trying to tell you that very thing for some time.

MR. CLAYTON—Only when your mother and I try to tell you, it is like pouring water on a duck's back. Sally's words at least made an impression.

MRS. CLAYTON—I feel very ashamed that Sally overheard such unkind words here in our home.

MR. CLAYTON—It is I who should feel ashamed. Here I am, president of the Men's Brotherhood Class, and did not know about Sally's father. I am going at once to tell some of the other men. Perhaps if a few of us talk to Mr. Miner, we can help him.

(*Exit* MR. CLAYTON.)

MARY LOU—We should be ashamed of ourselves for hurting Sally as we did. If we are honest with ourselves, we will admit she is right. I know I eat too much candy. I am going to start right now to do something about it. And you, Mary Ann—

MARY ANN—Yes, I know. I have let reading become a very bad habit because I have neglected other important things in order to read all the time. Sally is right. I have no self-control when it comes to reading. But I shall try to do better, beginning this very minute! (*Closes book and lays it on the table.*)

DICK—Same here. Drinking cokes is a very bad habit with me, because I drink too many. Watch me improve from now on!

LARRY—I guess I should feel the most ashamed. After all, it was I who said most of the unkind things about Sally, because I lost my temper. I feel we should go to Sally and apologize.

MRS. CLAYTON—An excellent idea! All four of you go and tell Sally how sorry you are for hurting her, and how grateful you are for what she has done for you tonight. Then bring her along home with you. We'll have a "rehearsal" wiener roast as soon as you get back! It will help Sally to understand how sincere you are when you invite her to the one you are planning for next Saturday night.

(*All exit, talking about their hopes to develop the self-control they know they are now lacking.*)

Prayer Hymn: Sing softly first verse of "My Prayer." Sing the second verse as the prayer response.

Prayer (by the teacher).

Offertory Service:

Shortly after David was anointed king, he called the children of Israel together for worship. He delivered a beautiful psalm of thanksgiving to God which we find recorded in 1 Chronicles 16:7-36. The "Call to Worship" which we read together at the beginning of this service is the first part of that psalm. Then David said, "Give unto the Lord the glory due unto his name: bring an offering, and come before him: worship the Lord in the beauty of holiness" (1 Chronicles 16:29).

That is how we worship God even today—by giving God glory, by bringing offerings, and by worshiping Him in the beauty of holiness.

(Play softly "O Worship the King" while the offering is taken, then have one of the students offer a short dedicatory prayer.)

Adult Leader:

This is the time of year when we watch the thermometer closely to see how hot the day is becoming. The hotter the day, the higher the mercury in the thermometer climbs.

Our tempers are much like thermometers. When we use self-control, we keep a cool and level head. This is just like keeping the mercury down to a cool and comfortable degree. The less self-control we use, the higher our temperatures rise. We had better take caution before we reach the danger point.

Have you ever noticed the word *danger?* It has *anger* inside it. Anger, we know, destroys all self-control. It causes our temperatures to rise and is just one letter from being *danger.*

We try to find ways of keeping cool during these summer days. There is one way we can always keep cool—use self-control.

(Have the students make the thermometer described in *Patterns for 52 Visual Lessons.*)

Benediction.

SERVICE NO. 27—JULY

Growing in Stature Through—

GROWING STRONG

(Taking Care of Our Bodies.)

Glorify God in your body, and in your spirit, which are God's.— 1 Corinthians 6:20.

Prelude: Use "Praise Him! Praise Him!" as an instrumental number played by as many students as possible.

Call to Worship:

Great is the Lord.
He laid the foundations of the world so they remain forever.
He sent the springs into the valleys to water the beasts of the fields and the fowls of the air.
He placed the moon and the stars and the sun in the heavens.
He created man in His own image, after His own likeness, and gave Him power over the birds of the air, the fish of the sea, and the beasts of the woods.
How great is the Lord!
Come, let us worship Him.

Hymn of Praise: "Jesus Is All the World to Me."

Thoughts on the Theme: (*An object lesson by one of the students.*)

(Provide the student with two copies of a magazine. They should be the same issue. Have one magazine clean and in good condition. Have the other magazine badly soiled. If possible, leave it outdoors all week.)

Here are two magazines. Once they looked exactly alike. The cover pictures were both bright and attractive. The inside pages of both magazines were clean and interesting. Now look at them. What a difference! And all because the one has been mistreated.

These magazines are like two men who started out with strong, healthy bodies just as these magazines started out with clean, interesting pages. One man took care of his body. He formed good health habits when he was a boy by eating the proper foods, drinking enough milk, playing out in the fresh air and sunshine, and getting plenty of rest. As a young man he continued his good habits. He did not smoke or drink. He ate wisely. He kept regular hours to be sure he had sufficient sleep.

This magazine is like the man who started off on the wrong foot as a child. He would not eat the proper foods. He would not drink milk. He pouted each night when bedtime came. As a young man, he smoked and drank. That led him to staying up so late every night he did not get enough rest.

If you had to choose one, there is no question which it would be. None of us would even want to touch, let alone thumb through, this magazine. No one wants to associate with a man who has ruined his body through carelessness, neglect, and bad habits.

Story: GOOD HABITS SPEAK FOR THEMSELVES.

It was a very important day in the life of Carl Fisher. He had been waiting for it since his graduation from college in June. Now at last he had an appointment to interview Mr. Benson Hilliard for a position which he felt sure was the one he wanted.

He dressed in his usual careful manner that morning. He must look his very best, for he had heard first impressions meant a great deal to Mr. Hilliard.

Carl was greatly disappointed when two other applicants arrived shortly after he had seated himself in Mr. Hilliard's outer office. At exactly three o'clock the buzzer on the secretary's desk sounded and the young lady looked up from her typewriter just long enough to say:

"Mr. Hilliard will see you three young men in his office."

The three looked awkwardly at each other. All three at once! What a strange interview this was going to be!

Mr. Hilliard arose to an amazing height as the three young men entered his office. He stood erect, holding his large square shoulders back like an athlete. He listened carefully to each of the three as they introduced themselves. Then, reaching for his soft gray felt hat which lay on the edge of his large, polished desk, he said:

"I have decided to take the afternoon off. Seldom do I have the pleasure of being away from the office with three young men. I shall take advantage of this opportunity. I have some property I would like to look over today. After that, we shall have dinner together at my club." So saying, he led the way to the door, the three puzzled young men following close behind.

Carl sat in the back seat with Frank Jackson. Roland Wendell sat in the front. As Mr. Hilliard drove along, he kept the conversation moving with questions. They finally reached Mr. Hilliard's club about six-thirty. As soon as they were seated at the table, Mr. Hilliard drew a full package of cigarettes from his pocket and offered one to each of the three young men. Frank took one and lit it immediately. He had been smoking almost constantly all afternoon. When Roland was offered one, he hesitated a moment. Then he glanced at Mr. Hilliard and took one. He toyed with it several moments before he finally lit it. Then he smoked it as if he did not enjoy doing so.

"Just smoking to please me," Mr. Hilliard thought.

When Carl was offered one, he said politely, "No, thank you, Mr. Hilliard. I never smoke." It seemed to Carl that Mr. Hilliard raised his eyebrows slightly. Carl also noticed that Mr. Hilliard himself did not smoke.

Then the waiter brought the menu and suggested various drinks with which to start the meal. Frank ordered one immediately. Roland ordered one hesitantly, after a brief pause. Carl shook his head. "Thank you," he told the waiter. "I never drink."

"You and Mr. Hilliard," the waiter smiled politely as he turned from the table without a word from Mr. Hilliard.

Carl thought, "That same waiter must serve Mr. Hilliard often. He seems to know his habits."

Roland thought, "Now, why did I order that drink? I don't enjoy drinking any more than smoking, but I always feel embarrassed to refuse."

Mr. Hilliard thought, "Hm-m-m-m. Frank drinks. Roland only smokes and drinks because he is not strong enough to refuse. Hm-m-m-m." Then he looked at Carl again.

After dinner they went into the lounge and chatted for a while. Finally, Frank said, "It is still early. Let's go somewhere for a show. I know a couple of good places we could go."

"It's quite all right with me if the rest of you want to go," Roland said, without too much enthusiasm.

Mr. Hilliard looked at Carl. Carl frowned. What a disappointing business this turned out to be! Mr. Hilliard must have a very poor opinion of him by this time.

"Well, it would be quite late by the time we got home," he said, glancing at his watch. "It is after ten o'clock now. If you will all excuse me, I think I shall start for home. I am not much of a hand for keeping late hours."

Mr. Hilliard decided he would leave, too. He shook hands with all three young men and assured each he would know the decision soon.

A half hour later, when Carl stepped into the living room, his mother and father both came hurrying toward him.

"Congratulations, son!" his father exclaimed joyously.

"Oh, Carl. We are so happy for you!" his mother cried. "Mr. Hilliard called a few minutes ago. He said you are to start your new job Monday! Isn't that wonderful?"

GROWING STRONG 137

Carl was dumbfounded. "Mr. Hilliard called!" he fairly shouted in excitement. "Why, why I thought he wasn't the least bit impressed with me!"

"Oh, how I wish you could have heard all the fine things Mr. Hilliard said about you!" his father said proudly. "It made us feel so good, son."

"The thing that made us feel the proudest," his mother added, "was when he said, 'This position calls for a strong body and a strong mind. Just looking at Carl tells me he has both. But if I had had any doubts, his good habits would have convinced me'."

It all seemed like a dream to Carl. He kept shaking his head and saying, "But Mr. Hilliard knows so little about me! I did not have an opportunity to really speak to him."

His father gently patted his shoulder. "Son," he said quietly, "good habits speak for themselves."

Prayer Hymn: "Take My Life and Let It Be."

Prayer (by the teacher).

Offertory Service:

God has blessed us with bodies which, if properly cared for, enable us to secure the necessities of life. One way to express our gratitude to God for this blessing is to return a portion of our money to work directly for Him.

(While the offering is being taken, play "Give of Your Best to the Master." After the prayer of thanks by a student, sing the first verse.)

Adult Leader: (Display suggested poster.)

All of you, I am sure, have seen a life preserver either on a boat, at a beach or public swimming pool, or those which are kept around the swimming pools at school. When some one is in danger of drowning, a life preserver is thrown out to him. If he holds fast to the preserver while those on shore pull him in, he will be saved.

Another word for life preserver is a life saver. Or, in other words, the purpose of a life preserver is to save a life. When we follow habits which will harm our bodies physically or mentally, it is the same as wasting a wonderful gift God has given to us, for our bodies are truly wonderful in many, many ways.

In 1 Corinthians 6:20 we read, "Glorify God in your body." There is only one way we can do this—by taking very good care of our bodies. Here are six good health habits which might be called six life preservers. If we follow them, we shall grow into strong men and women who will not be wasting their lives, but who will be capable of doing good work in the kingdom of God on earth.

(Display the poster described in *Patterns for 52 Visual Lessons*. Briefly mention the six health suggestions printed in the life preservers. Have the students make the life preservers described in the same book.)

Benediction.

SERVICE NO. 28—JULY

Growing in Stature Through—

CO-OPERATION

Now I beseech you, brethren, by the name of our Lord Jesus Christ, that ye all speak the same thing, and that there be no divisions among you; but that ye be perfectly joined together in the same mind and in the same judgment.—1 Corinthians 1:10.

Prelude: Play "The Lord Is in His Holy Temple." Sing it in unison while every one stands and remains standing during the call to worship.

Call to Worship:

The Lord is in His holy temple.
The earth stands silent as if bowed before His throne of justice and of love.
Let people everywhere rejoice and know that God is love. Amen.

Hymn of Praise: "Since Jesus Came Into My Heart."

Thoughts on the Theme: (*An object lesson by one of the students.*)

(Provide the student with a toy model passenger airplane.)

Our theme today is co-operation, or teamwork. Perhaps some of us do not fully appreciate what an important part co-operation plays in our everyday life. Practically everything we use or see represents co-operation. Let us take a passenger airplane, for example.

First of all, we might consider the co-operation of one part with another as an excellent example of mechanical teamwork. The propellers, the wings, the engines, the gas storage tank, the controls—all have a definite job to do. Working alone, they can not move the plane off the ground. Working together, the plane flies as smoothly as if it were a great bird floating through the air. If one of the engines suddenly stops working, the teamwork is broken and the plane suffers in some way.

Now let us think about other forms of co-operation which a passenger plane represents. Let us think of the crew. Usually there are the pilot, the co-pilot, the purser, and the stewardess. The pilot and co-pilot must co-operate in order to fly the plane safely. The purser must co-operate with the pilot and co-pilot in order that the passengers aboard are on the right plane and get off at the proper airports. The stewardess must co-operate with the pilot, co-pilot, and purser in order that meals are served on time and every passenger is ready to get off when the plane lands at the end of the flight.

Then there are the many workers at each airport along the way who help the pilot and co-pilot make safe landings and get the plane ready for the next part of the flight. The more co-operation there is between the workers all along the line, the safer and more pleasant the journey will be. This is not only true of passenger airplanes. It is true of everything we do in our everyday life at home, at school, or at play. The more we co-operate with others the better and quicker the job will be done.

Story: THE HURRICANE THAT SAVED OUR TOWN.

This is a strange story, because, first of all, most hurricanes ruin or destroy towns. But the hurricane about which I shall tell you saved Larksville. And in the second place this is a strange story because of Mr. Kettleby's strange promise.

Mr. Kettleby is the tall old gentleman with white hair who always stands as straight as an arrow and who always says, "It can't be done!" That is, he always said, "It can't be done," until the day after the hurricane ripped through Larksville. Although storm warnings had been posted that afternoon, the hurricane, which was already blowing furiously to the south, was expected to pass to the west of Larksville. Instead, quite suddenly it changed its course and struck Larksville shortly after we arrived home from the town-hall meeting.

That meeting upset my dad so much he talked as fast as he could all the way home. Mother scarcely had a chance to say a word, and I, comfortably settled in the back seat of the car, sat listening with wide-open ears. Even we boys knew how important it was to have the Bobbit Factories built in Larksville. Families were moving from Larksville every day because jobs were so scarce. If these factories moved to Larksville, it would mean plenty of work for all. But the owners could not decide between Larksville and Medina, a town some seventy miles away. While Larksville was the best location for the factories, the owners felt our town had not grown the way it should. For that reason they were thinking of locating in Medina.

Most people in our town knew the factory owners were right. Larksville still had many streets unpaved and some without any lights. The city hall was practically tumbling down for want of repairs. Even the bank building had not been painted in twenty years. And all because Mr. Kettleby always shouted, "It can't be done!" Every one knows that Mr. Kettleby is the richest man in our whole state. He owns the bank and most of the stores downtown. He owns many of the apartment buildings and much of the farm land. But every time some group tried to improve the town in any way, Mr. Kettleby would stand up at the meeting and shout, "It can't be done!" so loud and so long that every one became discouraged and went home feeling it was no use to try.

The factory owners sent a letter to the mayor, saying that at the end of two months they intended to pay a personal visit to both Larksville and Medina. They would see for themselves which town looked the best. Then they would start plans to have their branch factory built there. Every one knew Medina was much prettier than Larksville, for the people worked together and found more and more ways to improve their town. At the meeting that night, the mayor told of all the ways Medina was better than Larksville. Then he said:

"We need factories here. We will never get them unless we start right now and work hard. We must all spend every free minute the next two months improving and beautifying Larksville."

The people cheered and were ready to start right then and there. That is, all but Mr. Kettleby. He jumped up and cried, "It can't be done!" The longer he argued the more discouraged the people became. When the meeting ended, nothing was accomplished and every one (but Mr. Kettleby) went home unhappy and upset.

Then the hurricane whipped through Larksville. Almost all of the downtown buildings and half of the homes were ruined. The mayor called another meeting the following morning. There wasn't a town hall any more, so we met in what was left of the park, and used the fallen trees for benches. The mayor made a fine speech, telling all about the great damage the hurricane had caused. "But we must rebuild Larksville," he said. "And we must begin right *now*. We have but two months. If every man, woman, and child co-operates, we can build a new Larksville twice as beautiful as Medina!" Every one cheered and clapped. We boys whistled, we were so happy. Then Mr. Kettleby arose. "It can't be done!" he cried. "It can't be done!"

"It *must* be done!" cried the mayor, "and it *can* be done! You have suffered loss just like the rest of us, Mr. Kettleby. Financially, you have lost more because you had more to lose. If Larksville is not rebuilt, the Bobbit Factories will surely locate in Medina. More people will leave Larksville, for there will be less work, and you will lose even more. This time we shall not listen to you. We shall start right here and now to build a bigger and better Larksville." There was more cheering and whistling. Then Mr. Kettleby arose again.

"It can't be done!" he shouted. "And I am so sure it can't be done, I shall make you a promise. If you rebuild Larksville in time for the visit of the factory owners, and if they decide to locate their factories here, I shall build you the most beautiful library and high-school building in the entire state. I make this promise in spite of my losses in the storm, because I am so sure *it can't be done!"*

By sunset that day every man, woman, boy, and girl had been organized into teams and each had a definite job to do. Every one worked from sunrise until it was too dark to see. Every one co-operated with his neighbor. Before long, all the rubbish had been hauled away and buildings seemed to be springing up on every downtown street. Lawns were cleared. Homes were rebuilt and gardens replanted. When the factory owners arrived, they could not believe their eyes. That night at a meeting in the new town hall Mr. Bobbit said:

"When we learned that the hurricane had ruined Larksville, we decided to locate the factories in Medina without further delay. Then we received the wire from your mayor telling us of your plans to rebuild the town. Such a thing seemed impossible, but we decided to wait and visit both towns as we had planned. It is like a dream to see these beautiful buildings and beautiful homes. We know that you could not have done all this if you had not co-operated with each other. Such teamwork is just what we want in our factories. We feel honored to build our new factories here in Larksville!"

If you ever pass through Larksville, be sure to see our new library. It is truly the most beautiful one in the whole state. Over the door, carved in stone, you will read:

"The surest way not to fail is to determine to succeed."—*Sheridan.*

Then drive down Maple Street and see our new high school. Carved in stone above the front entrance you will read:

"Success in life is a matter not so much of talent or opportunity as of concentration and perseverance."—*Wendte.*

Mr. Kettleby selected both of these quotations!

Prayer Hymn: Sing the first verse of "Take Time To Be Holy" before the prayer, and the third verse as a prayer response.

Prayer (by the teacher).

Offertory Service:

(Play softly "This Is My Father's World" while the following poem is read and while the offering is taken.)

> Summer and winter, seedtime and fall;
> God in His mercy hath given us all.
> There's no better way to show Him our love
> Than by sharing the blessings received from above.

CO-OPERATION

(Conclude with a dedicatory prayer by one of the students.)

Adult Leader:

Have you ever thought what a wonderful blessing water is—plain, ordinary drinking water? We go to the tap and with a slight turn of our hand we have all the fresh, clear, pure water we need. It is such a vitally important part of our life we could not live without it. Yet it has become so much a part of our everyday life we take it for granted. For instance, how many of us ever think to thank God in our daily prayers for giving us water? Co-operation has become very much like water in our lives. It has grown to be such a vitally important part of everything about us that we take it for granted.

There was a time when people did more things for themselves than we do for ourselves today. They made all their own clothing from materials they had woven right in their own homes. The cotton used for weaving the cloth had been grown in their own fields. They raised all the food they ate, including the meat. They made their own furniture and built their own homes. But today we can not live alone. We need the help of others. We need the things others have grown or raised or made. Co-operation—or, in other words, men working together—has given to us all the conveniences as well as necessities we use and enjoy today. But when we butter a piece of bread or pour ourselves a glass of milk, we never think of all the people who shared or helped put them into our home. Since co-operation or the ability to work together is responsible for so many things in our everyday life, it should help us to understand better why it is so important for each of us to learn how to work with others.

(Have the students make the booklet described in *Patterns for 52 Visual Lessons.*)

Benediction.

SERVICE NO. 29—AUGUST

Growing in Stature Through—

OVERCOMING JEALOUSY AND ENVY

Jealousy is cruel as the grave.—Song of Solomon 8:6.
Let us not be desirous of vain glory, provoking one another, envying one another.—Galatians 5:26.

Prelude: "The Name of Jesus," sung as a solo or duet by students.

Call to Worship:

> Leader: *O come, let us sing unto the Lord: let us make a joyful noise to the rock of our salvation.*
>
> Students: *Let us come before his presence with thanksgiving, and make a joyful noise unto him with psalms.*
>
> All: *For the Lord is a great God, and a great King above all gods* (Psalm 95:1-3).

Hymn of Praise: "O Love That Wilt Not Let Me Go."

Thoughts on the Theme: (*An object lesson by one of the students.*)

(Provide the student with a pair of opera glasses.)

As you see, opera glasses have two sets of lenses. Or, in other words, there is a glass at each end through which we can look. When we look through the large lenses, with the small ones away from us, the objects look smaller. When we turn the glasses around and look through the small lenses with the larger lenses away from us, then objects are magnified, or look larger, clearer, and brighter than we can see them with the naked eye. They seem to be closer to us.

When we look about us through the eyes of love, it is like looking through the small end, with the large end away from us. All of our blessings look beautiful and bright. They are close to us. But when we look about us through the eyes of jealousy and envy, it is like looking through the other end. We do not see all our wonderful blessings for which we should be grateful. Instead, we look off in the distance and see only those things which belong to others.

Many times objects in the distance look much better than the ones we have. They look bigger and perhaps brighter. They seem more important, and we think if only I had those things to work with instead of the things I have, then I could really do good work. But when we get closer to the objects, we often find the things we have

OVERCOMING JEALOUSY AND ENVY

are much better in many ways. Jealousy and envy close our eyes to our many blessings and make us discontented. We covet and wish for things belonging to others. Love makes us realize how many things we have for which to be thankful.

Story: RIGHT IN HER OWN BACK YARD.

It seemed to Sue Ellen that she had hardly turned out the little blue china lamp at her bedside when she heard a tap at the window. She sat up in bed, peering across her room between the ruffled curtains.

"I am so sorry I could not come sooner," she heard some one say in a voice so soft and sweet it sounded more like silvery bells tinkling than some one actually speaking. And then Sue Ellen saw the little fairy gracefully waving a tiny golden wand. A sparkling light shone from the star at the end of the wand, which made the room seem as bright as day.

"I came as soon as I could, but I am kept so very, very busy these days. It seems there are so many discontented people."

Seeing Sue Ellen's wrinkled forehead and wide, staring eyes, the little fairy threw back her head and laughed merrily. "Oh," she cried. "I have not introduced myself! I am the I-Wish Fairy, the busiest fairy in Fairyland."

"I am certainly happy to know you," Sue Ellen said promptly, "but I am afraid there is some mistake. I am not expecting you. In fact, I did not even know you existed until this very moment."

"Oh, but you are one of the many people who call upon me all the time. Let me see," the little fairy paused as she drew a small gold notebook from her pocket. She flipped several pages and then said in a very serious tone, "You called upon me ten times today. Before you got out of bed you wished you would not have to go to school today. While dressing, you wished for Sarah Jane's new green jersey dress. During the history test you wished you had studied as hard as Beatrice Carter, for she always gets an A." The little fairy read the remaining wishes which Sue Ellen had made that day. They were all wishing for something that belonged to some one else. "And now," added the little fairy, "I have finally come to help you. Because you call upon me so often, I shall give you five wishes."

"Five wishes!" echoed Sue Ellen, in great surprise. "Really, I-Wish Fairy, one will be quite enough."

"We shall see," the little fairy smiled knowingly. "We shall see. Now make a wish. Any wish. And it shall be granted."

Sue Ellen's eyes opened wide. "I wish I were Sandra Wells, the richest girl in town, for then I should be completely happy."

Instantly, Sue Ellen found herself in Sandra's bedroom. There were no ruffled curtains on the tall, bare-looking windows. Instead, heavy, dark-colored drapes hung stiffly from the iron rods. The expensive old pieces of furniture gave the room a cold, unfriendly feeling.

Sue Ellen ate most of her meals alone, served by a maid in a stiff black uniform and a little white lacy cap and apron. The chauffeur drove her to school and called for her. As soon as she arrived home her tutor began where her teachers had left off for that day. From seven until nine every evening she had to practice the piano while her tutor stood near by, listening for mistakes. Before the first hour of practice was over, Sue Ellen said, "I wish I were Natalie Jarvis. She is so talented she can play the piano better than any girl at school." Instantly, Sue Ellen found herself seated before Natalie's shiny piano, practicing. Being Natalie meant practicing every free hour. She did not have time to read, to play, or even to spend much time on her hair or her nails. The class picnic was planned for the next day, but there was no time to put up her hair in pin curls before going to bed. So the next morning her unruly hair made her very unhappy. In despair she cried out, "I wish I were Wilma Bennet! She has such beautiful, wavy, auburn hair!" And instantly, Sue Ellen found herself to be Wilma Bennet.

Being Wilma meant putting in many extra hours studying, for Wilma found it very difficult to understand her school work. She had to work for hours in order to solve the simplest problem. No matter how hard she studied, she seldom passed a spelling test. And she usually received the lowest marks in her English classes. After struggling along one day as Wilma, Sue Ellen forgot all about Wilma's beautiful auburn hair and cried, "Oh, I wish I were Ruby Morgan! Ruby is so very smart, she never has to study. She seldom takes a book home with her, and always receives an A on all her tests." Instantly, Sue Ellen found herself to be Ruby Morgan.

But to be Ruby Morgan meant having a great deal of free time which other girls had to spend on studying their lessons. She read a great deal, but when tired of that she wandered about outdoors. But she had no brothers or sisters with whom to play, and no girls her age in the neighborhood. So Ruby spent many lonesome hours. Sue Ellen, now Ruby, sat alone on the wide front porch. "Oh," she sighed, "I wish I were Sue Ellen Martin. She has brothers and sisters, and they always seem to have such a happy time playing together!" Instantly, Sue Ellen became herself once more.

Mother was bending over her, shaking her gently and saying, "Come, dear. It is time to get up. Today is your class picnic, you know,

OVERCOMING JEALOUSY AND ENVY

and it is such a beautiful, sunny day for your trip to the park."

Sue Ellen sat up in bed and looked about her with wide, staring eyes. There were the dainty ruffled curtains. Here was the little blue china lamp. The room suddenly seemed more cozy than ever before.

"Oh, Mother!" she exclaimed, "I had such a strange dream! I dreamed I changed places with four other girls. But I did not like being them, so I finally wished myself to be Sue Ellen once more."

Mother smiled. "Sometimes people are really dissatisfied with the place God has given to them in this world, but that is because they close their eyes to all the blessings given to them and let jealousy and envy fill their lives."

"I have been one of those people, Mother," Sue Ellen said seriously, "for I have often wished to have something that belonged to some one else. I am not going to be one of the discontented people the I-Wish Fairy mentioned, for I shall always remember that I found real happiness right in my own back yard."

Prayer Hymn: Sing softly "I Am Coming, Lord."

Prayer:

Our loving heavenly Father, we come to Thee with hearts filled with thanks. Thou art always so kind and so loving to us, Thy children. Often we do not deserve Thy wonderful love, for we think unkind thoughts filled with jealousy and envy for those about us. But still Thou dost continue to send us blessings, because Thy love for us is so great and so beautiful. Forgive our many sins, we pray. Help us to overcome all forms of jealousy and to rid our lives of envy which often causes hatred and unkindness. May we ever remember the beautiful life of Jesus, how He went about doing good and helping those in need. Help each of us to live closer to Jesus by following His blessed example. In His name we pray. Amen.

Offertory Service:

> Which one of these gifts do you think was the best?
> Which gift do you think pleased the Lord?
> A little bit given by one who kept much
> As part of his own treasured hoard?
> Or a generous gift by a person who gave
> With a grudging, unwilling heart?
> Or a little bit given by some one who had
> Little but love to impart?

(Read the story of the widow's mite, Luke 21:1-4. Play softly "Leaning on the Everlasting Arms" while the offering is taken and while a student offers a prayer of thanks for the gifts received.)

Adult Leader: (Display the poster described in *Patterns for 52 Visual Lessons* and refer to it as you develop the following thoughts:)

According to ancient legends, what is supposed to be at the end of the rainbow? Yes, a pot of gold. There is an old story about a man who started out to find that pot of gold at the rainbow's end. He traveled for many weary years all around the globe, searching for it. Then one day he found it. But can you guess where? Right in his own back yard!

Of course, we know there really is not an actual pot of gold at the end of the rainbow. But there is something much better than all the gold in the world, for the rainbow is a sign that God will always keep the wonderful promises He has made to man. Let us see what some of these promises are. (Read and discuss the following verses: 2 Chronicles 7:14; Psalms 34:19; 37:3; 41:1; 91:10, 11; 121:3; Proverbs 3:5, 6; 3:9, 10; Isaiah 30:23; 41:10; 41:17; Daniel 12:3; Matthew 10:42; 11:28; Mark 9:41; 11:24; Luke 6:38; 11:9; John 3:16; 6:35; Romans 1:16; 10:13; 1 Corinthians 10:13; 15:58; James 1:5; 1 John 1:9.)

Unfortunately, sometimes we are so busy looking for the material pot of gold at the end of the rainbow that we do not realize the real pot of gold lies right in our own back yard. God's promises are meant for all of us. All we have to do is to accept them, believe them, and live so that we are deserving of such wonderful love.

(Have the students make the individual poster described in the book mentioned above.)

Benediction.

SERVICE NO. 30—AUGUST

Growing in Stature Through—

FAITHFULNESS TO GOD

Great is thy faithfulness.—Lamentations 3:23.

Prelude: "My Faith Looks Up to Thee," sung by a quartet (two altos and two sopranos).

Call to Worship:

> It is a good thing to give thanks unto the Lord, and to sing **praises unto** thy name, O most High:
> To shew forth thy lovingkindness in the morning, and thy faithfulness every night (Psalm 92:1, 2).
> Come, let us worship the Lord.

Hymn of Praise: "Faith of Our Fathers."

Thoughts on the Theme: (*An object lesson by one of the students.*)

(Arrange a light in front of the student so that his shadow **appears** on the wall behind him.)

Whenever we are in sunlight, in moonlight, or in artificial **light** (as we are in now), we can see our shadows. Our shadows **change** as we change. For instance, when I lift my arm, the shadow of **my** arm also lifts upward. When I move to the right, my shadow **also** moves to the right. When I bend over, my shadow also bends over. It is impossible for me to move to the right and have my shadow **move** to the left. It is also impossible for me to bend down and have **my** shadow remain in an erect, standing position. My shadow is **always** with me while I am in the light. The only way I can lose my shadow is to step out of the light.

God's blessings are just like our shadows. They are always with us as long as we walk in the light; that is, as long as we are faithful to God. Wherever we go, God's blessings follow us. When we **step** out of the sunlight, our shadow disappears. When we step out **of** the light of faithfulness, God's blessings disappear. God **does not** withdraw His blessings from us any more than He **withdraws our** shadow from us. As soon as we prove faithful once **again we receive** God's blessings, just as we have a shadow as soon as we step **back** into the sunlight.

Story: HE WOULDN'T TURN BACK.

Simon Crawford was a tall man with kind eyes and a gentle voice.

The summer sun, the winter winds, and now the spring rains had carved deep lines on his weather-beaten face. He glanced over his shoulders at the little clock ticking silently on the shelf above the kitchen stove. Then he glanced at the window which had a piece of cardboard tacked over a broken pane.

"It looks like an all-night rain," he said in his quiet way. "I might as well get started. It will take twice as long to walk the road in this wind and downpour."

"Oh, Simon," his wife said anxiously, "do you think there is much use to go to the schoolhouse tonight? Such a handful turn out for prayer meeting. In fact, so few come to Sunday services I can not help feeling discouraged at times. We have been in these mountains since last summer. And we have so little to show for all our hard work. We seem to be getting nowhere with these mountain folk. When they come to church or to prayer meeting, they just sit as if they were waiting for something."

"Yes, I know," Simon said quietly. "I can feel it each time I am with them. Sometimes I feel some of them are ready to accept Christ. Yet they seem to be waiting—waiting—waiting for what? If I only knew!"

Now Jane crossed the bare floor of the tiny log cabin and looked out of the window toward the road.

"It's raining harder, Simon. I have never seen such a storm. Take off your boots and stay home tonight. No one will come out in this downpour!"

But Simon shook his head as he reached for his raincoat.

"No, Jane," he said quietly. "I can not expect to teach these mountain folk to be faithful to God unless I am faithful to them. If just one person comes to the meeting tonight, I shall feel the trip worth while."

"Oh, Simon," Jane said as she took her raincoat from the peg behind the door, "you are so faithful. Surely your efforts will some day be well blessed."

Before they reached the road, Simon urged Jane to turn back.

"This wind is too strong for you to face," he said. "I'll go alone."

But Jane shook her head. She shielded her eyes with her upraised arm. They waded through water knee-deep. They climbed over fallen trees which blocked the narrow mud road. They splashed through cold, slimy mud. Twice they lost the road and stood huddled together waiting for the next flash of lightning to show them the way. Then the wind subsided. The rain gradually turned from a violent torrent into a gentle spring shower. As they turned the last bend in the road, they both saw it at once and cried together:

"A light! There's a light in the schoolhouse!"

A moment before, they had been close to exhaustion. But the light somehow gave them renewed strength. They fairly ran the remaining distance. Simon swung the door wide open. Then he and Jane stood as if petrified. The room was crowded with people, many of whom Simon had seen in church but once or twice in all the months he had been with them.

Barkus Wheeler stepped forward with an eager, outstretched hand. "Come in, preacher!" he cried. "Come in and be welcomed!"

And then Barkus told their story.

"It wasn't that we disliked you, preacher. Nor Jane here, neither. It was just that no one but us mountain folk stays here all year round. That is why our schoolteacher is always one of our own. Sure, these mountains are real pretty when it's summertime. The roads are dry and dusty, but the walkin' ain't so bad. Winters are pretty cold, and we have lots of snow. But the ground freezes so you can get around. But it's the spring, like now, that no one but mountain folks can take. When the snow on the peaks above begins to melt, we get flooded. Bridges git washed out. Roads git blocked. Strangers never stay in these parts through spring. Whenever we thought about asking some one to come as our preacher, we would be afraid he wouldn't stay. We decided we would just wait for some one to come along who would prove he'd be with us all the time. Even through storms like tonight. We've all been waiting for a storm to turn up on a prayer-meeting night. We promised each other we'd all turn out then. And if you turned out, too, then you are the one we want for our preacher. You and Jane have been kind to all of us in many ways. It wasn't easy to hold out. I've been praying for this storm tonight, preacher. For I knew you'd come. I knew you'd be faithful."

As Simon stood before the group to lead the worship service, his hands trembled from joy and excitement. He opened his Bible to Matthew 25:23. He had prepared a service on that text: "Well done, good and faithful servant; thou hast been faithful over a few things, I will make thee ruler over many things: enter thou into the joy of thy lord."

Then he gently closed his Bible as he said quietly:

"Let us give thanks to God for the wonderful blessings He offers to all who are faithful to His Word."

Prayer Hymn: "Bow Down Thine Ear."

Prayer (by the teacher, or by a pupil who has prepared a prayer).

Offertory Service:

Jesus said, "Well done, good and faithful servant; thou hast been faithful over a few things, I will make thee ruler over many things: enter thou into the joy of thy lord" (Matthew 25:23).

A good and faithful servant is one who takes good care of his master's belongings. Everything we have or use belongs to God. When we share with others the things God has given to us, we are proving good and faithful servants. Jesus promises that the more we share with others, the greater blessings He will send to us.

(Play "Count Your Blessings" while the offering is taken. Conclude with a short dedicatory prayer by one of the students.)

Adult Leader:

(Display a bunch of keys.)

Each key on this ring is for a certain lock. This one is for my front door. It will not open my back door. It will not open the garage door. But every time I put this key into the lock on my front door, it is sure to turn easily.

(Refer to the poster described in *Patterns for 52 Visual Lessons* as you conclude.)

We have been thinking about faithfulness this morning. There is a key that will unlock the door to faithfulness for us, just as this key will unlock my front door. It is a willing heart and a ready hand. If we keep our heart willing to *receive* the Word of God and our hands ready to *do* the Word of God, surely we shall be faithful.

"A faithful man shall abound with blessings" (Proverbs 28:20). The more we do for others and the more faithful we are to God, the greater shall be our personal blessings.

(Have the students make the key described in the book mentioned above.)

Benediction.

SERVICE NO. 31—AUGUST

Growing in Stature Through—

PERSEVERANCE

Be ye stedfast."—1 Corinthians 15:58.

Prelude: Play "Dare To Be Brave."

Call to Worship:

> O come, let us sing unto the Lord:
> For the Lord is a great God, and a great King above all gods.
> In his hand are the deep places of the earth: the strength of the hills is his also.
> The sea is his, and he made it: and his hands formed the dry land.
> O come, let us worship and bow down: let us kneel before the Lord our maker (Psalm 95:1, 3-6).

Hymn of Praise: "I Would Be True."

Thoughts on the Theme: (*An object lesson by one of the students.*)

(Provide the student with a small-eyed needle and three pieces of sewing thread—one too coarse to pass through the eye, one so fine it passes through very easily, and one that will pass through, but not too easily.)

There is a difference between trying to do that which is impossible and sticking to a difficult job which *seems* impossible. This needle has a very small eye. I could try for years to thread this needle with this piece of thread, but I could never succeed. This thread is much too thick to ever go through the eye of this needle, no matter how hard I try. This is like trying to do anything that is actually impossible to be done.

But if I try to thread this needle with this piece of very thin thread, I can do so easily. Compared to the thin thread, the eye of the needle is quite large. Perhaps I may have to try several times before the thread passes through the needle, but it can be done easily. That is like doing any ordinary job that merely requires our time and effort.

But this thread is thicker. It will pass through the eye of this needle, but not easily, because it is almost the same size. That means I shall have to try especially hard in order to thread the needle with it. I shall have to try again and again and again. It will take me a long time. I shall have to be very patient. No doubt, I shall feel like putting it aside many times. But if I stick to it long enough and try hard enough, I shall at length thread this needle with this thread.

That is like doing any job that is hard, but that is not impossible. If we stick to it, then we are exercising perseverance, or we are being steadfast. The harder the job, the more courage, will power, determination, and perseverance it takes.

Story: THE STORY OF CHARLES GOODYEAR.

The year was 1840 and the night was a cold, wintry one. Boston seemed to be quietly sleeping under a thick blanket of soft, white snow. A raw wind was blowing violently from the ocean. The streets were practically deserted. It was a good night to be home with your loved ones, comfortably settled around a blazing hearth fire.

But in one of Boston's poorest, humblest homes there was no cheerful hearth fire. For a hearth fire needs wood. And wood costs money. Many times Charles Goodyear did not have enough money to buy his family food. He never had money for fuel. So his wife and children sat huddled around the kitchen stove, wrapped in shawls and blankets worn thin through constant use. The fire was hardly more than a flickering flame. The wood box was completely empty. And there were bare places in the room where furniture had once stood, but which had been used for fuel to keep the small fire burning.

The tall, thin man looked around the drab, empty room. He reached for one of the few remaining chairs. It was easy to pull out several of the loose spindles. He placed them on the dying flame. While he waited for them to start burning, he glanced down at his feet. There lay a dark-looking substance. He must find a way to make it usable, he told himself over and over again. He must. He must. It was no good in the present form. All experiments had failed. Others had grown weary and had given up. But he would not. There was a way. He was sure there was a way. And he, Charles Goodyear, would find it. Yes, he would work and work and work until he found a way to keep rubber from cracking. Until he found that way, rubber would be useless for many things. Men had tried to use it for raincoats and boots, but they would become hard and stiff and would crack. They had tried to manufacture other items of rubber, but always the same thing would happen. As soon as the cold air struck them, they would become dry, hard, and stiff; then they would crack.

As Charles Goodyear stood there waiting for the fire to burn once more, he glanced at his wife and children. His wife had been loyal and steadfast. Even in the face of poverty and want she had encouraged him to continue with his experiments. And his children had been patient and understanding. They did without toys and clothing such as the other children had, but they did not complain. He would find the way, he would work—and work—and work—until he did.

Then the flames leaped up once more. He picked up the dark-looking substance and studied it carefully for a few minutes. Then, with a sigh, he moved to shift the wad of rubber from his right hand to his left. In doing so, it slipped from his fingers and fell upon the hot stove. Instantly a strong, unpleasant odor filled the room. With a startled cry Charles Goodyear moved quickly to snatch the scorched, half-burnt piece of rubber from the stove. His look of dismay turned into one of interest as he studied the parts that had touched the hot stove. His hands trembled. Had he at last discovered the way to keep rubber soft and flexible? After years and years of hard, steady work, was he at last near the gate to success? Would days of suffering and disappointment soon be ended for his family? He quickly stepped out into the raw night wind. If that piece of burnt, black substance would remain soft and flexible in the face of such extreme cold, then surely no element could harm products made of it.

The hours that followed were eager, anxious ones. But when morning came, the substance was still soft and pliable. Charles Goodyear had at last discovered the way to vulcanize rubber.

Others had started out with him. But when the road became hard they turned back. They were not brave enough to withstand the hardships of actual hunger and physical wants. They were unwilling to give up everything else and spend long hours every day trying—trying—trying.

We all have opportunities to be Charles Goodyears in one way or another. But when we fail to stick to the job until it is done, regardless of the time or physical effort required, and when we give up, we are like the ones who started out with him. They turned back because they lacked the perseverance to stick to a difficult job until it was done.

Prayer Hymn: "Take My Life and Let It Be."

Prayer (by the teacher).

Offertory Service:

(Play softly "Win the One Next to You" during the entire offertory service.)

Jesus said, "Verily I say unto you, Inasmuch as ye have done it unto one of the least of these my brethren, ye have done it unto me" (Matthew 25:40).

That means whenever we do any act of kindness to any one we are doing it for Jesus. The only way we can do things for Jesus is by doing deeds of kindness for those about us.

Bringing our gifts to Him is one way we can help, for part of our giving is used to help those in need, and part of our giving is used to help carry the story of Jesus to faraway places.

(Conclude with sentence prayers by several of the students.)

Adult Leader:

All of you, I am sure, know the story of the hare and the tortoise. The hare was so sure he could win a race with the tortoise that he played—and even napped—along the way. Compared to the hare, the tortoise was truly a slow-moving creature. But there was one important thing which the over-confident hare forgot to consider. The tortoise, while slow, was extremely persevering. He started the race knowing it was going to be a mighty hard task to win. But it was not an impossible one. He knew that he would have to make every minute count, and he would have to use every bit of effort and energy he had.

Now, the hare had many advantages over the tortoise. First of all, let us compare their legs. The rabbit's legs are long and slender. The legs of the tortoise are short and thick. That means the hare can cover more ground in one step than the tortoise can cover in a dozen steps. It also means that the hare could easily jump over many obstacles along the way with but one leap. But the tortoise would have to take the long way around. Then, too, the rabbit does not have a heavy shell to carry on his back.

Sometimes we look about us and feel that other people are like the hare. They seem to have all the advantages. It seems to us that everything has been made easier for them than for us. They seem to have been given everything necessary to succeed. We feel that we are like the tortoise, struggling along with nothing but disadvantages and handicaps. Perhaps we often think, "If I just had the things he has, what I could do!" Or, "If only I could be in his place, how I would use the things he has!"

But let us remember the story of the hare and the tortoise. With all his advantages, the hare lost. The persevering tortoise won, but not because he was swifter. He won because he had the determination to keep going even when it seemed hopeless for him to win.

There is an old hymn with a challenging chorus:

> Not to the strong is the battle,
> Not to the swift is the race;
> But to the true and the faithful
> Vict'ry is promised through grace.

(Have the students make the tortoise described in *Patterns for 52 Visual Lessons.*)

Benediction.

SERVICE NO. 32—AUGUST

Growing in Stature Through—

HONESTY

I exhort therefore, that, first of all, supplications, prayers, intercessions, and giving of thanks, be made for all men; for kings, and for all that are in authority; that we may lead a quiet and peaceable life in all godliness and honesty.—1 Timothy 2:1, 2.

Prelude: Have a student sing "I Would Be True."

Call to Worship:

>Hear our prayer, O God,
>And hear our joyful songs of praise.
>For we have come to worship Thee
>And learn more of Thy Word.
>Hear our prayer, O God,
>And bless us in this hour,
>So we may better understand
>The teachings of our Lord.
>   In Jesus' name we pray. Amen.

Song of Praise: "All Hail the Power."

Thoughts on the Theme: (*An object lesson by one of the students.*)

(Provide the student with a pair of glasses. Have one lens clean and the other covered with visible spots.)

Honesty is like the spotlessly clean lens of this pair of glasses. When I look through the clean lens, nothing mars my vision. I can see everything clearly. I can look all around me in any direction and everything looks bright and clean.

Dishonesty is like the other lens, covered with spots of dirt. When I look through that lens, I can not see clearly. Those spots keep me from looking directly into your eye. No matter how I turn my head, those spots remain between me and the world.

Those spots are selfishness, deceit, and greed. They are envying, coveting, the desire for wealth or fame or power. They are lies which we tell or all forms of jealousy which cause us to be dishonest in any respect.

The only way we can see clearly through this spotted lens is to clean it by removing all the spots. The only way we can rid our lives of all forms of dishonesty is to remove all the habits which lead to it. When we have done that, nothing will keep us from seeing clearly in all directions or from looking every one squarely in the eye.

Story: HOW HONESTY PAID MRS. MULLIGAN.

Mrs. Willett sat erect, peering out of the window of her large, shiny limousine while her chauffeur drove very slowly down Baxter Way. Mrs. Willett lived in a big house surrounded by rolling lawns and beautiful gardens, but she was often seen in alleys such as Baxter Way.

The houses on Baxter Way were old, and built so close together they seemed to be leaning on each other for support. Finally, the big car stopped in front of a small frame house with blackened shingles and a propped-up porch. There was no mistaking who lived here. Mulligan children were all over the tiny dirt yard. Ben and Jimmy were trying to swing on the gate, even though the hinges were pulled loose. Cora was sitting on the lower porch step, reading to Lucy and Peter. Thomas and Judy were tossing ball.

Mrs. Mulligan's eyes were wide with surprise as she opened the door even before Mrs. Willett's gloved hand tapped upon it.

"Good afternoon, Mrs. Mulligan. I am Mrs. Willett. I understand you are a very fine seamstress."

"Well," Mrs. Mulligan said shyly, "I do some sewing. That's how I manage to make ends meet since Mr. Mulligan took sick."

"So I understand," Mrs. Willett said with a kindly smile. "I have some sewing I would like you to do for me, and I shall pay you well."

"Just bring me your pattern and the material," Mrs. Mulligan said eagerly, "and I'll get right to work on it. I promise you a fine job."

"Well, you see," Mrs. Willett explained, "the sewing is not for myself. School will be starting very soon and I want you to make all the school clothing that a certain family will need."

"Just bring me the patterns and the materials," Mrs. Mulligan repeated, "and I'll get busy right away." She could not hide the gleam of excitement in her eyes. Such a big order! Her own children needed clothing badly. With so much work ahead, maybe she would be able to buy—but Mrs. Willett was speaking.

"I want this all as a surprise," she was saying, "so I can not bring the children here for fittings. But I shall tell you their sizes." She paused and glanced at the Mulligan children, who had all gathered around her. "They seem to be about the same size as yours," Mrs. Willett finally said, "and there are seven."

"Seven!" exclaimed Mrs. Mulligan. "Well, what do you know! I have seven, too!"

"Well," Mrs. Willett said, smilingly, "this will be much simpler than I had thought. Just make two complete school outfits to fit each of your children, and I am sure the sizes will be right. You know better than I what kind of patterns and materials to use for children's school clothing. So I am going to give you money to buy them for me. Buy good materials that will wear well, regardless of cost. As you finish them, pack them all in a big box. I am going on a trip and will not be back by the time the garments are ready. I shall send you the name and address of the family and would appreciate your sending the box to them. Here is money enough for the materials and patterns and also for your work." So saying, Mrs. Willett drew a large pack of folded bills from her purse and held them out to Mrs. Mulligan.

"You don't even want to see what materials I buy?" exclaimed Mrs. Mulligan in awe. "And you don't even want to see how much I pay for them? You don't want to look at my work to see that I made them all right?"

Mrs. Willett shook her head. "Why should I?" she asked. "I believe you are an honest woman, and I trust you."

That night when all the children were in bed, Mrs. Mulligan sat alone in her shabby little kitchen. The bills Mrs. Willett had given her were spread on the worn oil-cloth table covering. Never before had she held so much money at one time. How fortunate to be paid in advance for so much work right at this time, she thought! There were so many doctor bills, and Mr. Mulligan needed more medicine. Then, too, school would be starting in less than a month. That meant shoes and clothing for all her children. If the doctor bills were paid now, there would be no money left for school clothing. And doctor bills had to be paid in order to continue with the treatments for Mr. Mulligan. She would not have money for school clothing unless— unless— She gingerly touched the money spread before her. If she bought cheap materials instead of the best, there would be enough money for material for her children, too. Mrs. Willett would never know. She did not even want to see the finished garments. Or maybe —maybe if she just made one set of clothing for each of the children instead of two as Mrs. Willett had ordered, she would have money enough for one outfit apiece for each of her own. . . . And Mrs. Willett would never know. It was the only way. . . . And Mrs. Willett would **never know.**

As she gathered the money together she suddenly heard Mrs. Willett saying, "Why should I? I believe you are an honest woman, and I trust you." She slowly turned her head and looked over her shoulder, half expecting to find Mrs. Willett standing there. But she was quite alone. "Why should I? I believe you are an honest woman, and I trust you."

With a weary sigh she sank down on one of the scarred kitchen chairs and sat for a long time with her head in her hands. The next morning, as soon as the stores were opened, Mrs. Mulligan hurried to town. When the clerk in the yard-goods department asked, "May I help you?" Mrs. Mulligan stood her full height and said, "Yes! I have a long list of materials and patterns to buy. First of all, show me your *very best ginghams.*"

The next few weeks were busy ones at the Mulligan home. The older children did the housework and took care of the smaller ones, while Mrs. Mulligan sewed all day and late into the night. The materials were the best, so her sewing must be the very best, Mrs. Mulligan kept telling herself. And always in the back of her mind she could hear Mrs. Willett saying, "You are an honest woman, and I trust you."

As Mrs. Mulligan finished the garments, she folded them carefully and packed them in a large cardboard box, ready to be mailed to some fortunate family. Then one day, just after the last garment had been finished, the postman brought a letter. "It must be from Mrs. Willett," Mrs. Mulligan told her excited children who gathered around her. She hurriedly opened the letter with nervous fingers. Then her eyes became wide with excitement.

"Dear Mrs. Mulligan," she read aloud. "Please send the box of school clothing to the following address: The Mulligan Children, 57 Baxter Way."

Prayer Hymn: Sing softly the first verse of "Jesus, Saviour, Pilot Me."

Prayer (by the teacher).

Offertory Service:

Play softly "Something for Jesus" while the offering is taken and during the dedicatory prayer.

The great apostle Paul taught the early Christians many things about giving gifts to be used to carry on the work of God's kingdom. In a letter to the church at Corinth, Paul said:

"Every man according as he purposeth in his heart, so let him give; not grudgingly, or of necessity: for God loveth a cheerful giver" (2 Corinthians 9:7).

(Conclude with a short dedicatory prayer by one of the students.)

Adult Leader:

A ladder is a very handy article to have around the house. Sometimes it is necessary for us to store things on the top shelf of a closet. Without a ladder we could not reach that top shelf. A ladder, then, connects or joins us with some object which would otherwise be out of our reach.

Honesty is just like a ladder stretching from the earth up to heaven. It connects us with the heavenly home Jesus promised. Each rung of the ladder represents some form of honesty. One rung is for *truthfulness*. We can not be honest unless we tell the truth at all times. Another rung represents the way we *share* with others. If we keep the largest portion for ourselves, we are not being honest. Another rung represents the places where we should be honest—*everywhere*. Another rung represents when we should be honest—*now*. And another rung represents the ones to whom we should be honest—*others*.

If (when we climb a ladder at home to reach that top shelf) we miss a rung, or try to hurry to the top by skipping one, we fall. Sometimes we fall so hard we get hurt. That is just what happens to us when we try to get to heaven by skipping one of the rungs of the ladder called honesty. For instance, if we keep the largest share or cheat some one out of his rightful share, we are bound to be caught sooner or later. That is just like falling off the ladder because we tried to skip a rung. And we find we are not only hurt, but we must start our climbing all over.

(Use the poster described in *Patterns for 52 Visual Lessons* as you develop the preceding thoughts. Conclude by having the students read from their Bibles the various verses listed on the poster. If time permits, discuss each verse, encouraging the students to participate.)

(Have the students make the booklets suggested in the book mentioned above.)

Benediction.

SERVICE NO. 33—SEPTEMBER

Growing in Stature Through—

FAIR PLAY

And as ye would that men should do to you, do ye also to them likewise.
—Luke 6:31.

Prelude: "The Old Rugged Cross" sung as a duet by two of the students.

Call to Worship: (Read in unison).

> O praise the Lord, all ye nations: praise him, all ye people.
> For his merciful kindness is great toward us: and the truth of the Lord endureth for ever. Praise ye the Lord (Psalm 117).

Hymn of Praise: "When Love Shines In."

Thoughts on the Theme: (*An object lesson by one of the students.*)

(Provide the student with a small kitchen scale. A baby scale will do with the top part removed.)

When this scale is properly adjusted, it will tell us the correct weight of anything we place on it. When it is not properly adjusted, or when the hand does not point exactly to the zero when nothing is on the scale, all we need do is to turn this little knob. Now we know the scale is properly adjusted, because the hand is pointing directly to the zero. If we placed this book on the scale alone, we would find out its exact weight. However, if I kept my hand, or even just one finger, on the scale, the number to which the hand points is not the exact weight of this book. But you can easily see that I have my hand or a finger on the scale, so you would not be fooled. However, I could slip some loose papers in between the pages of the book which you would not see and which would add to the weight. Then, when you looked at the scale, you would think the book weighed more than it actually does. But that, we know, would not be honest. It would be dishonest.

This scale is just like the attitude we take when we play a game. First of all we must divide the teams evenly. That is just like adjusting this little knob to be sure we shall have the correct weight. Dividing teams evenly does not only mean placing the same amount of players on both sides. It means seeing that both sides have the same number of tall players, the same number of shorter players, and the same amount of skill.

When all the players play fairly and observe all the rules of the game, it is like placing the book on the scale in such a way that we shall see the correct weight. When we refuse to follow a rule because by doing so it will count against our side, it is like placing our hand or our finger on the scale. For every one can plainly see that we are not playing fair, that we are cheating. When we do anything during the game that will help our side to score, but not fairly, and purposely do it so cleverly or so quickly no one sees exactly what we have done, it is like weighing the book filled with loose papers. We would not be playing fair. We would not be honest.

Story: WINNING THE PENNANT FOR MADISON HIGH.

"Frankly, I don't think we have a chance," Bodie said, tossing his first-baseman's mitt into the air.

"Well! That certainly is a fine way to talk a week before the biggest game of the season!" Clifford said angrily. "If you keep talking that way, of course we won't win!"

"We won't win anyway," Bodie said.

"I'm not so sure about that," Duncan said over his shoulder. "We would have no trouble winning over Crescent High if Ivan Holloway could not play. Bodie is right, Cliff. We haven't a ghost of a chance to win the pennant game with Ivan Holloway playing."

"Ivan is the whole team," Arnold declared from his corner of the locker room. "He has been averaging two home runs a game and always comes to bat with the bases loaded."

"Not only that," Gerald added, "but Ivan is the best pitcher on any high-school team this year. He is an all-around star player."

"Ivan is the whole team," Arnold repeated. "If Ivan does not play, we will walk away with that pennant. But he will play. So we haven't a chance."

All evening Clifford thought of the conversation which had taken place in the locker room. He kept thinking of what Arnold said: "If Ivan does not play, we will walk away with that pennant." If Ivan does not play— If Ivan does not play. "But he will play. So we haven't a chance." Maybe something will happen to Ivan between now and Friday. Maybe he will get sick. Or maybe—

Clifford did not sleep well that night. He was the captain of the baseball team, and it meant a great deal to him to have Madison High School win the pennant. He planned it all carefully. It would look like an accident. Ivan might suspect, but that would not matter. He would not get badly hurt. Just enough so he could not play on Friday. He had better take care of it alone. If he told any of the other fellows, something might go wrong. Mr. Bromwell, the school coach, had a way of learning about such things. Yes, he had better do the job alone.

Having settled all the details of his plans, Clifford tried to find excuses to justify them. It was not fair to the other high schools to have such an exceptionally good player on one team. There should be a rule that no one would be allowed to play on a high-school team who could pitch or bat as well as Ivan. Finally he fell asleep, but he did not feel refreshed and rested in the morning.

He was a little nervous as he took his bike out of the garage after school that day and started pedaling toward Ivan's house. Everything was working fine. Ivan was at home when he called, and was quite eager to go bicycling with him. The game was tomorrow. He had to follow through with his plans now or Madison High would lose the pennant.

When Clifford reached Ivan's house he recognized Dr. Carter's car parked in front. Ivan was not waiting on the front porch as he said he would. Clifford parked his bike behind Dr. Carter's car and hesitated a moment before starting down the front walk. Ivan's mother came to the door, looking a bit concerned. Before she had a chance to speak, Ivan called from the next room, "If that's Cliff, Mother, tell him to come in."

Clifford was speechless as he stepped into Ivan's bedroom. Dr. Carter was winding the final layer of gauze around Ivan's right ankle.

"Look at this!" Ivan exclaimed, pointing to his bandaged leg. "What luck! Spraining my ankle the day before the biggest game of the year!"

Clifford was so surprised he could only stammer, "How—how—how did it happen?"

"I thought I had time to sweep the basement for Mother before you came," Ivan began.

"And instead of walking down the stairs," Mrs. Holloway interrupted, "Ivan decided to jump down in two leaps. He missed the halfway landing."

Clifford spent another restless night. It wasn't his fault, he kept telling himself. He had nothing to do with the accident. If he had not invited Ivan to go bicycling with him, the accident would have happened just the same. If only he could forget what he had planned. If only he had not planned it! He tossed and stirred restlessly all night.

The next morning Mr. Bromwell called a special meeting of the first and second baseball teams. It was about Ivan's accident, they knew, but why was the second team called to the meeting? Then the athletic coach raised his hand for silence.

"We have all heard about Ivan Holloway's accident," he began. "It is most regrettable that it had to happen at any time, but especially the day before such an important game. With Ivan playing, Crescent High stood an excellent chance of winning the pennant. Without Ivan the teams are so poorly matched that today's game will be a walkaway for us—if our first team plays. If our second team plays, Crescent will have a fighting chance. Without Ivan, Crescent's first team compares favorably with our second one.

"In the front entrance hall of this building are trophy cases filled with loving cups and pennants we earned in all sports during the past years. But we had to fight hard for each one. And we always fought fairly. If our first team won the pennant today, it would be under such unfair circumstances the award would seem out of place with the rest of the trophies. So in the big game this afternoon, our second team will play. Madison High has always stood for fair play. We want that trophy you boys of the second team win for us today to feel right at home with the rest."

Clifford was conscious of the boys cheering. Even the players on the first team were clapping.

"Cheer up, Cliff, old boy," Bodie said, tapping him lightly on the shoulder from his seat behind. "The second team will win for us. It will give us a chance to cheer for a change."

Clifford shook his head. It wasn't that. It was—it was the coach. How could any fellow have a swell coach like that and think he could do anything but play fair? The other players were all passing through the door to their respective classes. Clifford lingered behind. He started toward the door, then stopped. He turned and started for Mr. Bromwell's office. Then he stopped again. He would have to tell Mr. Bromwell. The sooner the better. You—you—you just had to play fair with a swell fellow like that.

Prayer Hymn: Sing softly "I Need Thee Every Hour."

Prayer (by the teacher).

Offertory Service:

The apostle Paul writes, "I have shewed you all things, how that so labouring ye ought to support the weak, and to remember the words of the Lord Jesus, how he said, It is more blessed to give than to receive" (Acts 20:35).

Let us remember these words as we bring our offerings to Him.

(Play softly "Open My Eyes That I May See" while the offering is taken and through the dedicatory prayer by a student.)

Adult Leader:

(Refer to the poster described in *Patterns for 52 Visual Lessons* as you develop the following thoughts:)

When we wish to balance anything, both sides must be equal. That is, both sides must weigh the exact amount. If you have ever tried to balance a seesaw (and I am sure most of you have), you will understand what I mean.

A balance scale works the same as a seesaw. If the weights on the one side weigh more than the weights on the other, the heavy side will drop lower and the lighter side will rise. But when both sides are equal, the crossbar will remain perfectly balanced.

Let us see what would happen to the crossbar if we kept the biggest share for ourselves and gave the smallest portion to others. Our share would far outweigh what we gave away, and the scale would look like this. The only way we can keep the scale of fair play perfectly balanced is to live by the Golden Rule and do unto others as we would have others do unto us. That means we would use the same rules for ourselves that we want others to use.

So in order to balance the scale of fair play, we would have to place our actions on one side, and the way we want others to act toward us on the other side. That means living by the Golden Rule at all times.

(Have the students make the scales described in the book mentioned above.)

Benediction.

SERVICE NO. 34—SEPTEMBER

Growing in Stature Through—

ASSUMING RESPONSIBILITIES

Let us not be weary in well doing: for in due season we shall reap, if we faint not.—Galatians 6:9.

Prelude: Use "Ivory Palaces" as a duet sung by two of the students.

Call to Worship:

Come, let us praise the Lord with a whole heart.
Let us worship in His holy temple.
For His mercies and His loving-kindness and His truth endureth forever and ever. Amen.

Hymn of Praise: "Help Me Find My Place."

Thoughts on the Theme: (*An object lesson by one of the students.*)

(Provide the student with an assortment of buttons ranging in size from the very smallest to large, heavy ones.)

As you see, these buttons are all sizes. No two of them are alike. Yet they were all made to do the same kind of work—hold two pieces of material together. But because of their size, and therefore their weight, some of them could hold very heavy materials together, like the two sides of a winter coat. We would not think of sewing this tiny button on the front of a coat. We would not even sew these middle-sized buttons on a heavy winter coat and expect them to hold the two sides of the coat together. Some of these buttons are so very small we would just use them for decoration.

People are like these buttons. No two of us are alike, yet we were all created to do the same work—further God's kingdom on earth. There are many ways in which God's work must be done, and it is up to us to find our place. The size of these buttons represents our growth as we accept responsibilities. We start out being small, and therefore capable of doing only small work. We are like these little buttons. But as we accept greater and greater responsibilities, we grow bigger. We are capable of doing more important work, just as the larger the button the heavier the cloth to which it can be sewed. The "I can nots" remain like small buttons. They never grow in size, for they are unwilling even to try to accept any responsibilities. The people who say, "I will try, but I know I can never do it," remain as middle-sized buttons. They grow bigger than the "I can nots," but they are unwilling to put forth all the energy and effort it takes to grow bigger through accepting added responsibilities. The people who say, "It is a big job, but I am willing to give it my very best." are the people who continue to grow. They are like the largest buttons which are used for heavy, strong, tough materials because they are capable of carrying a heavy load.

Story: VACATION WITH AUNT PEGGY.

Judy Ann was the main topic of conversation among all the students in the Junior class of Hamilton High. The first day of school you could hear girls whispering excitedly to each other, "Have you seen Judy Ann Sherman? What has happened to her?" But all any one could say in answer to that puzzling question was, "Judy Ann will say nothing but that she spent her vacation with her Aunt Peggy!"

Even the teachers noticed the change in Judy Ann. Like the students, they asked each other what had happened to her. For Judy Ann was no longer the whimpering, sulky girl who sat slouched in her seat and whined, "I don't know," to every question she was asked, or "I can't" to everything she was told to do.

"She seems to have grown so much taller since last June," Miss Boyd marveled at the end of the first week of school.

"Perhaps that is partly because she now stands with her shoulders thrown back and her head erect," Miss Williams suggested. "I was too astounded and too pleased for words when Judy Ann volunteered to go to the board and try to work a very difficult math problem. Until now, such a thing has been unheard of in the life of Judy Ann Sherman."

"Truly, I have never seen such a remarkable change," Mrs. Green said. "Last year I could never trust her to do her work carefully. I always had to check her stove and sink when the cooking lesson was over, for they were never cleaned thoroughly. Now she is the most efficient and responsible girl in any of my cooking classes. When I spoke to her about it, she just laughed and said, 'I spent my vacation with Aunt Peggy'."

And really that is all Judy Ann did—spent her vacation with Aunt Peggy. But what a vacation it turned out to be!

Judy Ann stepped off the train tightly clutching her traveling bag in one hand and her purse in the other and feeling bewildered and confused. This was her first trip alone. The day had seemed so long, for all she had done was to slouch in the seat and stare out of the window in her usual listless way. She had expected Aunt Peggy to come rushing to her the moment she stepped off the train. But Aunt Peggy was nowhere to be seen. After a few moments she caught sight of a white uniform. What a relief! Aunt Peggy at last! But no, it was not Aunt Peggy. It was another nurse coming toward her.

"This must be Judy Ann," the nurse said, smiling in a friendly way. "I am Kathleen Munson. Your Aunt Peggy has been delayed at the hospital and could not meet you. I am to send you to her apartment in a cab. She expects to be there by the time you arrive." So saying, she took Judy Ann's bag and led her toward the taxi stand.

Judy Ann swallowed hard. Never before had she done such things alone. At home, when she did not want to do anything, she would whine until her mother said, "Never mind. You do not have to do it." Or, "Stop that whining, and I shall do it myself." She puckered her lips and wrinkled her face getting ready to whine, but they were already at the taxi stand and Miss Munson was giving the driver the directions.

"Here," she said, turning to Judy Ann and placing a folded dollar in her hand. "Give this to the driver when you get out. I have given him your Aunt Peggy's address. Come to the hospital and see all of us one of these days!"

With that the driver helped her into the cab, and in another second they were winding their way through the heavy downtown traffic. No use to whine, Judy Ann thought. No one was around to hear.

A very sweet-looking gray-haired lady was waiting for her in front of the apartment building. "I am Mrs. Jenison," she said kindly. "I live in the apartment across the hall from your Aunt Peggy. She just phoned and said she has been delayed at the hospital longer than she expected to be. I am to let you in, and she will be home shortly."

As soon as Mrs. Jenison closed the door behind her, Judy Ann sank into the nearest chair. What a day! It seemed like weeks instead of just a day since she said good-by to her parents at the station. Now it must be close to six o'clock. She felt dirty and mussed from the train ride. And she was very hungry.

She looked about the apartment. Everything was spotless and in perfect order. Not even a book was out of place. Suddenly she pictured the cluttered, disorderly room she had left for her mother to tidy. Out of habit she puckered her lips ready to whine that she did not want to clean her room. Just then the telephone rang. It was Aunt Peggy.

"Darling, I am so anxious to get home to see you, but I will be delayed a little longer. Two of my nurses are on vacation and one went home ill today. You must be starved. You will find some cold cuts in the refrigerator. Also fresh vegetables for salad. And you will find a pan of rolls ready to be popped into the oven. Get a cold supper ready for us, and I shall be home in half an hour at the very latest."

Judy Ann stood for a moment with wide-staring eyes. Make a salad! Bake rolls! Prepare a cold supper! Why—why—why, she did not do such things at home! She puckered her lips. She did not *want* to prepare supper! Furthermore, she did not know how. She sank back into the chair, sulking and whining. She would go home on the next train! But suddenly she sat up straight. Aunt Peggy's voice had been gentle and sweet, but it had also been firm and definite. Aunt Peggy was used to giving orders and having them obeyed.

When Aunt Peggy stepped into the kitchen a half hour later, the table was neatly set, the tempting odor of baking rolls was floating from the oven, and Judy Ann, freshly bathed and with carefully brushed hair, was putting the finishing touches to the vegetable salad. All during the meal Aunt Peggy praised her. It was a strange new feeling for Judy Ann.

So began the three happiest and busiest weeks in Judy Ann's life. Before the end of the first week she was preparing breakfast, tidying the apartment, and catching an early bus for the hospital. There she helped the nurses' aides fold linen, change the water in the many vases of flowers for the patients, and do other odd jobs to help the busy nurses. To the nurses and the aides, Aunt Peggy was Miss Richardson. Judy Ann learned the first morning that everything had to be done as neatly, as quickly, and as carefully as possible to please Miss Richardson. Every one loved Aunt Peggy and tried hard to please her, for she was quick to praise any work well done.

Once again Judy Ann stepped off the train. This time her parents came hurrying toward her.

"Why, Judy Ann!" her mother exclaimed. "I do believe you have grown all of six inches during these three weeks!"

"We judged from your letters that you have had a fine vacation," her father began, after they had greeted each other.

"Fine is hardly the word, Dad," Judy Ann said seriously. "I have had a *wonderful* vacation. I have learned how happy we are when we are useful. I always felt that responsibilities were things to be avoided. Now I know that we only grow when we assume responsibilities. It has all been like a wonderful dream."

As they walked to the car Judy Ann talked excitedly about the first evening with Aunt Peggy. Her mother and father smiled happily and winked at each other. Judy Ann did not see that wink. If she had, she would not have guessed that it meant, "Our little scheme worked. And Peggy has done another wonderful job of helping others."

Prayer Hymn: "I Must Tell Jesus."

Prayer (by the teacher).

Offertory Service:

This is the time of the year when we realize anew how truly full of blessings the earth is. We see the signs of harvest—gathered fruits, the piles of pumpkins, the wheat and corn tied into sheaves, standing like tents in the fields. And we think, "The earth is the Lord's, and the fulness thereof; the world, and they that dwell therein" (Psalm 24:1).

May we show our thanks to God for His countless gifts to us by bringing our offerings to Him.

(Play "Bringing in the Sheaves" while the offering is taken and while a brief prayer of thanks is given by one of the students.)

Adult Leader:

(Display the poster described in *Patterns for 52 Visual Lessons* and refer to it as you develop the following thoughts:)

Football has come to be a popular and favorite sport. It seems that every one—even little fellows on the playground—understand the game and enjoy playing it. The object of football is, of course, to get the ball over the goal post. If we were playing football, we could not possibly win by merely kicking the ball from one person to another, because no one wanted to hold onto it. We would not kick the ball to each other very long, for the opposing team would be sure to take the ball from us and score.

Responsibility is much like a football. If we are unwilling to accept responsibility, but pass it on to some one else who passes it on, who passes it on—nothing is gained. In football, the longer the player practices and the harder he tries, the better player he will become. Responsibilities work the same way. The more responsibility we accept, the more we develop and grow, and the more we are capable of accepting. The bigger the responsibility we assume, the bigger the responsibility we are capable of assuming. If we are not willing to assume responsibilities, some one will come along who is, and he will take our opportunities away from us.

ASSUMING RESPONSIBILITIES

To win a game of football we must get in there and play hard. We can not be afraid to get the ball and carry it. To accomplish anything in life we must do the same thing. We must be willing to really work hard. We can not be afraid to carry our share of responsibilities.

(Have the students make the football described in the book mentioned above.)

Benediction.

SERVICE NO. 35—SEPTEMBER

Growing in Stature Through—

CHOOSING THE RIGHT

For the eyes of the Lord are over the righteous, and his ears are open unto their prayers: but the face of the Lord is against them that do evil.—1 Peter 3:12.

Prelude: "Follow the Gleam."

Call to Worship:

> *Blessed is the man that walketh not in the counsel of the ungodly, nor standeth in the way of sinners, nor sitteth in the seat of the scornful. For the Lord knoweth the way of the righteous: but the way of the ungodly shall perish* (Psalm 1:1, 6).
> Let us learn more about the righteous way of the Lord.

Hymn of Praise: "Yield Not to Temptation."

Thoughts on the Theme: (*An object lesson by two of the students.*)

(Provide the student with a ball of colored string which he will wind around another student. The second student will stand with his hands against his sides.)

This string is fairly tough, but I can break it if I hold a single strand of it firmly between my hands and give a hard tug. (Start winding around the other student, beginning around the chest.) If I wrapped this string around John just once, he could free himself by giving his arms a hard jerk. But let us see what happens when we wind the string around John many times. (Wind the string around him many times. One of the teachers might help, to save time.) Now let us see if John can break the string. Already the string has been wound around John too many times for him to free himself. And the more we wind the string the more securely John will be bound.

Bad habits are just like this string. At the very beginning we can overcome a bad habit very easily, just as we could break this string when it was a single piece or when it was wrapped just once around John. But the more we follow a bad habit the stronger it becomes. Soon it has wound itself around us so securely we are helpless. The sooner we break away from a bad habit the easier it is and the safer we are. Of course, it is best that we do not form bad habits. That means choosing the right at all times.

Have you ever seen a beautiful lawn ruined by a path across it? The first time a person wanted to make a short cut across the lawn, he thought, "It will not show." Then the second time, and the third, he thought the same thing. Before he knew it, there was an ugly mark on the lawn that could not be removed. Think twice before you do something harmful the *first* time.

Story: HE WHO CHOOSES RIGHT SHALL LEAD YOU.

The stalwart young braves stood like three straight arrows before Okechobe. The aged tribal chieftain gazed intently into first one pair of deep-set, dark eyes and then another. Finally he spoke:

"I am now old. I am tired. I am weary of being the tribal chief. You are the three most courageous young braves. One of you must take my place. But you shall decide for yourselves which one it shall be. Depart at sunrise. Travel together eastward until you come to a place where four roads meet. Then separate, each one traveling that road which he chooses. Return at the end of a fortnight. My departing words are, he who chooses right shall lead you."

The three young braves started on their journey at the very first break of dawn. They traveled steadily for two days before they came to the place where four roads met.

"Which shall it be?" each youth thought.

Just then a little old man bent low over a cane appeared from a hut almost hidden by the tall trees. "All who pass here stop and wonder which road to choose. Let me tell you what lies at the end of each. Then it will be easier for you to decide. They say gold lies at this trail's end. And this one leads to the home of him who is most famous in all the surrounding parts. This road runs downhill all the way. At its end is a place where people come to bathe and fish and hunt. This road climbs upward and is rocky. The traveling is hard. It stretches to the mountaintop. There are many buildings sheltering the sick and needy along it." With that the little man bowed and disappeared into the clump of trees.

The first brave turned toward the first path. "Gold lies at its end," he thought. "If I bring Chief Okechobe golden nuggets, he will surely choose me as the one to take his place." And so he waved farewell to his companions and started toward that road.

The second brave stood looking at the three remaining roads. He promptly turned his back upon the last one. "It is too steep a climb," he thought. "Besides, why should I tire myself just to see the ones not strong enough to stand alone? I am strong and have always provided well for myself. Why can not others do the same? Now this road—this road leads to him who is most famous. Perhaps I should seek him and learn his ways. But then such time would be but wasted, for surely fame is meant for me. Besides, that road lacks trees. It would be sunny all the way. But this road—this one looks inviting. The path winds downward all the way. That means the traveling would be fun. And see how cool and pleasant the overhanging branches make the road. There is a place for hunting, fishing, and bathing at its end. That means fun and play. No cares. No work. Ah, that road is the one for me! I shall take the easy way and return to Okechobe fresh and rested. He shall surely choose me for his place." So, waving a cheery good-by to Maniwakan, he started on the downward path.

All the while Maniwakan had stood with his eyes fixed on the upward trail. The aged one was right. Surely that road would be a steep, hard climb. Those rocks were sharp. They would cut his flesh if he but stumbled once along the way. But the sick and needy were up there. Time had always been precious to Maniwakan. He did not want to waste the remaining days that stretched before him. Perhaps in some small way he could be useful to some one up there. So, without a backward glance, he started to climb the steep, rocky road.

At first the traveling was rough and hard. He cut his hands on the jagged rocks. And once he lost his footing and bruised his face when he fell upon a fallen tree. The sun was so hot it seemed to scorch his body. But the higher he climbed the cooler the breeze and the smoother the way. Before very long he was traveling upon a broad, paved road swept clean by constant breezes. A sharp turn in the road brought him suddenly upon a village of white frame buildings. In each he found a warm, sincere welcome.

In time the three young braves met again where the four roads branched to travel homeward together. Okechobe watched them coming from afar. The first youth carried something slung across his back. His shoulders sagged from exhaustion rather than from the weight of the load. He walked with a tired limp.

"Ah!" thought the aged Okechobe. "He had been searching for gold. He carries the nuggets in the bag across his back. His shoulders sag and he limps because he is tired. He did not take time to eat or to sleep. He was so anxious to find more golden nuggets."

Then he watched the second youth approaching. "His gait is slow and leisurely," thought Okechobe. "He walks with downcast eyes. He no longer holds his head up high and looks straightforward. He has chosen the downward path and spent his time carelessly."

Now the three youths stood before their chieftain.

"Ah, Maniwakan!" cried Okechobe. "No prouder father ever was! Your quick, steady stride tells me you have breathed the pure, fresh mountain air. Those scars upon your hands and feet—they tell me you chose the hard, steep way. You hold your head upright and high. That tells me as you climbed you kept your eyes fixed upon an upward goal. And, son, that happy gleam tells me that your time was spent in helping others. Remember my parting words? He who chooses right shall lead you. What better path can any of us choose than that which leads us upward and helps us serve our fellow men?"

Prayer Hymn: "Give Me Your Heart."

Prayer (by the teacher).

Offertory Service:

God never expects us to do more than we are able. He does not expect us to give more than we have to give.

Every man shall give as he is able, according to the blessing of the Lord thy God which he hath given thee (Deuteronomy 16:17).

(Play "My Jesus, I Love Thee," while offering is taken and while a student gives a brief prayer of thanks.)

Adult Leader:

This is the time of the year when the leaves of the trees begin to turn beautiful colors. One of the most beautiful trees in any season is the sturdy oak. Have you ever thought, when you looked at some of the large oaks with wide-spreading branches and thick trunks, that it grew out of a tiny acorn? But the acorn had to be a good acorn. An acorn that is wormy or spoiled inside is of no use to any one.

Just as strong oaks grow from good acorns, so strong men grow from good habits. Good habits are just as important to our growth as good acorns are to the growth of an oak tree.

An oak that has grown strong can stand firmly against the hardest winter winds. And its spreading branches can shade a wide area all around it. A man that has grown strong because of good habits can stand firmly against wickedness, temptations, and troubles. His influence will be felt on all sides, no matter where he stands, just as the oak tree shades the ground all around it.

(Have the students make the folder described in *Patterns for 52 Visual Lessons.*)

Benediction.

SERVICE NO. 36—SEPTEMBER

Growing in Stature Through—

BEING A GOOD EXAMPLE

It is good neither to eat flesh, nor to drink wine, nor any thing whereby thy brother stumbleth, or is offended, or is made weak.—Romans 14:21.

Prelude: Use "Make Me a Blessing" as a duet by two of the students.

Call to Worship:

O Lord,
Thy word is a lamp unto my feet, and a light unto my path.
Thy faithfulness is unto all generations.
Thy hands have made me and fashioned me: give me understanding, that I may learn thy commandments (Psalm 119:105, 90, 73).

Hymn of Praise: "Win the One Next to You."

Thoughts on the Theme: (*An object lesson by one of the students.*)

(Provide the student with a mirror and a piece of cardboard. If it is a cloudy day or if the room does not have sunlight at that particular hour, use a flashlight. Otherwise, have the student stand so that he can reflect the sunlight by means of the mirror.)

When I hold this mirror so that the sunlight shines upon it, I can reflect the sunlight all about me by merely moving the mirror. It takes very little effort on my part. The sun and the mirror are doing all the work. I am merely making a few gestures with my hand.

Now, when I hold this piece of cardboard in the sunlight, nothing happens. It does not reflect the sunlight as the mirror does. I can try ever so hard by turning and twisting the cardboard, but still there is no reflection. When we are good examples, we reflect God's love to those about us. God's love is like the sunlight. It brightens the darkest lives, just as the sun brightens the darkest rooms. Our lives are either like this mirror or like this piece of cardboard. We either reflect God's love or we do not. If we do, then we are like the mirror, for we reflect God's love in everything we do and say. We do so with no effort on our part, for we are so ready and willing to follow God's Word.

If we do not reflect God's love, then we are like the cardboard. His light shines on us and for us just the same, but our souls are so dull and our lives so far away from Him we have not the power to reflect the light. We do not spread sunshine and happiness as we should.

When I move the mirror about in the sunlight, the reflection moves from place to place. It brightens every spot I focus it on. When we are Christians and truly follow the Word of God, we are certain to be good examples to others. Our influence for the good and the righteous will move from place to place and from person to person, wherever we go.

Story: A LESSON OUT OF SCHOOL.

Saturday afternoons were always dull on Oak Street. Freddie Bishop took his piano lesson and George McDonald his violin lesson. Jack Hall always went to his cousin's farm for the week-end. Jack Saunders went to the food market with his mother. So Ernie always found Saturday afternoons exceptionally long. To break the monotony, he often played with little three-year-old Willie Norton. Although Ernie was ten years older, he always enjoyed playing with Willie. And to Willie no boy was quite so wonderful as Ernie.

On school days, as long as the weather was pleasant, Willie would walk to the corner with Ernie every morning. And he would be waiting there after school. How excited he was the first day Ernie let him carry one of his books the length of four houses—from the corner to the house where Willie lived. Ernie lived next door. Willie thought it was truly wonderful to be able to do anything Ernie did.

So Ernie and Willie started for a walk that Saturday afternoon. Ernie decided to turn down Jackson Street when he saw the huge digging machines standing idle near the curb where the workmen had left them at noon. That's right, he thought. A new water main was being laid down Jackson Street. It would be interesting to see how the work was coming along.

Ernie stood for a long time talking to Willie about the mammoth machine. He explained how that great scoop with the big iron teeth swung into the ground and filled itself with huge rocks just as easily as if it had been lowered into soft sand. The more he explained the machine to Willie, the more interested he himself became. That scoop surely was a mighty big thing! He wondered how it would feel to sit in it. His eyes ran down the long crane shaft to the little gray metal house resting on the wide, flat caterpillar treads. Ernie knew the man who operated the crane sat in the little cubbyhole in the front. The rest of the little house must be for the engine and all the other machinery necessary to operate such a powerful crane. Then he spied the little metal ladder that reached from the footing around the little house to the roof. He glanced hurriedly down the street. No one was in sight. This was his chance to explore the big crane!

"Wait here, Willie," he said quickly. "Just wait here. I'll be right back."

He stepped from the caterpillar tread onto the narrow footing. Then up the ladder, across the roof, and started crawling on his hands and knees along the crane shaft to the huge shovel. He was so intent on crawling along the narrowing crane shaft that Willie was completely forgotten until he felt a tug on his left ankle. He glanced over his shoulder and into the smiling, upturned face of little Willie. "Willie right behind you!" he said happily. "Willie right behind you!"

Ernie was paralyzed with fear. Below them was a ten-foot ditch the workmen had dug just before quitting time that day. They were almost to the shovel end of the crane shaft, which meant they were in the air about ten feet. He did not dare turn around, for the shaft was the narrowest at that point. Beads of perspiration suddenly stood on his forehead. He tried to keep his voice calm as he said:

"Willie, hold tight. Hold real tight, Willie."

"O. K., Ernie," the little fellow smiled proudly. "I do what you do."

Ernie's hands were cold and clammy. He was hot and cold at once. All he could think of doing was to keep saying as calmly as possible, "Hold tight, Willie. Hold real tight."

Then there was a piercing squeak of breaks. A construction company's truck came to a sudden stop a few feet in front of the "Street Closed" sign. The watchman leaped from the truck. He threw up his arms wildly and was about to shout when he checked himself. Instead, he walked quickly, but as carefully as he could, toward little Willie, trying to smile in a friendly manner. Whatever happened, he must not frighten the little fellow.

"Hold tight up there, sonny," he called cheerfully. "I'll get a big ladder and get you right down!" Then he turned and raced toward the truck.

Ernie was so weak from fright and from the strain that when his feet left the last rung of the ladder and touched the ground once more, his legs simply folded beneath him. His head was spinning round and round, and his stomach felt as if he would never want any food again. Little Willie came running to his side, crying happily, "Willie big like Ernie! I hold on tight!"

Ernie looked up into the sober face of the watchman.

"Is he your little brother?" the workman asked.

"N—n—no, sir," Ernie managed to stammer. "H—h—he lives next door."

"Son," the watchman said in a serious tone, looking down at Ernie, "do you realize he could have been seriously hurt today? Maybe killed?"

Ernie hung his head. His lips quivered.

"And do you realize," the watchman went on, "that it would have been your fault? He is such a little mite. To him you are somebody really great. He wants to be like you. He wants to do the things you do. That puts you in a mighty important spot, son. If he is going to do just what you do, that means you must be mighty careful what you do. That means you must be a good example."

"Y—y—yes, sir," Ernie stammered. "I—I—I know. I don't know why I did it, sir. I guess I just did not think."

The watchman was ready to say more. But one look at Ernie told him nothing further needed to be said. There was no mistaking. Ernie had learned his lesson that day.

Prayer Hymn: Sing softly "Open My Eyes That I May See."

Prayer (by the teacher).

Offertory Service:

Jesus said, "Take heed, and beware of covetousness: for a man's life consisteth not in the abundance of the things which he possesseth" (Luke 12:15).

To covet something means to have a great desire for something. Jesus tells us to beware of having a great desire for worldly goods and putting the desire to own or possess things before the desire to do good. We can not be good examples when we are covetous. Nor can we be good examples when we fail to share. In the eyes of God, it is not how much we have, but how much we share that counts.

(Play softly "I'll Be a Sunbeam for Jesus" while the offering is taken. Conclude with a short prayer by one of the students.)

Adult Leader:

Last Sunday we thought about choosing the right. Today our theme is being a good example. These two lessons go together, for we can not be good examples unless we choose the right. And if we choose the right, we are bound to be good examples. There are certain things which interfere with our choosing the right, and therefore keep us from being good examples. What are these certain things? (Give the students an opportunity to express themselves.) They are *bad habits* which at first do not seem important, but gradually take hold of our lives.

This is the time of year when leaves are falling from the trees. The leaves are brown and dry. They are dead leaves. They are no longer beautiful to look at, nor are they a help to the tree in any way. So they drop from the branches and clutter the streets and lawns. We get rid of them by raking them together and burning them.

Bad habits are just like dead leaves. They make our lives as unsightly as dead leaves make a lawn. They are harmful to us. They keep us from living beautiful lives and being good examples. So, like the dead leaves, we must gather all our bad habits together and destroy them. We must rid our lives of bad habits as we rid our lawns of dead leaves.

Let us think about some of the bad habits we must get rid of if we are going to be good examples.

(Display the poster with the empty basket described in *Patterns for 52 Visual Lessons*. Fill it with leaves as you read the undesirable quality written on each, and discuss the accompanying verse of Scripture. Have the students locate the verses and participate in the discussion.)

(Have the students make the baskets described in the book mentioned above.)

Benediction.

SERVICE NO. 37—OCTOBER

Growing in Stature Through—

APPRECIATION

In every thing give thanks: for this is the will of God in Christ Jesus concerning you.—1 Thessalonians 5:18.

Prelude: Use "He's a Wonderful Saviour to Me" as a duet sung by two of the students.

Call to Worship:

> *I will lift up mine eyes unto the hills, from whence cometh my help. My help cometh from the Lord, which made heaven and earth* (Psalm 121:1, 2).
> *O Lord, how great are thy works!* (Psalm 92:5).
> *I will praise thee, O Lord, with my whole heart;*
> *I will shew forth all thy marvellous works* (Psalm 9:1).

Hymn of Praise: "Sunshine in the Soul."

Thoughts on the Theme: (*An object lesson by one of the students.*)

(Provide the student with a book or magazine containing a great many colored illustrations, such as a copy of *National Geographic*.)

If I turn the pages of this magazine slowly, one by one, you have plenty of time to see the beauty of each picture. You are able to see all the details and appreciate the pictures and the beautiful colors. The faster I turn the pages the less you see of the pictures. Therefore, much of the detail and beauty is lost. If I hold the book in one hand and merely run my thumb along the edge of the pages, you see nothing clearly. Everything is just a blur.

When we take time to appreciate the things given to us, it is like turning the pages slowly, one by one. Appreciating something means more than just voicing our thanks. It means looking at it carefully so as to enjoy all its beauty. It means using the gift. In some instances it means learning how to make the most use of it or better use of it.

But when we accept things done for us as a matter of fact without showing sincere appreciation, it is like turning the pages of this magazine so rapidly we can not possibly see or understand all the beauty of each individual picture. And when we take everything given us for granted, it is like running our thumb along the edge of the pages so that we see nothing but a blur.

In order to receive the most good from a picture, we must study each detail carefully. In order to get the most good from what is given to us, we must prove our appreciation by using the gifts the very best way we can.

Story: LOVE IS A POWERFUL THING.

Luckily a beautiful, full moon shown brightly that October night, otherwise little Mrs. Dawson might not have seen 864 painted on the gatepost of Dr. Richard's home. The nights were already chilly, and she held her thin, shabby coat closer to her as a rough autumn wind suddenly raced through the valley. Twice she almost rang the bell, but twice she hesitated. What could she say to Dr. Richards? How could she begin? After all, why bother him with Jerry? It would be different if Dr. Richards was the only doctor who could help him, but more than a half dozen other doctors had told her the same thing. Jerry would walk again if he had a series of operations, but they would cost well over a thousand dollars. A thousand dollars! They might as well ask for the moon. How could she possibly pay a thousand dollars? Again she withdrew her hand from the bell. It was no use. No use to bother Dr. Richards—and yet every one of the other doctors had ended by saying, "Why don't you see Dr. Richards? Maybe he can help you." She thought of Jerry's little twisted legs. She thought of his patient smile and of the longing in his eyes as he watched the other children at play. Then, with one quick movement, she rang the bell. The door opened almost instantly and a cheery voice said:

"Come in! Come in! It's a chilly night to be out in the wind."

When she was comfortably seated before a crackling fire, the young man said in a friendly tone:

"I am Dr. Richards. How can I help you?"

Mrs. Dawson showed her surprise. Somehow she expected Dr. Richards to be an older man. Why waste his time? Surely he would not be interested when he learned how poor they were. She felt embarrassed and ill at ease.

"I—I—I—I came to tell you about Jerry," she stammered. "That is, the other doctors told me—I mean—you see—"

Dr. Richards smiled kindly. "Take off your coat," he said quietly. "Then tell me all about Jerry."

While Mrs. Dawson spoke, Dr. Richards nodded silently. Several times he interrupted by asking a question. Finally, he said, "I shall stop by and see Jerry tomorrow. Then perhaps we can make plans for his first operation as soon as possible."

"Dr. Richards," Mrs. Dawson said in a trembling voice, "we are poor, but we are honest. We have paid so much for doctor bills for Jerry these past ten years that we never have an extra penny. In fact, we are always in debt. We could never pay you even a small amount, let alone a thousand dollars. There is nothing Mr. Dawson nor I would not do for Jerry. Yet we could not promise to pay such an amount, knowing we could never do so."

Dr. Richards leaned forward so that the lively fire in the hearth lit his face.

"There will be no charge for any of the work I do for Jerry. In fact, not even while he is at the hospital. You see, it is my way of showing appreciation for the things done for me. When I was a very small child my parents died, leaving me an orphan. I was placed in a children's home even before I could walk. Had it not been for the great kindnesses others did for me, I would not have lived, let alone become a doctor. The people who gave generous gifts to the children's home so that the home could take care of needy children, and the people who sent me through college and medical school, do not need money. They do not want any part of their generous gifts returned. But my appreciation is too great to forget such wonderful kindnesses. Since I have become a doctor, I have helped many children the way I will help Jerry. You see, it is the only way I can really show how much I appreciate what others did for me when I needed help. Love is a powerful thing when it gets rolling, and true appreciation is the best thing I know to send it off to a good start."

Mrs. Dawson was too excited to think clearly. Her one thought was to hurry home and tell the wonderful news to Mr. Dawson and Jerry, who she knew would be sitting in front of the window in Jerry's room, eagerly watching for her return. She thanked Dr. Richards again and again. Then she buttoned her worn, old coat around her and hurried down the drive. As she passed through the stone gateposts, she paused. Tears of happiness filled her eyes. Dr. Richards was going to do all this for Jerry just because others had been kind to him when he was a helpless child! Maybe she should have told Dr. Richards more about Jerry. Maybe she should have told him that she and Mr. Dawson took Jerry into their home when he was a very small, neglected boy for the very same reason. Others had been kind to both of them in many ways, so they had felt they could best return such love by loving another needy child.

"Love is a powerful thing when it gets rolling," Dr. Richards had said, "and true appreciation is the best thing I know to send it off to a good start." Truly, love is a powerful thing, Mrs. Dawson thought as she braced herself against the wind and hurried toward the little frame house on the other side of town—so powerful that it was going to turn two little twisted legs into two sturdy ones. It was going to make a little boy walk again!

Prayer Hymn: "More Love to Thee." Use the first two verses as a prayer hymn and the last two verses as a prayer response.

Prayer (by the teacher).

Offertory Service:

As Jesus entered a certain village, ten lepers who stood off in the distance saw Him. They lifted up their voices, saying, "Jesus, Master, have mercy on us." When Jesus saw them He said, "Go shew yourselves unto the priests." When they did as Jesus had told them, they were healed of the disease. All ten lepers were healed, but only one returned to thank Jesus. He showed his deep appreciation by falling on his knees before Jesus and giving Him thanks. "Were there not ten cleansed?" Jesus asked. "But where are the nine?" (Luke 17:11-17.)

God gives us wonderful gifts each day. When we forget to show our appreciation for His wonderful love, we are like the nine lepers who were healed, but who forgot to say thank you. God gives us many ways each day to say thank you. Sometimes it is helping an old person. Sometimes it is caring for a small child or some one ill. Sometimes it is by running errands. Sometimes it is by sharing with others the things we are given.

(Play softly "Do a Deed of Kindness" while the offering is taken and while one of the students offers a brief prayer of thanks.)

Adult Leader:

Every evening before she went to bed, Lucy sat at her desk for a long time, writing. Her mother asked about it one night.

"You write so earnestly, Lucy," her mother said. "Tell me, what is it you write?"

"Each night before I go to bed," Lucy replied, "I make a list of all the things for which I am thankful. When I see all my blessings written down, it makes me appreciate them more."

Often when some one does something kind, we merely say a quick thank you and fail to appreciate fully what has been done for us. One of the best ways to make ourselves fully appreciate any type of gift is to sit down and write a letter of appreciation.

Benediction.

SERVICE NO. 38—OCTOBER

Growing in Stature Through—

DOING OUR PART

Well done, thou good and faithful servant: thou hast been faithful over a few things, I will make thee ruler over many things.—Matthew 25:21.

Prelude: Use "Does Jesus Care?" as a soprano solo sung by one of the students.

Call to Worship:

>Did you pause and thank your Father
>Since the dawning of this day,
>For the countless blessings sent you?
>For His love which lights your way?
>If you have, then come and join us.
>Sing again your thankful songs.
>If you have not, come and worship,
>For to God all praise belongs.

Hymn of Praise: "Glorious Things of Thee Are Spoken."

Thoughts on the Theme: (*An object lesson by one of the students.*)

(Provide the student with a blooming potted plant and a flower pot of hard, dry soil.)

Our lesson theme today is doing our part. We have learned the importance of having faith and trusting in God at all times. But along with our faith and trust in God we also must be willing to do our part if we expect God to bless us and provide for us. These two flower pots show us what happens to a life when a person is willing and when he is unwilling to do his part.

A seed was planted in each of these pots. The person who planted the seed in this pot immediately forgot about it. He did not water the seed. He did not place it in the sunlight. So, now he has nothing but a pot of hard, dry soil. But this person cared for the seed. He watered it. He placed it in the sunlight. And he cared for the plant which grew from the seed. Now he has a beautiful flower to enjoy.

God gives all of us talents, abilities, and opportunities. The person who says, "God will take care of me"—and means God will provide for his every need, so all he intends to do is to sit back and wait—is like the person who did not take care of the seed.

But when we say, God will take care of me and provide for me *if* I do my part, then we are like the person who took care of the seed which God gave to him and from which this beautiful flower grew. God has given us hands with which to work. He has given us minds to use, eyes to see, and talents and abilities so that we can do certain things well. If we expect God to continue to bless us, we must prove worthy of doing our part.

Story: THE PRIZE PILE OF SCRAPS.

"But Joyce!" exclaimed Marcia. "It's the Halloween party! The big fall event of the Freshman year! Surely, if you wrote home explaining *that,* your folk would send you the money for a costume. You simply *must* go to the party!"

Joyce smiled faintly. Somehow these girls did not quite understand that every one did not come from a wealthy home. Just to be able to attend college was more than she had dreamed. She knew what a sacrifice her family was making for her. She was too grateful to ask for anything but her actual needs. But why bother to explain it to these girls? Most of them would not understand. So she simply shrugged her shoulders and said lightly, "Of course, I would like to go, but since I can not, I shall not waste my time feeling sorry for myself."

She sounded quite convincing, but as the Halloween party drew closer and every one talked about nothing else, Joyce could not help but wish that she, too, might go. But it was out of the question to buy a costume. Then she happened to pass Patrica's door the afternoon a half dozen girls gathered in Patrica's room to try on their costumes. Patrica stood in the middle of the room dressed in a beautiful flowing hoop skirt with ruffled flounces showing beneath the lacy edge.

"I still do not like it," Patrica said as she viewed herself in the mirror of her dresser. "I think I'll change it."

"Oh, Patrica," said Marilyn, fearfully, "if I were you, I would not change it one bit. It is really beautiful."

"I distinctly told my mother to send me a gypsy costume," Patrica complained in a peevish way. "I don't know why she sent this thing."

"But, Patrica, this is simply beautiful," Carrie Anne assured her. "And it fits you perfectly. I feel sure you will win first prize in it."

"No," insisted Patrica. "I think I shall change it."

With that she opened her dresser drawer and whisked out a pair of scissors. She handed them to Rosemary, saying, "Here. Cut off the skirt to my knees." The girls all pleaded, but in the end Rosemary cut the skirt according to Patrica's orders. As soon as the piece fell to the floor, Patrica decided to make other changes. "I shall cut the whole skirt off. Then I'll use the bottom white flounces around the waist. And I'll change the blouse."

The girls stood by pleading with Patrica, but when Patrica decided to do a thing, Patrica did it no matter what others said. Soon the costume lay in a hopeless heap in the middle of the room.

"It's no good now," she said lightly. "I might as well finish the job." So saying, Patrica held up the larger pieces and merrily cut them into odd shapes. Most of the girls watched her without comment. They were used to Patrica's unreasonable ways. This, however, was too surprising for words. Then Julia looked at Patrica disgustedly.

"If you ask me," she said sternly, "I think that was a terrible thing to do."

"But I didn't ask you, Julie," Patrica said sweetly. "So you need not worry. I'll wire my mother right away. She will send me a gypsy costume the first thing in the morning, and I shall have it in plenty of time for the party Saturday night."

Joyce was still standing in the doorway, watching silently. Patrica paused beside her long enough to say:

"Why don't you take that pile of scraps and make yourself a costume out of it, Joy? Then you can go to the Halloween party, too."

Joyce's eyes fairly beamed. "Do you really mean it?" she cried.

"Of course, I mean it. What will I do with that junk?" With that she was down the hall on her way to send the wire.

Saturday night finally arrived. A beautiful, bright harvest moon shone as if it were special decoration. Such excitement! Such fun! And such lovely costumes—but none as lovely as the peasant outfit Joyce wore. So the judges said, as they awarded her first prize. Of course, they did not know that it was once a beautiful old-fashioned costume with a hoop skirt and a white ruffled flounce. To them it was a clever little peasant skirt with a white ruffled blouse. Nor did they know that Patrica was sitting alone in her room, staring at her mother's letter which read:

"I am sorry, dear, but you must learn to show appreciation by taking care of the things given to you."

Perhaps if the judges had known about Patrica and about the pile of scraps from which Joyce made the prize-winning costume, they would have praised her even more.

Prayer Hymn: "I Need Thee Every Hour."

Prayer (by the teacher).

Offertory Service:

If we wrote down all the things God has given to us (or, in other words, all the things we call ours), we would have a very long list. Some of us would have such long lists that we might become vain, feeling that we have so much more than others. In his second letter to Timothy, Paul warned the people of that day about feeling vain or conceited over earthly possessions. Paul wrote: "Charge them that are rich in this world, that they be not highminded, nor trust in uncertain riches, but in the living God, who giveth us richly all things to enjoy; that they do good, that they be rich in good works, ready to distribute, willing to communicate" (1 Timothy 6:17, 18).

Let us always remember that it is more blessed to give than to receive.

Adult Leader:

We know that God made all creatures, even the little squirrels. But God did not create them and then forget about them. God provides for them. He takes care of their needs. This time of year He gives them enough food to last during the long winter ahead. But the squirrels must do their part. They must spend time and energy gathering and storing acorns and nuts for use when ice and snow cover the ground.

God provides for us in exactly the same way. He sends us all our needs through His continuous blessings. But it is up to us to do our part. If the squirrels do not do their part and gather the nuts and store them, they will not have enough food to last them until spring. If we do not use our energy and abilities and time making use of the opportunities God gives to us, then, like the squirrels, we will not have sufficient to carry us through times of need.

(Have the students make the squirrel described in *Patterns for 52 Visual Lessons*.)

Benediction.

SERVICE NO. 39—OCTOBER

Growing in Stature Through—

SELF-DENIAL

Whosoever will come after me, let him deny himself, and take up his cross, and follow me.—Mark 8:34.

Prelude: Have a group of students sing "My Saviour First of All."

Call to Worship:

    Leader: *And he said to them all, If any man will come after me, let him deny himself, and take up his cross daily, and follow me* (Luke 9:23).

        For what shall it profit a man, if he shall gain the whole world, and lose his own soul? Or what shall a man give in exchange for his soul? (Mark 8:36, 37).

    Group: *I will extol thee, my God, O king; and I will bless thy name for ever and ever.*

        Every day will I bless thee; and I will praise thy name for ever and ever (Psalm 145:1, 2).

Hymn of Praise: "Praise Him! Praise Him!"

Thoughts on the Theme: (*An object lesson by one of the students.*)

    (Place nickels in three stacks of ten, five, and one.)

Self-denial means doing without something we need or want in order to give to others. For instance, let us pretend I am on my way to the store to buy myself a box of cookies and I meet some one who is in great need of a nickel. I have ten nickels in my pocket, so I readily give him one of them. Now I have nine nickels left. I can still buy my cookies and have eight nickels left for myself. Giving such a small part of what I have left is not self-denial.

If I have these five nickels in my pocket and give one away, I can still buy my cookies. Again there would be no self-denial.

But if I have just one nickel with which to buy cookies and I give it to some one I meet who is in great need of a nickel, that is self-denial. When I gave the nickel away, I had none left. That is what self-denial really means—giving something to some one at a sacrifice to myself.

Story: PENNY PURSE.

My name is Penny—Penny Purse. My friends now call me Happy Penny. I say *now*, because not very long ago they called me Penny Lag-Bag. But, really, it was not my fault. I did not mean to lag behind the others all the time. In fact, I often hid my face in shame —especially in church. There I was, stuffed so full I was rapidly losing my shape. And Mr. Gordon never took me from his pocket! Lag-Bag, indeed! I did not want to lag behind. I did not want to be idle and just grow fatter and fatter all the time. But what could I do? Mr. Gordon was too fond of his money to part with even a penny. And then Linda changed everything.

You will like Linda the moment you see her. I did. Grandfather Gordon had just taken me from his pocket to lock me up in the deep, dark desk drawer where I always spent the night, when the front doorbell rang and almost instantly Linda breezed into the room. It was like a breath of refreshing air, or perhaps more like a brilliant, dazzling sunbeam.

"Hello, Grandfather Gordon," she cried. "I was so afraid you had gone to bed, and I just had to see you tonight."

"Huh," grunted Mr. Gordon. "It seems to me young ladies should be home, asleep, at this hour."

"But it is only nine o'clock, Grandfather!" Linda cried. I could tell from her sparkling eyes that she was bubbling over with excitement. "Grab your hat and coat. I have a cab waiting outside. They are holding up the meeting until we get there."

"Who? What meeting?" demanded Grandfather Gordon. Linda was always doing something unexpected. She graduated from college last June, and since then has been doing social-service work in the thickly populated tenement district across town. "Come along. We haven't time now for talking. I shall tell you all about it on the way."

For a moment I held my breath for fear I would be forgotten in all the rush. Grandfather Gordon had already placed me in the top desk drawer. Linda hurried him halfway across the room. Then he turned back to the desk, placed me in his pocket and mumbled unpleasantly, but followed Linda out to the waiting cab.

"I knew you would not mind, Grandfather," Linda began, as soon as they were seated inside. "In fact, I knew you would want to do it. I can not understand why I did not think of you sooner. I do hope you will forgive me for being so thoughtless."

"Where are we going? And what is this all about?" Grandfather roared.

"We are going to the meeting."

"What meeting?"

"The meeting of the workers who put on the drive for funds for the new children's hospital."

"What's that got to do with me?" I could tell from his voice that Grandfather Gordon was anything but pleased.

"The workers were divided into two teams," Linda explained as calmly as if she did not know that Grandfather was about to explode. "Our team has been ahead all the time. That is, our team has received more contributions than the other team. Then tonight at the meeting, without any warning, Mr. Cahill stood up and said he would make a contribution of five hundred dollars and give the other team credit for it."

"Huh," grunted Grandfather Gordon. "Old Sid Cahill did that? Why didn't he give his contribution to your team?"

"His niece is on the other one."

"Huh," grunted Grandfather Gordon.

"Our team has worked so hard, Grandfather. I myself have called on over a hundred persons and received a contribution from each. We have been far ahead all the time. And then this! So, Grandfather, do you know what I did? I stood right up and said, 'Ladies and gentlemen, one of our gifts is not in as yet. If I may have a half hour, I shall get the person who will match Mr. Cahill's gift and bring him to the meeting in person'."

"Huh," grunted Grandfather Gordon. "So now we are going to get him? Who is he?"

"Why, you, of course, Grandfather!"

For a moment I thought Grandfather Gordon was going to have a heart attack. He mumbled and sputtered and grunted and groaned all at once. Just then the taxi stopped suddenly, and instantly the door was opened by one of the crowd standing near the curb, waiting for us. Grandfather was almost lifted out and noisily escorted across the sidewalk and into the building by at least a dozen people. They hurried us down the hall, all talking at once. I could just hear a jumbled chatter about the gift being so wonderful and Mr. Gordon being such a fine, generous gentleman. When we entered the meeting room all the people on one side stood up and cheered. Linda and three other young women hurried Grandfather to the front of the room. She raised her hand for silence.

"Ladies and gentlemen," she said eagerly, holding fast to Grandfather's arm as if she was afraid he would start running home any minute, "this is my grandfather, Mr. Clyde Gordon. He is going to give a generous gift to the children's hospital fund." Grandfather Gordon must have frowned and scowled or started to mumble, for she quickly added, "He is happy to match the gift Mr. Cahill just made."

That remark, as Linda well knew, caused Grandfather Gordon to grunt out loud. He and Mr. Cahill have been business rivals for some forty years. Neither one would let the other fellow get ahead of him.

"Match Mr. Cahill's gift, indeed," roared Grandfather. "I shall double it!" I thought the crowd would go wild. I did not know people could make so much noise. They clapped their hands. They whistled and cheered. It even sounded to me that some one was jumping up and down on the bare floor. I could tell the way Grandfather was standing that his chest was out, his head was held high, and he was smiling.

Then Mr. Cahill started shouting and the crowd quieted down.

"Double me, will you, old Clyde Gordon!" he thundered. "I'll double your gift and add an extra hundred dollars!"

That set the crowd cheering like mad once more. I felt Grandfather Gordon stiffening, so I knew he was about to explode again.

"Huh!" he grunted. "A hundred dollars extra! I'll double your gift, old Sid Cahill, and I'll add *five* hundred dollars!"

That broke up the meeting. Newspaper photographers sprang up in all corners. Such excitement! Every one rushed forward to shake Grandfather's hand—the mayor, the chief of police, and half of the Chamber of Commerce. Finally, our minister gripped Grandfather's hand firmly and said:

"This is wonderful, Mr. Gordon! Simply wonderful! The need for a children's hospital is so great, you know. Surely your generous gift will be a challenge to many others who have not as yet given."

Then the most wonderful thing happened. Grandfather pulled me from his pocket. I was so fat I felt ashamed, but only for a moment. For Grandfather Gordon opened my clasp and drew out a large portion of the bills crowded inside. He handed them to the minister, saying, "Here is something for the work of the church. I have grown careless about my contributions, Mr. Brighton. Let me know when something special is needed in the Bible school or church."

I can not begin to tell you how happy I was. I looked about me. The little brown suede bag dangling from Lucy Milton's arm smiled at me so sweetly. So did the red-leather purse Doris Wilkinson was carrying. They go to church often and have no doubt been wondering why they never see me there. I am so glad they were at the meeting that night and saw how happy I was. For now they call me Happy Penny. And we often meet each other in church these days, for Grandfather Gordon has become a most generous giver. Just yesterday on the way home from church Grandfather said:

"I am a happy old man these days, Linda, and I have you to thank. You showed me the great happiness which comes from helping **others.**"

Linda smiled. "That makes two of us happy, Grandfather," she said.

"That makes three of us happy," I whispered. For truly I am a very thin, but very happy, little purse these days.

Prayer Hymn: "Praise the Name of Jesus."

Prayer (by the teacher).

Offertory Service:

> Praise the Lord with songs of gladness
> Praise the Lord with prayers sincere,
> Praise the Lord with deeds of kindness
> Done to others far and near.
> Praise the Lord by bringing offerings
> Given gladly out of love,
> So God's kingdom here on earth
> Might be more like heaven above.

(Play softly "Willing Am I" while the offering is taken. Conclud with a brief prayer of thanks offered by one of the students.)

Poem (by a student):

> Give of your best to the Master,
>   Give Him first place in your heart;
> Give Him first place in your service,
>   Consecrate ev'ry part.
> Give, and to you shall be given;
>   God His beloved Son gave;
> Gratefully seeking to serve Him,
>   Give Him the best that you have.

Adult Leader:

(Display the poster described in *Patterns for 52 Visual Lessons* and refer to it at the conclusion of the following thoughts:)

Through our object lesson we learned that self-denial means to give to others by doing without ourselves. Jesus said, "Whosoever will come after me, let him deny himself, and take up his cross, and follow me. For whosoever will save his life shall lose it; but whosoever shall lose his life for my sake and the gospel's, the same shall save it" (Mark 8:34, 35). What did Jesus mean when He said that whosoever saves his life shall lose it, but whosoever loses his life for Jesus' sake and for the gospel's, he shall save his life? (Encourage the pupils to express their thoughts on these questions. Then explain the meaning.)

At the beginning of our story today, Grandfather Gordon was

hoarding his money. He was living for himself alone, helping no one and closing his eyes to ways of helping others. Had he not changed, he would have died a very unhappy old man, without friends and disobedient to God's Word, which teaches us to share and help others. However, at the end of our story he had changed completely. He no longer hoarded his money, but he shared with the needy. He spent his money and used his life to help others. Therefore he was really saving his life, for he was proving worthy of a reward in heaven.

Penny Purse says, "I am always happy when people give, denying themselves so others might live."

Let us try to remember those words and follow the teachings of Jesus by serving God through helping others.

(Have the students make the purse described in the book mentioned above.)

Benediction.

SERVICE NO. 40—OCTOBER

Growing in Stature Through—

OBEDIENCE

We ought to obey God rather than men.—Acts 5:29.

Prelude: "Trust and Obey" sung as a solo by one of the students.

Call to Worship:

> Teach me, O Lord, the way of thy statutes; and I shall keep it unto the end.
> Give me understanding, and I shall keep thy law; yea, I shall observe it with my whole heart.
> Make me to go in the path of thy commandments; for therein do I delight.
> Behold, I have longed after thy precepts: quicken me in thy righteousness
> (Psalm 119:33-35, 40).

Hymn of Praise: "Have Thine Own Way, Lord."

Thoughts on the Theme: (An object lesson by one of the students.)

(Use the electric-light wall switch.)

An electric-light switch is an excellent illustration of perfect obedience. When we press the button (or flip the switch, depending upon what kind it is), the light goes on immediately. There is no questioning. There is no arguing. There is no hesitation. We do not have to coax or beg or threaten. The light goes on instantly. When we press the other button, the light goes off just as quickly.

Once in a while, something goes wrong with the wiring and breaks the connection between the light bulb and the wall switch. When that happens, the light sometimes flickers, then goes out. Sometimes the button must be pressed several times before the bulb will light. Sometimes it must be pressed a certain way before the bulb will light. And sometimes, no matter how we press the button, the bulb will not light.

When we are disobedient we are like the wall switch that will not work. When we must be coaxed to be obedient, we are like the switch that must be pressed a certain way in order for the bulb to light. When we are partly obedient and partly disobedient, we are like the bulb that flickers on and off, but does not give a steady, bright light.

In Colossians 3:20 we read, "Children, obey your parents in all things: for this is well pleasing unto the Lord." This does not mean we should obey our parents part of the time, or halfway some of the time. It means all the time. When we do so we are like the good switch that lights the bulb instantly without questioning, without arguing, without hesitation, and without being coaxed.

Story: OUR DENNIS DILLWORTH.

I suppose there is a Dennis Dillworth in every group—the kind of person who always knows better; who laughs at signs and then pays no attention to them; and who thinks he is just too smart to be told anything. If you have a Dennis Dillworth in your group, I hope he reads this, so he can change his ways before it is too late. For this is the story of what happened to our Dennis Dillworth.

Honestly, it is surprising that he has not been hurt before. Seriously hurt, I mean. For he has been inviting trouble for a long time. Like last winter when we were all ice skating. The sign at one end of the lake clearly said in bold red letters DANGER—THIN ICE. But Dennis only laughed. He would show us what fancy skating was on any part of the lake. And so he fell in. Of course, we pulled him out, and all that happened was he caught a bad cold from having to go all the way home in wet clothing.

Then at school, Dennis spoiled every game we tried to play. He simply would not obey the rules. It wasn't much fun trying to play baseball with Dennis on one team. We would catch the ball he batted high in the air, far off the ground, and tag him, but still he would argue that he was not out. And there was no use to argue with Dennis. He was always right. So we stopped playing baseball.

He was always disobeying our teachers and being punished by having to stay after school. Sometimes the whole class had to stay fifteen minutes because of him. That did not help his popularity any.

He was in my Bible-school class, and really I felt sorry for Miss Smith. She always prepared such an interesting lesson for us, and then had to put up with Dennis! He would whisper and often talk out loud all the while she was trying to teach. Sometimes he would hit the boys over the head with books or tease the girls. We were pretty disgusted with Dennis.

Then came the last week of school. A picnic was planned for our entire class. We all brought our lunches and went to Quinlan's Wood. Dennis started out by spoiling our fun on the slides as soon as we arrived. Miss Dorn told him several times to be more careful, and then, when he pushed Mabel so hard she went over the side and skinned her elbow, we all had to stay away from the slides. Then he caused Leroy to get hurt on the swings. We all held our breath, but Miss Dorn said the rest of us could go on swinging, but Dennis was to sit at the end of the bench until lunch. I was close enough to Dennis to hear him mumble under his breath, "If she thinks I'm going to sit there, she is crazy." He pretended he was slowly making his way over to the bench until Miss Dorn was out of sight. She was taking Leroy to the park's first-aid office to get the nick in his forehead taken care of.

"Nobody's going to make me sit on a bench!" he scowled. And with that he was off in the opposite direction. Even Miss Dorn thought he had gone home. I believe most of us thought "good riddance." I know I did, and I am sorry now. We surely had a fine time at that picnic.

It was not until the next day that I learned about Dennis. He had not come home that night. In fact, he was still missing when the noon dismissal bell rang. We all felt sorry for Miss Dorn, she was so upset, but no one felt she was really responsible in the slightest way. I guess we were all pretty worried about Dennis, because when the word came about three o'clock that afternoon that he had been found, we all whistled and cheered and stamped our feet. Ordinarily, none of us would have acted like that in Miss Dorn's room. She had rules about whistling and cheering in class. And she was very strict about no feet-stamping. But she did not mind that day. She was so happy, she sat right there in front of the class and cried.

When I arrived home from school I learned the whole story. My father had been one of the men who had found Dennis—in a ravine about two miles from Quinlan's Wood.

"He is quite badly hurt," my dad told me. "There is a deep cut on his head and one arm seemed broken. He was a mighty sick boy when we arrived at the hospital."

We all felt sorry for Dennis, but most of our sympathy went to Miss Dorn. She was the most popular teacher in school. Every pupil wanted to get into her class, and then, like us, did not want to leave.

"This settles it for me," I told Charlie at recess the next day. "As soon as Dennis is well again, I am going to tell him plenty."

"Same here!" exclaimed Earl, as he joined our group. "I feel like telling him plenty every time I think of Miss Dorn."

"Just give me a chance at him," Charlie said. "Just one chance. I'll show him. He has been doing things his own way too long."

We really felt that way, too, until we stood in an awkward group around the white, iron hospital bed, looking down at poor Dennis. You could tell he had been pretty sick. His head was still bandaged so that he looked top-heavy. And his left arm was in a cast. We just stood there on one foot and then the other, looking at poor Dennis.

He smiled weakly and said in a very quiet, subdued tone of voice:

"Gee, it was swell of you fellows to come. I was afraid nobody would want to see me again."

I was about to say we had not thought of coming until Miss Dorn suggested it. In fact, she was waiting for us in her car right then. But Dennis said:

"I—I—I guess I sort of ruined the picnic."

"Oh, no," Joe quickly assured him. "We had a fine time after you left. That is—I mean—"

"I know," Dennis said quietly. "I know how I have been acting, but I have learned my lesson. I want to start all over again. I was thinking this morning I hope I pass so I can go on with you fellows and show you how good I can be. But on the other hand, I hope I do not pass. Then I could be in Miss Dorn's room another year and show her how sorry I am."

"It's time to lie down now, Dennis," the nurse said quietly.

I fully expected at least an argument, but Dennis said quickly, "Yes, nurse," and immediately settled back. I looked at Charlie. Charlie looked at me.

"Don't worry about that," I tried to assure him. "Even if you do not pass, you still can be one of us outside of school hours." Then we filed out of the room. I was last. I paused and glanced back as I passed through the door. I wondered why I had said such a thing. Then I was glad—not glad just because I had said it, but glad because, as I looked at Dennis, I suddenly knew that I really meant it.

Prayer Hymn: First verse of "O Jesus, Thou Art Standing."

Prayer (by the teacher).

Offertory Service:

To be obedient to God means following His Word. It means living, loving, and giving according to His commands. God has told us a great deal about giving. We are to share with the poor and needy. We are to give so the orphans and widows are cared for. We are to give so that the work of His kingdom may grow. We are to give so that every man, woman, and child all over the world may be taught about Jesus and how He has died to save them, too. We are told to bring our gifts to God the first day of each week. We are told to give freely and wholeheartedly. We are told that it is more blessed to give than to receive. Let us be obedient to God's Word as we bring Him our offerings with glad hearts and willing hands.

(Play "Something for Jesus" while the offering is taken and while

OBEDIENCE

one of the students gives a short prayer of thanks in conclusion.)

Adult Leader:

The owl has come to be a symbol of wisdom as the eagle stands for strength. When some one is wise (or intelligent or smart), we often refer to him as "a wise old owl." One of the wisest things any of us can do is to obey God's Word. God has given to us many wonderful promises. One of the most wonderful promises is that we shall have life everlasting—BUT only if we are obedient to His laws. We must OBEY God by living as He has commanded us. Therefore, it is of greatest importance that we learn to obey or be obedient. In both the Old and the New Testaments much has been said about obedience. Let us turn to our Bibles and learn more about obeying our parents, our teachers, those in authority over us, and obeying God.

(Have students locate, read, and discuss the verses listed in the moon around the owl on the poster described in *Patterns for 52 Visual Lessons*. Be sure to encourage every student to participate in the discussion.)

(Have the students make the owl described in the book mentioned above.)

Benediction.

SERVICE NO. 41—NOVEMBER

Growing in Stature Through—

HUMBLENESS OF MIND

For I say, through the grace given unto me, to every man that is among you, not to think of himself more highly than he ought to think; but to think soberly, according as God hath dealt to every man the measure of faith.—Romans 12:3.

Prelude: Have a group of students sing "Some One Is Watching Your Light."

Call to Worship:

> *I was glad when they said unto me, Let us go into the house of the Lord* (Psalm 122:1).
>
> *The Lord is in his holy temple: let all the earth keep silence before him* (Habakkuk 2:20).

Hymn of Praise: "O Master, Let Me Walk With Thee."

Thoughts on the Theme: (*An object lesson by one of the students.*)

> (Provide the student with a deflated balloon. Use one that has been blown previously, so the student will have no difficulty blowing it during the object lesson.)

A balloon, we know, is capable of stretching. The more air we blow into it, the more the rubber stretches, and the bigger the balloon becomes. Until we put air into it, the balloon is not useful. It can not do the things for which it was made. So, in order to use the balloon, we must blow it up. (Blow balloon to safe size.) The rubber will stretch farther and the balloon will, therefore, hold more air, but this is the safe size. If we blow it any higher, it will be sure to break.

Our minds are very much like balloons. When we do not use our minds, they are as empty and flat as a balloon with no air in it. So we must stretch our minds through learning, working, and growing, just as we must blow air into a flat balloon. As we study and learn how to do more things, our mind enlarges. It is necessary for us to develop a certain amount of self-confidence and self-importance. If we do not, then we will not try to do new things. We will feel we are incapable of learning how, and will not even try. At the same time we must always be humble. The more we learn the humbler we should become, because the more we learn the more we realize how much more there is to learn, and therefore how little we really know. When we keep growing in self-importance and self-confidence, and stop growing in humbleness, then we are like a balloon that is blown too big. We are sure to end up being very unhappy. No one will want to associate with us in the same way that no one wants to play with a broken balloon.

Story: THE LITTLE BUN MAN.

There was a short lull in the usual afternoon rush which gave the three young clerks an opportunity to restock the shelves in the glass cases with more tempting-looking rolls, pies, cakes, and breads. The door had just closed behind a neatly dressed, little, gray-haired gentleman.

"Who is he?" Delores asked as she filled the shelf with creamy lemon pies.

"I don't know. Do you, Estelle?" Alma asked over her shoulder.

"Whom do you mean?" Estelle asked, without turning from the row of chocolate cakes she was arranging. "That little man who just bought six buns?"

"Yes," Delores replied. "He comes in here every day about four o'clock and buys six buns. He seems like such a fine old gentleman."

"I've noticed him, too," Estelle said, "but I have no idea who he is. He is such a kind little man."

"No doubt he lives alone in one of those cheap rooming houses on the next street," Delores suggested. Then the door opened and customers kept coming until six o'clock.

Sure enough, every day the kind little gentleman came into the bakery and purchased six buns. He stood quietly at the edge of the constant row of customers and patiently waited his turn. Many times other customers elbowed their way next to the counter and got served long before him. The girls noticed this.

"He stands so patiently and quietly at the edge of the customers, I am afraid he always waits longer than he should," Delores said several weeks later.

"Yes," agreed Alma, "but no matter how long he must wait, he never complains like some customers."

"Why don't we put his six buns into a bag earlier in the afternoon?" suggested Estelle. "Then we could just hand him the bag. He always has correct change."

"That is an excellent idea," Delores exclaimed. "Let's put the bag right here on the shelf under the cash register. Then it will be handy for all of us."

That is how the quiet little gentleman always received such prompt service at Emil's Bakery when he called daily for his six buns.

Some months later, the daily papers were filled with plans for an art exhibit which would display the works of three internationally famous artists. One was a local artist, Graham Penbrook, who had painted the murals in the new airport depot, the library, and the civic auditorium.

"Wouldn't it be wonderful if we just caught a glimpse of the artists themselves?" Alma said as the three young bakery clerks entered the Jefferson Galleries.

"I should like to see Graham Penbrook," Delores said. "I can not even imagine how it would feel to actually see some one as famous as he."

The next hour passed quickly for the girls as they viewed the wonderful display of masterpieces. A line seemed to be forming at the opposite end of the galleries.

"Graham Penbrook just arrived," the girls overheard some one say. "So many wanted to meet him that he consented to spend the remaining time meeting people."

The three girls hurried to the end of the long line. Delores was eager to get a glimpse of the great artist. She stood on her tiptoes and peered over the crowd. Then she gave a muffled exclamation. "Why—why, he is our little bun man!" she whispered excitedly. "He is our little bun man! Why, I can't believe it!"

Alma and Estelle stood on their tiptoes and peered over the many heads before them. Sure enough! There was no mistaking! Graham Penbrook was the quiet little man who came into Emil's Bakery around four o'clock every afternoon for six buns.

"I—I—I simply can not believe it!" Alma whispered in amazement. "He is so ordinary. So—so—"

"So humble," Estelle added. "Imagine us putting six buns in a bag every day for the famous Graham Penbrook!"

"I guess that is what makes him so great," Delores said. "He is so ordinary. So unassuming. So quiet. So—so humble."

Then the line moved forward and Graham Penbrook's kind eyes smiled warmly as he recognized the three young clerks from Emil's Bakery.

Prayer Hymn: First verse of "Just as I Am."

Prayer (by the teacher).

Offertory Service:

(Play softly "How Can I But Love Him?" while the Scripture is read, while the offering is taken, and while a student offers the dedicatory prayer.)

But this I say, He which soweth sparingly shall reap also sparingly; and he which soweth bountifully shall reap also bountifully. Every man according as he purposeth in his heart, so let him give; not grudgingly, or of necessity: for God loveth a cheerful giver (2 Corinthians 9:6, 7).

Adult Leader:

(Display the poster described in *Patterns for 52 Visual Lessons* and refer to it as you develop the following thoughts:)

In our object lesson John explained how our minds are like balloons. We all know what happens when we blow a balloon too big, when we stretch the rubber too far by blowing too much air into it. Let us think what happens to our minds when we let conceit, self-importance, egotism, or self-confidence stretch them too far.

Let us think about conceit. What is conceit? How can it harm us? Is it all right for us to be conceited about any outstanding talent we might have? (Answer these questions by means of a class discussion. Discuss self-importance, egotism, and self-confidence by means of similar questions. Encourage all students to participate. Conclude by reading Romans 12:3 in unison.)

(Have the students make the balloon described in the book mentioned above.)

Benediction.

SERVICE NO. 42—NOVEMBER

Growing in Stature Through—

SERVING OTHERS

Be kindly affectioned one to another with brotherly love.—Romans 12:10.

Prelude: Use "O Day of Rest and Gladness" as an instrumental played by as many students as possible.

Call to Worship:

> Sing unto the Lord with thanksgiving; sing praise upon the harp unto our God:
> Who covereth the heaven with clouds, who prepareth rain for the earth, who maketh grass to grow upon the mountains.
> He giveth to the beast his food, and to the young ravens which cry.
> The Lord taketh pleasure in them that fear him, in those that hope in his mercy (Psalm 147:7-9, 11).
> Praise ye the Lord.

Hymn of Praise: "This Is My Father's World."

Thoughts on the Theme: (*An object lesson by one of the students.*)

> (Provide the student with eight birthday candles, each in a holder, and two small empty boxes. Arrange seven candles on one box and one single candle on the second box. Arrange the seven so there is plenty of room between each to take it from the box, light it, and replace it without touching the other candles. As the student begins talking, he lights the single candle and one of the seven candles with the same match. Have an older student give this object lesson so there will be no danger of an accident.)

Each of these candles represents a person. When I light these two candles with this same match, it is like God giving life to two people. This candle off by itself is like the person who lives for himself alone. He has the light in his life which God gave to him, but he does nothing to share it with others. So his light burns alone and gives but a small glow.

I can take the other lighted candle and light another one with it without putting out the flame. Now I have two candles burning brightly, giving twice the light given by the one burning all alone. I can take the second candle and light a third one, and again neither flame is put out. Now I have three candles burning brightly, giving three times as much light as the single one. And again I can take the third candle and light a fourth, and the fourth and light a fifth, and the fifth and light a sixth, and the sixth and light a seventh. Each time another light is added the glow is brighter without putting out the flame of the candle which gave the light. These seven candles all burning brightly are like seven lives. One person was willing to serve his neighbor by doing a deed of kindness. That neighbor, in turn, helped some one else, who, in turn, helped some one else, and so on. They each served others, but none of them took any light from his own life. In fact, by serving others, each one made the world a brighter place in which to live.

Now these two candles which were lighted first are almost completely burned. They are like two old people whose life on this earth is almost ended. This person will die without leaving a light behind—without any good deeds by which he shall be remembered—for he has lived alone and only for himself. But when this person dies, the good that he has done will be long remembered, for the good deeds that he started were carried on by others, and the world, therefore, has been made more beautiful because he lived.

Story: THE DAY GOOD DEEDS CAME HOME.

When Bob Benton broke his hip and was told by Dr. Johnson that he would have to remain in bed two months, he was the most unhappy boy in Middleville.

"Two months!" he groaned. "Why, that means I will be in bed for Thanksgiving and for Christmas! And I will miss two months of school work, to say nothing of sledding and ice skating! These will be such long, lonely days just lying here alone."

But the news of Bob's accident spread so rapidly, by evening it seemed every one in town knew about it. That very afternoon things began to happen. Leslie stopped on his way home from school.

"Just heard about your accident, Bob," he said as he seated himself on the chair near Bob's bed. "I am going to deliver your papers for you until you are able to do so. I am doing it for nothing, Bob. I won't take one cent pay."

Bob's eyes opened wide.

"Gee, Leslie!" he exclaimed. "That will be great! It will be wonderful! All day I have been trying to figure out what to do. I do not want anything to happen to my paper route. But you must keep all the money you earn. Just keeping my route in good shape for me means a great deal."

"I should say not!" exclaimed Leslie. "I will not take even a penny. You have been a real friend to me. I am glad to have this opportunity to do something for you in return for your kindness."

"All I ever do for you," Bob objected, "is to help you with your homework."

"And that's enough!" exclaimed Leslie. "I would never have passed my English or math last year but for your help. I am doing this to repay you for the many hours you spent helping me."

Then Joe and Henry stopped by. "We're coming over every afternoon to bring you the assignments and to tell you what we studied that day," they said. "Then every morning Kenneth and Jim will stop by to pick up your homework and take it to school for you. Jerry said he is going to be your librarian and get any books you want from the library and return them for you."

"Gee, fellows!" Bob exclaimed. "That will be great! I hope I can do something for you some day."

They both laughed out loud. "What about the time I broke my arm last spring and you carried my books to and from school and to every class all day?" Joe reminded him.

"And what about the time my dad was sick and you helped me take care of some of his work for more than a month? I never could have done it alone."

"That was nothing," Bob said modestly. "I have forgotten all about those times long ago."

"Well, we haven't," Henry assured him. "And neither has Jerry forgotten how you helped him fix his bike and paint it like new."

Then the bell rang and little Mrs. Schultz brought in a big, beautiful pumpkin pie.

"I'm going to bake one for you every Friday," she said, smiling at him.

"Gee, Mrs. Schultz, that's wonderful," Bob said. "But that would be too much trouble for you."

"Trouble, indeed!" she exclaimed. "That's little enough to do for all you've done for me." Then she turned to Bob's mother and said, "Every day when Bob brings my paper, he carries a basket of wood up three flights of stairs so I can have fire in my living-room fireplace. Then he carries the ashes down. Trouble, indeed!"

No sooner had Mrs. Schultz gone when Mr. Benton stopped by. "I'm going to keep you well supplied with fresh fruit," he said, placing a basketful on the table near Bob. "It's just to say thanks for all you've been doing for me."

"Gee, Mr. Benton, that's wonderful!" Bob exclaimed. "But I haven't done that much for you."

"Oh, no?" Mr. Benton said with a twinkle in his eye. "What about the help you give me every day when you deliver my evening paper? Why, you have helped me unload more boxes of fruit than you will eat in your whole lifetime."

Just then the phone rang.

"It is Mrs. Milton," Mother told him. "She said to tell you that she and Mr. Milton are sending you a radio for your room. She said it is to show their appreciation for all you have done for them."

Bob frowned. "That's wonderful of them," he said, "but all I ever do is to shovel the snow off their walk every day when I deliver their paper. Any one would do the same for two old folk as nice as they are."

Shortly after dinner, Mrs. Anderson and about half of Bob's Sunday-school class stopped in. They brought candy, nuts, and magazines. "We're going to hold all our class meetings and parties right here in your room," Mrs. Anderson told him. "Your mother and I planned it over the phone this morning. As soon as the class heard of your accident, they all wanted to plan some way so you would not miss the Thanksgiving and Christmas parties."

"Gee, Mrs. Anderson, that's wonderful!" Bob said, smiling at the group of high-school boys gathered around his bed. "But I don't want to inconvenience any one."

"I guess the class has inconvenienced you enough," George assured him. "You are always doing so much work to make every class project a success that we would not think of having a party without you."

Just before bedtime Mother brought in a scrapbook. "You said you wanted to keep an account of everything that happened while you were home in bed with a broken hip. So here is a scrapbook. Why don't you begin by writing down all the things that happened today?" she asked.

"That's a good idea," Bob said as he reached for his fountain pen. "So many wonderful things have happened to me today. I am going to give each page a title. What do you think I should call the happenings of today?"

"Why don't you call it 'The Day Good Deeds Came Home'?" Mother asked with a smile. "And if there is room at the bottom of the page, I should like to write, 'Son, I am very proud of you'."

Prayer Hymn: "Did You Think to Pray?"

Prayer (by the teacher).

Offertory Service:

One day Jesus said to His disciples, "The harvest truly is plenteous, but the labourers are few; pray ye therefore the Lord of the harvest, that he will send forth labourers into his harvest" (Matthew 9:37, 38).

The whole world is like God's great field, overflowing with much grain to be harvested. We are the laborers or workers who have been sent here by God to do His work. We learn how to do God's work by coming to Bible school and church. We help with God's work when we share with others the things that God has given to us.

(Play softly "Fairest Lord Jesus.")

Adult Leader:

(Display the poster described in *Patterns for 52 Visual Lessons* and refer to it as you develop the following thoughts.)

This time of year in store windows, in newspaper ads, in magazine illustrations, and on greeting cards we often see the horn of plenty. Usually we find all kinds of vegetables and fall fruits tumbling from the horn as a sign of a plentiful harvest just gathered.

A plentiful harvest means, first of all, rich blessings received from God. If God had not made the seeds and the fertile land and sent the rain, the sunshine, the winds, and the seasons, there could be no harvest, for there would be no fruits and vegetables.

Next, a plentiful harvest shows that certain people have worked hard to make use of the blessings that God has given to them.

Just as the horn of plenty is a sign of a fruitful harvest, so serving others is the sign of a fruitful life. Just as God provides the means of a fruitful harvest by sending the rain, the sunshine, and so on, so God provides the means of a fruitful life. God offers to each of us certain good qualities which will help us to help others. Some of these good qualities are listed on our poster. (Discuss each briefly.)

But just as the workers must do their part in order to use God's blessings and prove worthy of a plentiful harvest, so we must use the blessings God offers to us. We can not serve or help others if we are thoughtless. So if we know we are thoughtless, then we must try hard to think about the needs of others. We must speak kind words and show love at all times to every one, be patient and sincere, and willing to share. The more we serve others the more fruitful will be our own lives, and the greater love we will be showing for Christ.

(Have the student make the horn of plenty described in the book mentioned above).

Benediction.

SERVICE NO. 43—NOVEMBER

Growing in Stature Through—

SERVING GOD

Seek ye first the kingdom of God, and his righteousness, and all these things shall be added unto you.—Matthew 6:33.

Prelude: Have a student quartet sing "Count Your Blessings."

Call to Worship:

> *O give thanks unto the Lord; call upon his name: make known his deeds among the people.*
> *Sing unto him, sing psalms unto him: talk ye of all his wondrous works.*
> *Glory ye in his holy name: let the heart of them rejoice that seek the Lord* (Psalm 105:1-3).
> *For the Lord is good; his mercy is everlasting; and his truth endureth to all generations* (Psalm 100:5).

Hymn of Praise: "Come, Ye Thankful People."

Thoughts on the Theme: (*An object lesson by one of the students.*)

(Provide the student with twenty-four flat, thin pieces of wood. Tongue depressors would work very well and can be purchased in any drugstore for about ten cents a dozen. Turn to the contents and select twenty-four titles of previous lesson themes. Write one on each stick.)

We have learned about many things which will help us to grow in stature and become better Christian boys and girls. Some of these things are faith, work, courage, reverence, prayer, patience, co-operation. (These and others are read from the sticks.) If I take any one of these sticks alone, I can easily break it. (Break one as you speak.) But when I put them all together, they become such a strong bundle of sticks I can not break them, no matter how hard I try.

Each of these sticks is like a life that has just one of these many qualities about which we have studied. Because the life has not grown to include all these Christian qualities, but just one of them, that quality can be easily destroyed, just as we can break any one of these sticks when it is apart from the rest. For instance, if a person has faith, but if that faith is in material things rather than in God, or if that person has faith, but is unwilling to work and do his part, he will not grow into a strong Christian character. And his faith, standing alone, can be easily destroyed.

Or if a person has courage, but has no patience or perseverance and is unwilling to co-operate, his courage can easily be destroyed because he lacks the other necessary Christian qualities.

But if we grow in stature in all of these qualities, we shall become such strong and useful Christians that nothing will be able to destroy or weaken us.

Story: SERVE THE LORD WITH GLADNESS.

Peter placed his uncle's letter on his desk and walked to the window. He stood for a long time looking down into the valley. It was a cold, unpleasant day in late November. A snow so wet it was almost rain was falling drearily from the dark, low clouds and melting as soon as it touched the ground. The wind sounded lonely as it shook the leafless trees. Everything in the valley looked cold and bare and bleak. But then winter had come once again to the West Virginia mountains, and the mining towns spotting the hills and valleys all looked forgotten and dismal this time of year. There were no paved streets in the town below. Miners waded through cold and slimy mud to get from their old, battered cars to their houses. The flimsy houses were built so close together they looked like one continuous shed from where Peter stood.

The five years spent here as one of the mining superintendents seemed like a century to Peter. But it had been a necessary training period, so his Uncle Ben had said. Now at last the word had come that the position was open in one of his uncle's steel mills, for which he had been training. He returned to his desk and reread his uncle's letter. He was to leave at once. Peter glanced at his watch, then reached for the phone. There was still plenty of time to make reservations and leave on the train that pulled out at nine forty-five that night.

He packed hurriedly and returned to his office to give last-minute instructions to the works there. Then he reached for his hat, intending to use the rest of the afternoon and all evening to say brief good-bys to some of the miners. But the phone rang, so he hurried to Dr. Bailey's office instead.

"It's Bobby Hawkins," Dr. Bailey said, bending over a four-year-old who had been hit by a truck. "He is badly hurt, and, of course, the family has no money."

"Put him in my car," Peter said, without hesitating, "and I'll drive him to the hospital in Bloomington."

When Peter returned about two hours later, he drove directly to the Hawkins' home. He rolled up his trousers legs before stepping out of the car into the mud. Mrs. Hawkins met him at the door.

"Oh, Mr. Allen!" she cried. "We have been watching for you! We knew you would come right here! How is Bobby?"

Another hour elapsed while Peter comforted the Hawkins family and assured them that Bobby would receive the very best care at no cost to them. When he returned to his car, he found a group of boys waiting for him, all dressed in their Boy Scout uniforms.

"That's right!" Peter thought. "Today is Tuesday." In all his packing, he had forgotten about the meeting. Well, there was plenty of time for it.

"Hop in!" he called gaily as he wiped the cold, mushy snow from his windshield.

Before the meeting was over, Peter began to hear dishes rattling in the adjoining room of the community house. Of course! It was the third Tuesday in the month—the night for the community supper. He chuckled as he thought of forgetting about something that he himself had started.

Every one turned out for these community potluck suppers which had become a most important part in the lives of many of the mining families. After supper the tables were hurriedly cleared. Then Peter led them in an hour of community singing. He had taught them to read music and was constantly supplying them with new and beautiful songs. Their favorite was "The Holy City," sung in four parts, which they always used to climax the singing period.

Then the chairs were pushed against the wall and Peter led them in playing group games. Every one joined in. And every one had fun. At nine-thirty the chairs were again placed in large semicircles around the pot-bellied stove. Mrs. Haggerty, seated at the piano, played the introduction to "The Old Rugged Cross." Then every one joined in singing. No songbooks were needed. Even little Sarah Jane Watkins knew all four verses by heart.

After the song, Peter arose, his Bible in hand. These monthly meetings always ended with a hymn, a prayer, and the reading of a passage from the Bible. As Peter was ending the prayer, a forlorn train whistle sounded in the distance. The nine forty-five! His reservation! His bags all packed, waiting for him by the door of his room! He had forgotten all about catching that train! He stood bewildered for a moment, then said quickly, "Let's sing another hymn tonight."

"Let's sing 'In the Service of the King'!" cried Willie Blackhurst.

Peter sank down to his chair, feeling limp. His uncle would be expecting him. How could he have failed to catch that train? For five years he had been looking forward to this very night when this basic-training period would come to an end and he could leave the mud holes and dismal shadows of every mining town behind him. He looked about. Every one was singing from the bottom of his heart. Old men. Old women. The miners and their wives. Young men. Young women. Boys. Girls. This would probably be the last time he would see them all together. He would be gone on the first morning train.

Who will lead them when I am gone? he thought. Who will be the Scout leader? Who will order new music from Chicago for them, and then teach them the new songs? Who will take little fellows to the hospital for them, and go to their homes all hours of the day and night to comfort the families in times of sickness and death? Who will plan their summer picnics? Or take the boys swimming in Brady's Creek when summer finally comes to the mountains again? Who will be their preacher three Sundays each month when Mr. Montgomery is preaching at one of the other four mountain churches where he ministers?

The song ended. Peter stood up. This was the first time he had come without a definite passage of Scripture in mind to read and a few comments to make pertaining to its meaning. He opened his Bible, intending to read the first passage his eyes fell upon.

"Serve the Lord with gladness," he read. Then the whistle sounded again, warning all the latecomers the train was ready to leave.

"Serve the Lord with gladness," Peter said again more slowly. "These words are found in Psalm 100. Listen while I read the rest to you." And as he read that Psalm he knew within his heart that he could never disappoint the faith and trust these simple people placed in him.

Prayer Hymn: "My Prayer."

Prayer (by the teacher).

Offertory Service:

This week we shall celebrate Thanksgiving—the day set aside for giving special thanks to God for His many blessings to us. It is fine for us to give special thanks to God on this special day, but actually every day should be thanksgiving day. Giving thanks means more than offering special prayers of thanks. Giving thanks means showing our love for God in every way we can to every one we meet. That is why every day should be thanks-giving day. Sharing generously and unselfishly is one of the best ways to show our thanks to God for His great blessings and His wonderful love.

(Play "Count Your Blessings" while the offering is taken. Conclude with three or four sentence prayers of thanks by students.)

Adult Leader:

(Display the poster described in *Patterns for 52 Visual Lessons* and refer to it as you conclude the following thoughts:)

Thursday we shall celebrate Thanksgiving. We shall feast on special foods like turkey and cranberry sauce and pumpkin pie. But with all our merrymaking and feasting we want to be sure we do not forget this day has been set apart as a time for giving special thanks to God for the many blessings and wonderful loving care He has given to us all during the year.

The Pilgrims were the first to celebrate Thanksgiving Day. Because they were so grateful for God's help and guidance during their first winter in a new world, they planned a special celebration as a time for giving thanks.

It is important for each of us to give thanks, but it is even more important for each of us to *live* thanks. For Thanksgiving really means thanks-living.

(Have the students make the table decorations described in the book mentioned above.)

Benediction.

SERVICE NO. 44—NOVEMBER

Growing in Stature Through—

JOY

Your joy no man taketh from you.—John 16:22c.

Prelude: Play "He Keeps Me Singing" as an instrumental number, using as many students as possible.

Call to Worship:

> O come, let us sing unto the Lord: let us make a joyful noise to the rock of our salvation.
> Let us come before his presence with thanksgiving, and make a joyful noise unto him with psalms.
> For the Lord is a great God, and a great King above all gods (Psalm 95:1-3).

Hymn of Praise: "Joy to the World."

Thoughts on the Theme: (*An object lesson by one of the students.*)

(Provide the student with a musical powder box.)

This powder box looks just like any other one until we lift the lid. Then we find it plays a lovely melody. Other musical powder boxes may sound something like it. They may even play the same tune. But each box has a certain sound all of its own. When we replace the lid the music stops. The box remains silent until some one lifts the lid.

No matter how closely we examine the box, we can not see any actual signs of the music. It is somehow bottled up inside this box, waiting to be released or set free. When we lift the lid, every one who is close enough to hear enjoys the cheery little melody.

We are all much like a musical powder box. There is a happy song bottled up inside of us, waiting to be released. Some people go through life like a musical powder box that has never had its lid removed. That is, they never share a happy song with others. They are always gloomy or unhappy about something. Yet, like a musical powder box, they have a joyous song hidden within, ready to cheer all close enough to hear.

There is only one way we can lift the lid and release the happy song inside of us. That is to live close to Jesus. When we do this, we shall find we have joyous songs in our hearts all the time. And we shall want to release these joyous songs by spreading as much cheer and happiness as we can to all the people we meet each day, no matter where we may be. Think how far-reaching our small deeds might be!

Story: NO ONE CAN TAKE YOUR JOY.

Mrs. Montgomery Wilbert Clayton, Senior, stood like a cold, pale statue staring out of the big, square window. She was a tall, slender woman with thin lips that seemed to disappear because she closed them so tightly. Matilda thought she looked lonelier than ever that day.

"It's this house," Matilda decided. "When these bare floors are covered with rugs and these cold-looking windows covered with ruffled curtains, it will seem more like home to her. She won't look so lost and so unhappy then."

Heavy steps sounded on the wooden porch. Matilda automatically opened the door and held it ajar while the movers brought in another piece of furniture.

"It's your secretary, Mrs. Clayton," Matilda said. "Where would you like it?"

Without turning, Mrs. Clayton made a sweeping gesture with her right hand. "Over there," she said crisply. Her voice sounded hollow and penetrating, like the damp air and piercing wind of that late November afternoon.

"She's tired," Matilda thought. "She's tired and she's so—so unhappy. She is used to a big house full of servants. Now she has just a little house with no one but me to look after her. She has grown cold and bitter since her investments failed and she had to sell almost everything to pay her debts. She said she hated this house before she even saw it. She said she hated this street and all the people who live on it. But somehow—somehow I feel she will find understanding and friendship and happiness here."

The dreary November days turned into snowy December ones. Finally, the whirling, blustering March winds arrived. Now it was April, with warming days and gentle spring showers. But still Mrs. Clayton sat motionless in front of her big square window. She spoke only in reply to Matilda's household questions and moved only when Matilda said a meal was ready or when it was time for bed. So you can well imagine why Matilda almost dropped the vase she was dusting one morning in late April when Mrs. Clayton suddenly said:

"Who lives in the house next door?"

Matilda managed to hide her great surprise and stammer, "I—I don't know, Mrs. Clayton. I have kept so close to the house, to be with you if you needed me, that I do not know any of the neighbors."

"People go in and out of that house all day long," Mrs. Clayton continued. "All kinds of people. Old people. Young people. Children. Sometimes they carry something in. Sometimes they carry something out. Some of them go in looking sad. They come out looking—well, looking joyous. I have been watching them for months."

Matilda purposely forgot to phone her grocery order to the market in time for the afternoon's delivery. So she had to make a trip to the store herself. As Matilda walked along in the warm spring sunshine, she hummed a gay little tune. It was hard for her to be so quiet and never sing around Mrs. Clayton's home, for Matilda loved to sing. She also loved to laugh. She had a jolly laugh that sounded like a group of tinkling bells all ringing at once. An hour later, she hurried into the living room and said:

"A Mrs. Shaw lives next door with her housekeeper, a Mrs. Morgan."

"Why do people go in and out all the time? Just to see her?" Mrs. Clayton questioned.

"I did not wish to appear too inquisitive," Matilda replied. "I shall learn more tomorrow."

"I shall learn more right now, Matilda. Bring my hat and gloves."

It would have been hard to decide whether Matilda was more pleased than she was astonished, or more astonished than pleased as she watched Mrs. Clayton walk up the path next door. Then she hurried to the kitchen, and all the while she baked Mrs. Clayton's favorite cake she sang at the top of her voice.

Mrs. Clayton's finger was still on the bell when the door opened. Before she had time to say a word, Mrs. Morgan grabbed her hand, shook it in a sincere, friendly way, saying:

"Come in, come in, Mrs. Clayton! How did you know we needed help today? Go right upstairs. Mrs. Shaw is in the front bedroom."

The next thing Mrs. Clayton knew, she was standing at the bedside of a frail, thin woman, slightly older than herself in years, but one who seemed radiantly young in spirit. She stretched out her thin, soft hand in an eager, friendly way as she exclaimed:

"I am so happy to know you, Mrs. Clayton! Nora and I have wanted to invite you to tea these many months, but each day is busier than the one before. How grateful I am you came today! I need help so badly. See that pile of children's garments? They must be patched and have buttons sewed on. Mrs. Barkley just received word that her mother is very ill. They are leaving as soon as Mr. Barkley arrives home from work. Her mother lives some two hundred miles from here on a farm. There is no telling how long they will be away, so I told Mrs. Barkley to bring over all her mending. I promised to have it mended and packed for them to pick up as they pass by here about six o'clock this evening. She broke her wrist about a month ago, and, of course, fell behind in her mending. Take off your hat and gloves. Pull up that comfortable chair. Here is a needle. We can talk while we sew."

But there was little time for talking. Mary Ellen Jackson arrived right then. After her came Theodore Nelson. Then Billy Hendricks, whose arm was still in a cast. Then Mr. Westley, owner of a large department store. Then Sarah Barker. Mrs. Shaw seemed to know just what to say. Her voice was soft and gentle and sweet. Her smile was warm and relaxing like the hot tea she served from her bedside table. She listened patiently to the troubles of others, and then talked them over as earnestly as if they were her own. Each entered the room with a worried frown, but left it with a smile. As she said good-by to each one, she always added:

"Keep a smile on your face and a song in your heart. Always remember that no one can take your joy."

All afternoon Mrs. Clayton sat quietly, rocking and sewing and listening. The troubles she heard made her own look small and insignificant.

Hours later, as she noiselessly stepped into her own kitchen once again, Matilda stopped singing abruptly in the middle of a song. Mrs. Clayton's voice sounded strange even to herself as she said with a radiant smile:

"Keep singing, Matilda. Always keep a smile on your face and a song in your heart. Always remember that no one can take your joy."

Prayer Hymn: Sing softly the first verse of "Prayer Is the Soul's Sincere Desire."

Prayer (by the teacher).

Offertory Service:

As the shepherds watched their flocks in the field that night, an angel suddenly appeared before them and said, "Fear not: for, behold, I bring you good tidings of *great joy*" (Luke 2:10). And when the Wise-men saw the star in the east, they rejoiced with *exceeding great joy* (Matthew 2:10). When God gave to us the wonderful gift of His only Son as our Lord and Saviour, He did so with joy. When we give our gifts to God we should do the same. We should give them joyously, with a joyful song in our hearts.

(Play "In My Heart There Rings a Melody" while the offering is taken. Conclude with a short dedicatory prayer by one of the students.)

Adult Leader:

Whenever we think of bells, we think of a joyful ringing sound that gladdens the hearts of all who hear. We think of bells in connection with happy, joyous occasions—wedding bells, Easter bells, Christmas bells. A bell, we might say, has become a symbol of joy. Just as the bells add joy to an occasion, so joy adds happiness to the life of a Christian.

How can we find and then keep joy in our lives? (Display poster described in *Patterns for 52 Visual Lessons* and refer to it as you go along.) There are three simple rules: (1) Put Jesus first in your life. (2) Then put others. (3) Finally, think of yourself. If you put Jesus first, you will say only those things which you would say in His presence, and you will do only those things which you would want Jesus to see you do. If you put others before yourself, you will learn to be unselfish, generous, and thoughtful. Surely, then you will have a joyous song in your heart at all times.

(Have the students make the bell described in the book mentioned above.)

Benediction.

SERVICE NO. 45—DECEMBER

THE SHEPHERDS WHO HEARD A MESSAGE

And there were in the same country shepherds abiding in the field, keeping watch over their flock by night. And, lo, the angel of the Lord came upon them, and the glory of the Lord shone round about them.—Luke 2: 8, 9.

Prelude: Play softly "Angels From the Realms of Glory."

Call to Worship:

>*And there were in the same country shepherds abiding in the field, keeping watch over their flock by night. And, lo, the angel of the Lord came upon them, and the glory of the Lord shone round about them: and they were sore afraid.*
>
>*And the angel said unto them, Fear not: for, behold, I bring you good tidings of great joy, which shall be to all people.*
>
>*For unto you is born this day in the city of David a Saviour, which is Christ the Lord* (Luke 2: 8-11).

>   Come, let us worship Christ, the Saviour,
>   Let us worship Christ, the Lord.

Hymn of Praise: "While Shepherds Watched Their Flocks."

Adult Leader:

Instead of an object lesson for the next three Sundays, we shall learn how some of the Christmas customs which we observe came into being. Some of them you may already know; some may be new to you.

WHY WE HANG ORNAMENTS ON OUR CHRISTMAS TREES

(Presented by one of the students.)

Trees were not decorated at Christmas time until the tenth century. Then an Arabian geographer named Georg Jacob made a journey to western Europe and told a strange, but beautiful, story. Because of this story, people began to decorate trees growing in their gardens at Christmas time in honor of the Christ-child's birth. Here is the story George Jacob brought to Europe from the faraway land of the Orient:

The night that Jesus was born was no ordinary one. As the shepherds watched their flocks, the skies were suddenly brilliant with a radiant light. A choir of heavenly angels sang, "Glory to God in the highest, and on earth peace, good will toward men." Then the shepherds heard the wonderful tidings that a child had been born whom God had sent to be the Saviour of the world. And then, according to this ancient Arabian legend, another miracle happened. All the trees, both large and small, burst forth with blossoms and ripened fruit. The trees were so covered with fruit and flowers that their branches hung low, some even touching the ground.

The people in western Europe thought this old legend so beautiful that they began to tie fruits and flowers to their trees at Christmas time. As years went by, novelties and other decorations were made which would last longer than the fruits and flowers. So our Christmas-tree ornaments grew out of this beautiful Oriental legend of the trees that burst into blossom and ripened fruit the night that Jesus was born.

Story: I SAW THE STAR.

"What troubles you, Bariah?" my elder brother asked. "You keep turning and looking behind you as if some one else is near."

We stood together on the knoll overlooking the broad, flat, grazing plains. It was sunset. And a more beautiful sunset I have never seen.

"I—I—I do not know," I told Malcham, looking up at him. "All day I have had the feeling that something wonderful was going to happen—the way I feel the day before my birthday." Malcham smiled at me and patted my head. He always pats my head. Because he is ten years older, he sometimes forgets that I am almost twelve.

But I did have a strange feeling that day. I found it hard to remember to do my work. My father had given me certain tasks about the sheepcote and my mother about the tents, but I wandered about most of the day looking for something, and not knowing what it was.

Finally bedtime came. Carshena, my little sister who is just ten years old, and I sat quietly with my mother for our bedtime devotions. After our prayer I said:

"Mother, do you think the Messiah is coming soon?"

"We are all hoping He will come soon, Bariah," my mother answered.

"Do you think I shall be able to see Him when He comes?"

"Oh, no, Bariah!" Carshena cried. "When He comes He will be a great person. He will be too busy to bother with a little boy."

I tossed back my head proudly. "I am no little boy!" I said angrily. "I am almost twelve!"

"Well, He still will not have time to spend with children," Carshena said.

My mother smiled at both of us. "Perhaps Carshena is right,

THE SHEPHERDS WHO HEARD A MESSAGE

Bariah. Perhaps the Messiah will be too great and too mighty to even notice a boy of twelve. Then, again, perhaps the Messiah will love children and will bless them. We know not how or when He will come. All we know is that God has promised to send us a Messiah who will save the world.''

"When He comes," I said, looking at the quiet skies through the open tent flap, "I should like to be among the first to hear."

Carshena clapped her hands and laughed out loud.

"Oh, Bariah, Bariah!" she cried. "You are such a funny boy to wish such a foolish wish. How could *you* be among the first to hear? The only way we learn what is happening in the world about us is when caravans cross our plains. Often they are from places we never heard of. And it takes such a long time for news to reach us even from Bethlehem."

"I know," I told Carshena, with a toss of my head. "But I still wish I could be among the first to hear when the Messiah comes."

It took me a long time to go to sleep. I kept thinking about everything—what Carshena had said; what my mother had said; what I had heard my father and the other shepherds say about God's promise of a Messiah. Finally, I became sleepy and was just dozing off when I suddenly remembered my two little lambs. Father had given them to me. I had cared for them tenderly for many months. Today I had forgotten them! I sprang from my cot and grabbed my mantle off the hook. "Oh, how could I forget them!" I thought. "My two poor little lambs out in the open fields on this cold night! I must hurry and carry them safely into the sheepcote. What if I am too late!" I cried, as I raced across the open field.

In the distance I could see the small glow of the watch fire. I knew my father, Malcham, Ispah, Gozan, Ezer, and the other shepherds whose turn it was to watch by night, were gathered around it. Maybe Malcham saw my little lambs and carried them inside the sheepcote for me.

Suddenly the skies seemed to open and pour out brilliant light! The rays were so bright I fell to the ground, covering my eyes and shaking with fear. "What is happening?" I cried. "Oh, my lambs! My little lambs!"

Then I heard a voice say, "Fear not." I looked up and saw an angel in the midst of the radiant light. Then the angel said, "Behold, I bring you good tidings of great joy, which shall be to all people. For unto you is born this day in the city of David a Saviour, which is Christ the Lord. And this shall be a sign unto you: Ye shall find the babe wrapped in swaddling clothes, lying in a manger."

Suddenly there appeared a great many other angels. They were all singing praises to God. It sounded so beautiful coming from above the open fields that clear, cold night. "Glory to God in the highest," they sang, "and on earth peace, good will toward men."

Then, as suddenly as they came, the angels disappeared. The skies were quiet and clear once more. The stars were twinkling silently overhead.

I jumped to my feet and started running toward the watch fire. I saw my father and Ispah still kneeling upon the ground. Malcham and the other shepherds were scrambling to their feet. "I have seen the angels, too!" I cried. "I have seen them! I heard their singing! I heard what they said!" Then I stopped. I turned and raced back to the tents. "I must tell Carshena!" I cried. "I must tell Carshena that the Messiah has at last come! And that I, Bariah, almost twelve, was surely one of the first to know!"

Prayer Hymn: Sing softly first and third verses of "Saviour, Like a Shepherd."

Prayer (by the teacher).

Offertory Service:

"He gives not best who gives most; but he gives most who gives best. . . . If I can not give bountifully, yet I will give freely, and what I lack in my hand, I will supply by my heart."—*Warwick.*

Let us give unto God as God has given unto us, remembering that He gave us His very best through his own Son, Jesus Christ, our Lord.

(Play "O Worship the King" while the offering is taken and while a student gives a short prayer of thanks.)

Adult Leader:

Even today the shepherds of the Orient are very humble people who live simple, quiet lives with their flocks in the open pasture lands.

Why, then, do you suppose God sent His angels to the shepherds with the wonderful tidings that the Saviour of the world had been born in Bethlehem? Why not to the rich? Or to the powerful? Or to the persons who held high positions of authority? (Encourage students to express themselves. Lead the discussion so it revolves around answering these questions.)

In the sight of God, which of these are most important? Wealth. Power. Authority. High positions. Haughtiness. Vanity. Humility. Sincerity.

THE SHEPHERDS WHO HEARD A MESSAGE

Yes, humility and sincerity. That answers our questions. God sent the angels to the shepherds because in their hearts they truly believed that He would keep His promise and send a Saviour to the world. They believed so sincerely that they were eagerly waiting for Him to come. And they were humble and lived close to God. (Refer to the poster described in *Patterns for 52 Visual Lessons*. Read the verse aloud to the class.)

The very same things are important to God today. Those who are humble and sincere and live the closest to Him receive His greatest blessings.

(Have the students make the Christmas angel described in the book mentioned above.)

Benediction.

SERVICE NO. 46—DECEMBER

THE WISE-MEN WHO FOLLOWED THE STAR

Where is he that is born King of the Jews? for we have seen his star in the east, and are come to worship him.—Matthew 2:2.

Prelude: Have a quartet of students sing "We Three Kings."

Call to Worship:

    Leader: *Now when Jesus was born in Bethlehem of Judaea in the days of Herod the king, behold, there came wise men from the east to Jerusalem, saying,*

    Group: *Where is he that is born King of the Jews? for we have seen his star in the east, and are come to worship him.*

    Leader: *When Herod the king had heard these things, he gathered all the chief priests and scribes of the people together and demanded of them where Christ should be born.*

    Group: *And they said unto him, In Bethlehem of Judaea: for thus it is written by the prophet.*

    Leader: *Then Herod enquired of the wise men what time the star appeared. And he sent them to Bethlehem, and said, Go and search diligently for the young child; and when ye have found him, bring me word again, that I may come and worship him also.*

    Group: *When they heard the king, they departed; and, lo, the star, which they saw in the east, went before them, till it came and stood over where the young child was.*

    Leader: *When they saw the star, they rejoiced with exceeding great joy. And when they saw the young child with Mary his mother, they fell down, and worshipped him: and when they had opened their treasures, they presented unto him gifts; gold, and frankincense, and myrrh.*

    Group: *And being warned by God in a dream that they should not return to Herod, they departed into their own country another way* (Adapted from Matthew 2:1-12).

Story: IF I HAD NOT FOLLOWED THE STAR.

    It was early morning. Nathan sighed wearily as he swept the courtyard of his small inn. "This is going to be another busy day," he thought. "We have not had a moment's rest since the day the

THE WISE-MEN WHO FOLLOWED THE STAR

Romans required us all to register in the town of our birth. That was quite a while ago, but the dust has not settled since that day. *Surely,* the heaviest traveling will soon be over. We aren't equipped, in our little village, to take care of so many.''

Just then his helper, Reuben, rushed into the court. ''Send Jacob to be sure our best rooms are in readiness!'' he cried. ''Three travelers are but a short way off on the Jerusalem road. And *these* travelers we want to house! Their garments—I have never seen such costly robes! They dress as those who journey from the East. They speak as learned men. Their camels are the very best! They have sent word ahead that they will stop here for the day. It seems they travel just by night. I tell you, Nathan, these are no ordinary travelers!''

Nathan hurried into the inn. ''Leah,'' he called to his wife, ''prepare a special meal for three unusual guests. Reuben saw them in the distance. He says they are richly dressed and ride upon the finest camels. Jacob, find Naomi, and the two of you be sure that all is in readiness for these three. They will have our best rooms, of course. Oh, happy day for us to have such special guests!''

Reuben had not been mistaken. When the three Wise-men arrived every one looked at them in awe. It was not only their costly robes which caused so much excitement among the other guests as well as among Nathan's household and servants, but the strange things they were saying. They talked about seeing a star in the East and about their long journey following the star.

''These are Wise-men from the East!'' Nathan whispered to Reuben in excited tones. ''Why should Wise-men travel by night to follow a star?''

''They must be searching for something,'' whispered Reuben, as the two stood off in one corner of the room.

''Searching for what?'' Nathan asked. Reuben shrugged his shoulders.

Nathan motioned for Reuben to follow him. He made his way to the spot where the special guests were seated. Then he introduced himself as owner of the inn and welcomed the three in the name of his whole household. Reuben, he said, was his helper. If there was anything either of them could do for the three Wise-men, they would, indeed, be greatly honored to be instructed accordingly. Then Nathan said:

''I beg your humblest pardon, sirs, but we could not help but overhear your conversation. You speak of seeing a star. And of following this star. We can not help but wonder what it is you are seeking.''

"We seek a newborn babe," the first Wise-man said, and paused.

"A newborn babe!" exclaimed Reuben, in great surprise. Nathan looked disappointed.

"Ah, but a very special one," the second Wise-man said. "He is the Messiah, God's own Son, sent as He promised to save the world."

Then the three Wise-men told Reuben and Nathan about the star they had seen and about the prophecies which were at last being fulfilled. They showed the gifts which they had brought for the Christ-child. One had gold. One had frankincense. One had myrrh. The Wise-men said they would gladly travel twice as far in order to worship the newborn King.

Later, when the three Wise-men had retired to the special rooms prepared for them, Nathan and Reuben sat together in the open court.

"What do you make of their strange talk?" Reuben asked.

Nathan leaned closer and said in a low whisper, "I do not believe them. I do not think they are telling us the truth. Why should three Wise-men journey all the way from the East just to see a newborn babe? Of a truth, they are searching for something very precious, but mark my word, they are too clever to tell us what! And so they have made up this foolish story."

Reuben shook his head. "I believe everything they told us," he said solemnly. "Think what that means, Nathan. The Messiah has come! The Messiah for whom we have been waiting for generations! Wise-men such as these would not be mistaken. They have not traveled so far just to see a newborn babe, Nathan. They have traveled from the East to worship the newborn King, as I, too, should like to do!"

Nathan chuckled. "You have always been a dreamer, Reuben," he said. "When the true Messiah comes we shall know of it. There shall be trumpets and drums and bugles! His coming will be announced with marching soldiers and great armies. A newborn babe! Reuben, I would not travel even to Bethlehem, our nearest neighboring city, just to see a newborn babe. Surely, these Wise-men will return to the East over this same road. We are a convenient distance from Jerusalem and from Bethlehem. They are certain to stop here on their way home. Perhaps then they will have found their treasure and will tell us the truth."

"But, Nathan," Reuben insisted, "if this newborn babe is truly the Christ, wouldn't you travel that far to worship Him, too?"

"Aye! That I would!" exclaimed Nathan. "I would travel even farther to worship Him. But mark my word, Reuben, the Messiah will not come as a helpless, newborn babe. I for one am willing to

THE WISE-MEN WHO FOLLOWED THE STAR

wait here until the three Wise-men stop on their way home. Surely, then we shall learn the truth."

As soon as it was dark, the three Wise-men started on their journey once again. Reuben stood alone in the courtyard of the inn. There was the star. Truly, it was the most brilliant one he had ever seen. He watched the Wise-men slowly disappear from view. Then he looked up at the radiant star again. "That is no ordinary star," he thought. "Surely, no one but God alone could have placed it there in the heavens to guide the Wise-men to the cradle of the newborn Christ." He looked about him. Every one had gone to bed. Quickly he crossed the court and hurried through the quiet inn. When he reached the road he started to run.

He followed the Wise-men all the way to Bethlehem, watching the star as he hurried along. Finally, the star stood still directly over a stable behind an inn. The Wise-men hurried into the stable and fell upon their knees before the manger bed of Christ, the newborn King. They bowed their heads and thanked God for His wonderful gift to the world which fulfilled all His promises to mankind. Then they offered their gifts to the newborn King.

Reuben stood quietly in the shadows of the stable, feeling too humble to make his presence known. Then the Wise-men left and returned to their native land over a road different from the one over which they had come. Reuben did not know that God had warned them in a dream not to return the same way they had come, for the jealous King Herod was waiting in Jerusalem to learn where he might find the Christ-child.

Reuben turned and started on the long homeward journey from Bethlehem to the inn. He hurried, for he was eager to tell Nathan all he had seen.

"If I had not followed the star," he thought, "I would have waited in vain for the return of the Wise-men, for they are going home a different way. And if I had not followed the star, I would not have seen the Christ!"

Prayer Hymn: Sing the first verse of "Follow the Gleam" as the prayer hymn; the second verse as prayer response.

Prayer (by the teacher).

Offertory Service:

> The Wise-men traveled from the East
> Their gifts of love to bring.
> May we, in turn, bring gifts of love
> For Jesus Christ, our King.

(While the offering is taken, play "A Mighty Fortress Is Our God." After the prayer of thanks by one of the students, mention that this hymn, which is one of the oldest and most beautiful sung in Protestant churches, was written by Martin Luther.)

THE FIRST INDOOR CHRISTMAS TREE

(Presented by one of the students.)

First I shall tell you about the man who is credited for cutting down the first Christmas tree, taking it home, and decorating it with candles. As I tell you about his life, see if you can guess his name.

He was born November 10, 1483, in Eisleben, Germany. His parents were simple, religious peasant miners. His father was more ambitious than most peasants and moved to Mansfeld in the hopes of giving his son the advantages of higher education. When he was a young man, he entered the University of Erfurt, with the hopes of becoming a lawyer. But he soon discovered that he was more interested in religion and music than law. After years of earnest religious studies he became deeply distressed because the Catholic church had become so corrupt. He led the great religious revolt known as the Reformation. He and his followers were called Protestants, because they protested against the Catholic church. His love for music gave the world many beautiful hymns. "Away in the Manger," one of the first Christmas carols most of us sing, was written by this great man. Have you guessed his name? It was Martin Luther.

One Christmas Eve, over four hundred years ago, Martin Luther was returning home. The night was cold and clear. He glanced up into a sky crowded with hundreds of brilliant, glistening stars. As he looked at the tall, stately pine trees which lined both sides of the road, it seemed as if dozens of glimmering stars were clinging to the outstretched branches.

"If only I could share this beautiful sight with my family," he thought. And then he saw a small pine by the side of the road. That gave him a sudden idea. He took it home and decorated its branches with candles. So Martin Luther is not only remembered as the great religious reformer and the writer of many beautiful hymns, but also as the one who cut the first Christmas tree and decorated it with candles.

Adult Leader:

Turn to the index and select about ten of the topics used for previous lessons. List them on the blackboard, together with the opposite of

THE WISE-MEN WHO FOLLOWED THE STAR

ten other topics. For example, list: Sharing. Telling lies. Purity. Kindness. Unwilling to forgive. Overcoming difficulties. Living for yourself alone. Peace. Laziness. Courage. Being ungrateful. Insincerity.

Make two columns, heading one WISE MEN; the other, FOOLISH MEN. Have students select the traits of the wise men and the traits of the foolish men, and write them under the proper heading. Discuss each as you go along. This will offer a brief review of previous lesson themes.

Conclude by referring to the poster described in *Patterns for 52 Visual Lessons* and explaining that the Wise-men of old followed the star and wise men of today follow Christ.

Have the students make the star described in the book mentioned above.

Benediction.

SERVICE NO. 47—DECEMBER

GOD'S GIFT TO THE WORLD

For God so loved the world, that he gave his only begotten Son, that whosoever believeth in him should not perish, but have everlasting life.—John 3:16.

Prelude: Play a recording of Christmas chimes.

Student Duet: "Silent Night! Holy Night!"

Call to Worship:

> *For unto us a child is born, unto us a son is given: and the government shall be upon his shoulder: and his name shall be called Wonderful, Counsellor, The mighty God, The everlasting Father, The Prince of Peace* (Isaiah 9:6).

Hymn of Praise: "It Came Upon the Midnight Clear."

Solo: "O Holy Night," by Adams.

Listen to recorded Christmas chimes.

Story: PLACE A LIGHTED CANDLE IN YOUR WINDOW.

Lucy closed her book slowly. "That was such a beautiful story," she said. "It was about placing a candle in your window at Christmas."

"A candle in the window?" questioned Mother. "As a Christmas decoration?"

"No," Lucy replied. "As an invitation for the Christ-child to stop at your house. It seems to be an old custom, but it sounded so beautiful in the story."

"It does sound beautiful," Mother agreed.

"Do you suppose the Christ-child would stop *here* if we placed a lighted candle in *our* window?" Lucy asked eagerly.

Lucy's father put aside the evening paper and said, "He might. Why don't we try it, Lucy?"

That is why the girls from Lucy's Sunday-school class saw a tall white candle burning brightly in the large front picture window when they arrived that evening for their class Christmas party. When all the girls and their teacher, Mrs. Reamer, were there, Lucy explained why the lighted candle had been placed in the window.

"What a beautiful story!" Mrs. Reamer said. "What a beautiful thought! To place a lighted candle in your window as an invitation for the Christ-child to stop at your home."

"Do you suppose such a thing could be true?" Annabelle asked.

"Of course not," Ruth quickly replied. "It's just a Christmas story."

"Maybe He will stop, Ruth," Barbara said as she watched the candle's flickering flame.

"If He does stop," Jo Ann cried, "I hope it will be tonight while we are all here!"

And then the party began. Mrs. Reamer always planned interesting games. Class parties were always gala affairs. In the middle of one of the most exciting games the side doorbell rang. It was Betty Jean Rollins and her mother carrying a large basket of carefully ironed clothes between them.

"We are sorry to be so late, Mrs. Flemming," Betty Jean's mother said, "but it is so hard to walk in the snow."

"Come in!" cried Lucy's mother. "Come in and warm yourselves. You should not have carried this heavy load. Mr. Flemming could have called for the laundry tomorrow."

"But I promised you would have it today," Mrs. Rollins said. "Our car broke down this morning. It is so old, you know. And there has been one thing after another to delay me all day. Bobby has such a cold, and I do believe Billy is getting the measles."

An open archway separated the living room from the hall. Betty Jean stood quietly in the shadows of the stairway, looking into the living room. What a beautiful Christmas tree! What beautiful ornaments and lights! And so many presents piled on the floor under the branches! There were never many presents for her. She was the oldest of a family of seven, and money was always scarce in their home. She looked at the group of girls, all about her own age. How much fun they must have together! And how beautifully they all were dressed! Betty Jean suddenly backed farther into the shadows. They must not see her torn shoes. And her coat two sizes too small. The sleeves were inches above her wrists, and she had no gloves. Her hands looked red and chapped and raw. She hid them behind her.

Then Lucy stood close by.

"Betty Jean," she said, holding out her hand, "come and join us. We are having such a happy Christmas party. We want you to stay and join in the fun."

But Betty Jean crowded closer to the stairway.

"No, no," she murmured, her cheeks growing hot with embarrassment. "No, thank you, Lucy. I—I must go right home with Mother."

Lucy turned to Mrs. Rollins. "Please," she said earnestly. "Please may Betty Jean stay for the rest of the party?"

Mrs. Rollins' face broke into a happy smile, but only for a moment.

All the girls had crowded into the hall. Mrs. Rollins looked at them and then at Betty Jean. They all looked so pretty in their plaids and jersey dresses, with hair bows and socks to match. She blinked the tears from her eyes.

"Thank you, Lucy," she said quietly. "Perhaps some other time. We must hurry home now."

Lucy turned again to Betty Jean.

"If you can't stay for the party," she said quickly, "then you must take a Christmas gift home with you."

She hurried to the pile of presents underneath the Christmas tree. She reached for the one she had wrapped and tied that afternoon. It contained a pair of bright-red woolen mittens and was tagged for Martha Parker. She had drawn Martha's name, but surely Martha would understand! No sooner had Lucy given Betty Jean the gift than Doris cried:

"Wait! I have a gift for you, too!" Then she darted to the pile of gifts underneath the tree. She found hers immediately—the one wrapped in the holly paper. It was a pair of warm woolen socks which she had bought for Audrey. But surely Audrey would understand, especially if she, too, had noticed that Betty Jean wore no boots and that her shoes were badly torn.

A hurried scramble followed as the other girls rushed into the living room and came hurrying to Betty Jean, each with a gift beautifully wrapped with bows and ribbons. Betty Jean stood wide-eyed and speechless. Such a wonderful thing had never happened before!

After Betty Jean and her mother had gone, the girls sat around the Christmas tree. Somehow they did not want to play any more games. A wonderful feeling of Christmas seemed to have suddenly filled the room.

"This has been the most beautiful Christmas party we have ever had," Lucy said softly.

"And do you know why?" Mrs. Reamer asked. "Because you placed the lighted candle in the window."

"But the Christ-child has not come!" cried Beatrice.

"Oh, yes, He has!" Mrs. Reamer said gently. "He came to our party tonight in such a beautiful way."

"When?" cried Barbara. "Where was I? I did not see Him!"

Mrs. Reamer smiled. "You were too busy giving your gifts to Betty Jean. When you gave your own gifts to Betty Jean because she needed them and because you wanted to make her Christmas a happy one, the Christ-child accepted your invitation and stood in the midst of you. Whenever we do acts of love, we are bringing the

Christ-child into our lives. As Lucy just said, this has been the most beautiful Christmas party we have ever had."

Prayer Hymn: "As With Gladness Men of Old."

Prayer (by the teacher).

Offertory Service:

God so loved the world that He gave His only Son as the Saviour and Redeemer of all who will believe.

Let us show our love for God through our willingness to share with others and in that way help carry on His work of love here on earth.

(Play "Joy to the World" while the offering is taken. Sing the first verse after the prayer of thanks given by a student.)

Adult Leader:

The world is a mighty big place. And yet we know that God created every part of it—every country, every ocean, every river, every mountain. God created every kind of bird and plant and animal. He created every person of every color in this world. When we know and believe this, we can understand more fully our text of today: "God so loved the *world*, that he gave his only begotten Son." (Refer to the poster described in *Patterns for 52 Visual Lessons*. That means Japan, India, China, Sweden, Holland, Alaska, Egypt, Canada. That means France, Tibet, Mexico, the United States, Italy, Germany, Africa, Spain, England, Russia. That means even the smallest, most insignificant part of the farthest-away place.

Recently we learned through one of our lessons that God offers us many wonderful blessings. But there is always a part for us to fulfill in order to make ourselves worthy of these blessings. Offering us a Saviour and Redeemer is the greatest blessing possible. The remaining portion of John 3:16 tells what our part is to be—"Whosoever believeth in him should not perish, but have everlasting life." Our part, then, is to believe with all our heart that Jesus Christ, who was born in Bethlehem of Judea and whose birthday we are now celebrating, is truly the divine Son of God, and was sent by God to save us from sin.

WHY WE HANG UP OUR STOCKINGS

(Presented by one of the students.)

The custom of hanging up our stockings by the chimney or fireplace comes to us from the Netherlands. Like many of the southern

European peasants, the Dutch wear wooden shoes called sabots. During the rainy, wet winter season these wooden shoes were placed on the hearth before the open fireplace to dry.

Every Christmas season a jolly villager was chosen to be St. Nicholas. He dressed in a fur-trimmed costume, wore a beard, and gave toys and candy to all the children in the village. The children first shortened his name to Ni-K'Laus, and then to Claus. Spain is not far from Holland, and the Spanish influence changed "saint" to Santa. So St. Nicholas was, in time, changed to Santa Claus.

On the night St. Nicholas went through the village with toys and candy, the children would be sure to place their wooden sabots before the open fire. In the morning they found them filled with toys and sweets.

When the Dutch came to America and settled in New Amsterdam, they brought their Old World customs with them. When wooden shoes were no longer worn, stockings were hung by the chimney instead.

(Have the students make the sabot described in *Patterns for 52 Visual Lessons*.)

Benediction.

SERVICE NO. 48—DECEMBER

Growing in Stature Through—

KEEPING CHRISTMAS ALL YEAR

Let the word of Christ dwell in you richly in all wisdom; . . . and whatsoever ye do in word or deed, do all in the name of the Lord Jesus, giving thanks to God and the Father by him.—Colossians 3:16a, 17.

Prelude: Have a group of students sing "O Come, All Ye Faithful."

Call to Worship:

> O come, all ye faithful, and worship the King.
> O worship our Saviour and Lord.
> Come, worship with songs and with prayers and with gifts,
> And by studying more of His Word.

Hymn of Praise: "Joy to the World."

WHY WE CELEBRATE OPEN HOUSE AT CHRISTMAS

(Presented by one of the students.)

One of the happiest customs of Christmastide comes to us from England. It is the custom of "open house." Between Christmas and New Year's Day our friends drop in to visit us, and we, on the other hand, spend special effort to visit our friends.

Long ago in England the noblemen owned great tracts of land which were farmed by peasants. These peasants lived in little cottages right on the manors, as these large estates were called. Some worked in the fields. Some worked in the stables and took care of the many horses which the noblemen and lords kept. Some worked as cooks and servants in the large manor houses.

Each Christmas the noblemen threw open the doors of their great halls and invited all the peasants to come and celebrate. This was the one time of the year when the noblemen and lords mingled with the peasants. A great feast was prepared and there was much merrymaking and singing and folk dancing. The older men would gather in groups and tell tales of adventure.

At the very beginning of the celebration a huge yule log was dragged into the great banquet hall, accompanied with a wild burst of shouting and cheering. It was rolled into a fire pit so large it occupied the most part of one wall. The Christmas celebration lasted until this great log had been completely burned and was nothing but a pile of smoldering embers.

Out of this manor-house celebration of ancient England has come the custom of opening our homes at Christmas time to all our friends and neighbors.

Story: HOW GRANDMOTHER TAYLOR TAUGHT THE TOWN.

Grandmother Taylor is a frail little lady with twinkling gray eyes and soft white hair curling around her dainty, smiling face. She lives in the white frame cottage with a little picket fence and an extra large mailbox hanging near the front door. The extra-large mailbox is needed to take care of Grandmother Taylor's extra heavy mail. You see, Grandmother Taylor never forgets any one's birthday or anniversary. She sends dozens of cards every week. If you are ill, the first card you receive comes from Grandmother Taylor. If you are going on a trip, a little card will come from her hoping you will have a fine journey and return home safely. If you graduate from Junior high, high school, or college, you will receive a beautiful card from Grandmother Taylor congratulating you upon your achievement. So, on Grandmother Taylor's birthday or on Christmas or Easter or Valentine's Day, or when she is ill, the extra-large mailbox will not even hold all her mail. Every one in town knows and loves Grandmother Taylor.

But she not only sends cards, she is always among the first to call upon the sick. And if any one needs anything, you can count upon Grandmother Taylor hearing about it and helping. Perhaps that is why she was so disturbed when she returned home from a shopping trip the week after Christmas one year. Her last trip to town had been in the midst of the Christmas shopping and Christmas preparations. Every one had been so happy and jovial. Clerks were saying "Thank you," and customers, "Yes, please." That was before Christmas. Now, just a week later, Grandmother Taylor found frowns instead of smiles; irritable complaints instead of friendly words; and even though the holly wreaths and Christmas decorations were still in store windows and on each light down Main Street, all of the Christmas spirit had vanished.

She stepped into an elevator just as one woman accidentally brushed against another. The second woman scowled and glared at the first. That seemed to be the last straw. Grandmother Taylor quickly stepped from the elevator and hurried to the counter where left-over Christmas cards were being sold at half price.

"I'll take all the cards you have left," she told the clerk.

She waited patiently a whole month. Then, on the 25th of January, she sent a Christmas card to every one on her long mailing list. She enclosed a little note inside each which read:

> "A month ago today we celebrated Christmas. We hung wreaths in our windows and bells on our doors. Our hearts were filled with Christmas cheer. What are YOU doing to help keep Christmas in the hearts of men all year?"

Then, on February 25, Grandmother Taylor sent every one another Christmas card with another little note reminding her many friends that God gave Jesus to the world all the year, not just for the Christmas season. "Let us show our thanks to God," she wrote, "by serving others every day."

And on March 25 every one received another Christmas card. It made the whole town conscious of trying to do things for others. When Grandmother Taylor's Christmas cards arrived, every one was certain to make a special effort to do something to make somebody else happy.

Soon every one in town was using the slogan, "Let's keep Christmas all year." Now our town is known as the friendliest and happiest town in the whole county. But when people keep Christmas in their hearts all year, how else can they be but friendly to every one and happy because they are serving the Christ-child through serving others?

Prayer Hymn: Sing softly the first verse of "Silent Night! Holy Night!" as a prayer hymn. Sing the last verse as a prayer response.

Prayer (by the teacher).

Offertory Service:

God gave to us the love of Jesus, not only for the brief Christmas season, but for every day throughout the entire year. And for every year still to come.

Let us thank God each day for all His blessings and bring our gifts of love throughout the year.

(Play softly "O Come, All Ye Faithful," as the offering is taken. Conclude with a brief prayer of thanks by one of the students.)

Adult Leader:

Soon we shall be taking down our Christmas trees and packing away all the ornaments. We shall place the boxes on the top shelf of the closet, out of the way, until next year. We shall forget all about them and shall not open them again until we decorate for the next Christmas season.

Some people seem to pack away all their Christmas spirit the same as they pack away their Christmas decorations. They forget to be kind and thoughtful as soon as Christmas is over. They forget the poor and needy. They overlook opportunities where they might help some one else. They forget to sing, now that the jubilant Christmas carols are no longer sung. In short, they are entirely different people all through the year than they are during the brief holiday season. They even forget the Christ-child when His birthday celebration has passed.

If every one kept Christmas in his heart all year, then Christ would live in the hearts of all men all year. Let us do our part to spread the love of Christ by keeping the meaning of Christmas alive in our hearts.

(Read aloud the verse from the poster described in *Patterns for 52 Visual Lessons*. Have the students make the tree described in the same book.)

Benediction.

SERVICE NO. 49

EASTER

He is not here: for he is risen, as he said.—Matthew 28:6.

Prelude: Use "Resurrection Morn" as a solo or duet sung by students.

Call to Worship:

When Mary Magdalene and the other Mary came to the sepulcher early the first Easter morning,

There was a great earthquake: for the angel of the Lord descended from heaven, and came and rolled back the stone from the door, and sat upon it.

"Fear not ye," the angel said, "for I know that ye seek Jesus which was crucified. He is not here: for he is risen, as he said." (Adapted from Matthew 28:1-6.)

Let us worship a risen Lord.

Let us worship a living Saviour.

Hymn of Praise: "Christ the Lord Is Risen Today."

Prayer Hymn: After the prayer, sing all three verses of "Christ Arose."

Prayer (by the teacher).

Offertory Service:

Let us remember Jesus—

How He went about doing good.

How He lived for others.

How He loved all people, everywhere, even the little children.

How He was crucified for us so that our sins might be forgiven and that we might have eternal life.

And remembering Jesus, let us praise Him with hymns, with prayers, and by bringing our gifts of love so that His name may be glorified among men forever.

(Play softly "I Know That My Redeemer Liveth" while the offering is taken and while a student gives a short prayer of thanks.)

Adult Leader:

(Display the poster described in *Patterns for 52 Visual Lessons.*)

We know that Jesus entered Jerusalem riding on a humble ass, before unmounted by any man, on the Sunday before His crucifixion. Crowds of people lined the streets. They cheered and shouted loud hosannas. Some cut branches off the palm trees and spread them along the road. Others spread flowers in Christ's path. And yet

Jesus rode into Jerusalem that day with a heavy heart. He knew that the friendship and loyalty these people were showing now would soon be forgotten; they would cry, "Crucify Him!" He knew that God had sent Him to save the world, and He was willing to so suffer, but He was sorry to experience the fickleness of the mob. Jesus, riding to Jerusalem, pondered about His Father's will and mankind's cruelty.

Scripture: (*Read by one of the students.*) Matthew 21:1-9.

A Reading: (*By one of the students.*)

THE TRIUMPHAL ENTRY

>Great crowds of people lined the road that day,
>All eager for a glimpse of Him
>Whose name was known throughout all Galilee.
>All knew the wondrous things He did.
>Some said He healed ten lepers. Others said
>He caused the lame to walk. And there
>Were some who knew a man named Lazarus
>Whom Christ had raised from the dead.
>"Such power never hath been seen," said one.
>"I saw Him touch two blinded eyes.
>The beggar saw! Who else can do such things?"
>"Lo, here He comes!" the shouts rang out,
>>"Hosanna to the Son of David: Blessed is
>>he that cometh in the name of the Lord;
>>Hosanna in the highest."
>Then branches from the stately palms were cut
>And spread upon the dusty road,
>Together with a myriad of blooms.
>The Christ must ride in glory all the way
>Into Jerusalem!
>>But Christ is sad! He does not seem to hear
>>The joyous shouts, or see the blooms
>>The crowd has spread upon His way.
>>Behold, His solemn face and eyes
>>So quiet, with a searching gaze—
>>He seems to look beyond the walls
>>At something far away—a hill—
>>Christ looks up to a distant hill—
>>The one called Calvary.—*I. W. V.*

Adult Leader:

Then followed a week filled with suffering and agony for Jesus. Judas betrayed Him. Peter denied Him. False witnesses accused Him unjustly. He was finally condemned to die on a cross, the most shameful and physically cruel punishment.

On the day we call Good Friday, three crosses could be seen on that part of Calvary's hill called Golgotha. On two crosses hung men who were condemned to die because they had lived sinful lives. On the cross between them hung Jesus Christ, the Saviour of the world, who had committed no sin in His whole life, but who had taken upon Himself *our* sin, that we might live.

Scripture: (*Read by a student.*) Mark 15:1-39.

A Reading: (*By one of the students.*)

THE CRUCIFIXION

The week of lying and deceit was over.
One of the twelve had first betrayed His Lord.
And then another had denied Him thrice.
With hidden bribes men falsely testified.
And Pontius Pilate, weary and afraid
That blame would come to him if he decreed
That Christ be killed, declared he washed his hands
Of any further part in crucifying Christ.
Thus Christ was given to the soldiers sent
From Rome who were, in turn, to see that He
Was crucified upon Golgotha's crest.
They pressed a crown of thorns upon His brow,
And struck Him with a rod upon His head.
They spat at Him and mocked and hissed and sneered.
And then they led Him up the sloping steep
Of Calvary and nailed Him on a cross to die.
A Roman soldier took a spear and pierced
His side as final proof that Christ was dead.
Then suddenly an earthquake shook the hill.
The sun was overshadowed by black clouds.
The lightning flashed. The mighty thunder roared.
The world seemed lost. And frightened men cried out
That truly He was Christ, the Son of God,
Whom they had crucified in shame upon a cross!

—I. W. V.

Adult Leader:

Three days later, on the first day of the week, Christ arose from the dead as He had promised. His body had been laid in a tomb in the garden of a man named Joseph of Arimathea. A great stone had been rolled in front of the tomb to prevent any one from entering. Roman soldiers were placed on guard before the tomb. But in spite of the stone and in spite of the guards, Christ arose.

When a group of women came to the tomb early Easter morning, they found the stone rolled away. "Be not afraid," an angel said. "Ye seek Jesus of Nazareth, which was crucified: he is risen; he is not here: behold the place where they laid him."

Scripture: (*Read by one of the students.*)   Mark 16: 1-6.

A Reading: (*By one of the students.*)

WHAT DOES IT MEAN?

What does it mean to you and to me
  That Jesus was crucified?
What does it mean that He suffered and bled
  And was nailed to a cross where He died?
What does it mean that His body was laid
  In the cool of Joseph's tomb,
In a quiet garden near Golgotha,
  When lilies were fragrant with bloom?
What does it mean that a stone sealed the tomb
  And soldiers were placed there to guard
To see that the body of Jesus remained
  Enclosed in the tomb they had barred?
What does it mean that Jesus arose
  In spite of the guards and the stone?
What does it mean that, though buried as dead,
  He walked from the garden alone?

It means that through Christ we are saved from our sins.
  He died on the cross in our place.
It means that Christ died to save all mankind,
  Regardless of color or race.
It means that He died for us both—you and me—
  So we may have life without end.
It means He's our Saviour, Redeemer, and King,
  Our Comforter, Lord, and our Friend.

SERVICE NO. 50

MOTHER'S DAY

Honour thy father and thy mother: that thy days may be long upon the land which the Lord thy God giveth thee.—Exodus 20:12.

Prelude: "Let Jesus Come Into Your Heart," played as an instrumental special number by as many students as possible.

Call to Worship:

> Let us learn more of God's Word
> Which tells us we should love each other,
> And teaches us to honor both
> Our father and our mother.
> Come and worship,
> Come and pray;
> Come and serve
> Your Lord today.

Hymn of Praise: "Tell Me the Story of Jesus."

Prayer (by the teacher).

Prayer Response: "Bow Down Thine Ear."

Offertory Service:

God has given each of us a great many blessings. One of the greatest blessings is our mother's love. Before we were able to take care of ourselves, our mothers spent countless hours caring for us. They taught us how to walk and how to talk. They taught us how to use a spoon and then a fork. They taught us nursery rhymes and told us stories. Our mothers did all these things because of their great love for us.

But our mothers did not stop loving us when we could stand alone or walk alone. Their love for us grows deeper every day. And so God loves each one of us. He tenderly cares for us and sends us blessings too numerous to count.

We give our mothers special gifts because today is Mother's Day. Let us bring our special gifts to God upon His special day.

(Play softly "Make Me a Blessing" while the offering is taken and while a student concludes with a short prayer of thanks.)

Solo: "Lullaby and Good Night"—Brahms.

Adult Leader:

(Display the poster described in *Patterns for 52 Visual Lessons* and refer to it as you develop the following thoughts:)

For the past several weeks we have been seeing attractive window displays of special gifts for Mother's Day. Some of the gifts, like flowers, are beautiful, but last only a short time. There are other gifts, however, which all of us can give to our mothers and which will last the whole year through. The first of these special gifts for Mother is *lots of love.*

LOTS OF LOVE

(A reading by one of the students.)

> For special people such as mothers
>   Nothing else will do
> But special gifts all wrapped and tagged
>   Especially for you.
> The gift that heads this special list
>   Is one we all should give.
> It's lots and lots and lots of love
>   Shown by the way we live.

Adult Leader:

The next special Mother's Day gift is one that she will appreciate very, very much. If we give it to her all the year, it will save her time and patience, and it will bring her much happiness. The second special gift we all can give our mothers is *obedience.*

LET'S BE OBEDIENT JUST THE SAME

(A reading by one of the students.)

> On days when we feel that we know everything
>   Much better than even our mother,
> And that we are certainly grown up enough
>   To do everything just like big brother—
>   Let's be obedient just the same.
>
> On days when we feel that our way is the best
>   Of any that ever was tried,
> And we feel so abused when we're found to be wrong
>   That we want to run outdoors and hide—
>   Let's be obedient just the same.

On days when we feel we are quite big enough
   To make our decisions alone,
And when we are certain our parents forget
   To consider how much we have grown—
     Let's be obedient just the same.

Adult Leader:

Our next special gift is courtesy. Sometimes in our homes we forget to be courteous. We forget to express our thanks for something received or for something done for us. Our mothers do so many things for us each day, we often fail to remember to say thank you. Being courteous to our mothers every day is one of the very best Mother's Day gifts we can possibly give.

COURTESY

(A reading by one of the students.)

Just to remember to say, "I thank you";
   Just to remember to say, "Yes, please";
Just to remember to say, "You are welcome,"
   And forget how to pout or be stubborn or tease;
Just to remember to run all the errands
   And save steps for Mother whenever we're near—
These little courtesies all tied up together
   Make a Mother's Day gift that will last through the year.

Adult Leader:

Somehow willing hands, happy hearts, and sunny smiles all go together. We can not give one without giving the other two. So, giving our mothers willing hands is like giving them a three-in-one gift. For if we give them willing hands, we shall also be giving them happy hearts and cheerful dispositions.

WILLING HANDS

(A reading by one of the students.)

Have you heard of some one who has two willing hands,
   And yet has an unwilling heart?
Who is willing and ready to help all he can,
   But unwilling to shoulder his part?

I am sure you have never met any like this,
　Because I am sure you agree
That two willing hands mean a heart filled with love
　And a smile that is pleasant to see.
So, two willing hands which are given to Mother,
　On this day set apart from the rest,
Will mean giving a heart that is willing to serve
　And a smile that is always our best.

Adult Leader:

    Although consideration is last on our list, it is certainly not the least of the special Mother's Day gifts. For giving our mothers consideration is very important for many reasons.

    In the first place, we are no longer little tots, unable to do things for ourselves. We are about to enter into adolescence, which marks the beginning of young womanhood and young manhood. So it is very important that we learn to do things for ourselves. If we do not begin by learning how to do the little things well, we shall not be able to take care of larger responsibilities as we grow older. If we take care of all the many little jobs around the house, we will not only be giving our mothers a special Mother's Day gift every day of the year, but we shall also be helping ourselves become more efficient and more responsible. This special Mother's Day gift is, of course, consideration. We shall be more considerate of her time and her energy when we learn to do more things for ourselves. And at the same time we shall be helping ourselves grow into finer, more capable young people.

CONSIDERATION

(A reading by one of the students.)

When we hang up our clothes and tidy our room,
　And stack all our books away;
When we help wash the dishes or vacuum the rug,
　Or run all the errands each day;
When we help Mother save a step or an hour,
　And do all of these with a smile,
We are giving our mothers a gift they deserve,
　And one that will last quite a while.

(Have the students make the kitchen memo pads described in the book mentioned above.)

Benediction.

SERVICE NO. 51

FATHER'S DAY

My son, hear the instruction of thy father, and forsake not the law of thy mother.—Proverbs 1:8.

Prelude: "Faith of Our Fathers" sung by a boys' quartet.

Call to Worship:

>Let us give thanks to God
>   And praise His holy name,
>And through this worship hour
>   His wondrous works acclaim.
>For God is good and kind,
>   And God is just and fair.
>Come, let us worship Him
>   Through songs of praise and prayer.

Hymn of Praise: "This Is My Father's World."

Solo: "My Task," by Ashford.

Adult Leader:

(Display the poster described in *Patterns for 52 Visual Lessons.* Make large placards from stiff white poster paper. Tack them on slats made from the sides of orange crates. After the students recite their lines, they stand in a row before the group so their placards can be read from left to right.)

A parade is given in honor of a special event or to honor a special person. Father's Day is a very special event, because our fathers are very special people. So let us have a Father's Day parade right now to honor all our dads.

A parade never seems complete without a number of placards telling about the special event which it honors. So we have placards, too, telling about our dads.

First Student: (Carrying placard reading LET'S SHOW OUR LOVE ON FATHER'S DAY.)

>Let's show our love on Father's Day!
>   The best way that we can
>Is growing into a Christian fine
>   Young woman or young man.

Second Student: (Carrying a placard reading LET'S HONOR DAD IN EVERY WAY.)

> Let's honor Dad in every way,
>   Let's make him proud of us,
> And willingly obey his word
>   Without delay or fuss.

Third Student: (Carrying a placard reading LET'S TELL OUR DAD WE THINK HE'S GRAND.)

> Let's tell our dad we think he's grand—
>   And grand in every way—
> And that we're mighty proud of him
>   Today and every day.

Fourth Student: (Carrying a placard reading LET'S GIVE OUR DAD A HELPING HAND.)

> Let's give our dad a helping hand.
>   There's lots that we can do
> To help him so he can enjoy
>   A little spare time, too.

Fifth Student: (Carrying a placard reading LET'S BRING HIM JOY IN ALL WE DO.)

> Let's bring him joy in all we do,
>   And honor to his name,
> So we will never cause him grief
>   Or bring him any shame.

Sixth Student: (Carrying a placard reading NOT JUST TODAY, BUT ALL YEAR THROUGH.)

> Not just today, but all year through
>   Let's show our love for Dad,
> For he's the very finest that
>   A fellow ever had.

Adult Leader:

Let us read together all the placards and we shall learn the final thought for this special day:

> Let's show our love on Father's Day.
> Let's honor Dad in every way.
> Let's tell our Dad we think he's grand.
> Let's give our Dad a helping hand.
> Let's bring him joy in all we do—
> Not just today, but all year through.

Prayer Hymn: "More Like the Master." Sing the first verse softly as a prayer hymn and the last verse as a prayer response.

Prayer (by the teacher).

Offertory Service:

One day is set aside each year as a day to give our earthly fathers special honor. That day is Father's Day, which we are celebrating today.

One day is set aside each week as a day to give our heavenly Father special honor. That day is the Lord's Day, which we are also celebrating today.

Just as we give our earthly father gifts on each Father's Day, so we bring our gifts to our heavenly Father on each Lord's Day.

Let us remember the words of Jesus when He said, "It is more blessed to give than to receive" (Acts 20:35).

(Play softly "Give of Your Best" while the offering is taken and while a student gives a brief prayer of thanks.)

(Have the students make the Father's Day card described in the book mentioned above.)

Benediction.

SERVICE NO. 52

MISSIONS

Go ye therefore, and teach all nations, baptizing them in the name of the Father, and of the Son, and of the Holy Ghost.
—Matthew 28:19.

Prelude: Have a group of students sing "Tell It Wherever You Go."

Call to Worship:

> Truly my soul waiteth upon God: from him cometh my salvation. Trust in him at all times; . . . pour out your heart before him: God is a refuge for us (Psalm 62:1, 8).

Hymn of Praise: "We've a Story to Tell to the Nations."

Prayer (by the teacher).

Prayer Response: Sing softly the first verse of "If Jesus Goes With Me."

Quartet: "Send the Light."

WHO IS MY NEIGHBOR?

(A reading given by four students.)

First Narrator:

> A certain lawyer came to Christ and said,
> "What shall I do to gain eternal life?"
> Then Jesus said, "How do you read the law?"
> The lawyer said, "I read that I should love
> The Lord my God with all my heart and soul
> And with my strength and mind, and that I, too,
> Should love my neighbor as I love myself."
> "You have answered right. Do this," Christ said,
> "And you shall live." The lawyer then asked Christ,
> "Who is my neighbor?" Jesus said to him,
> "A certain man was on the road between
> Jerusalem and Jericho when thieves
> Molested him and stripped him of his clothes.
> They wounded him and left him there half dead.
> By chance a priest passed by that way, but when
> He saw the wounded, bleeding man, he crossed
> The road and passed by on the other side.

Soon afterward a Levite did the same.
He, too, passed by, but on the other side.
A Samaritan was next to pass that way.
His heart was filled with grief when he beheld
The suffering, helpless man. He bound the wounds
And placed him on his beast and took him to
An inn. 'Take care of him,' he said, 'and when
I come again I will repay if you
Need more than these two pence'." Then Jesus asked,
"Which one of these was neighbor unto him
That fell among the thieves?" The lawyer said,
"The one who showed great mercy unto him."
Then Jesus said, "Go, then, and do the same."

(Taken from Luke 10:25-37.)

Second Narrator:

A certain young man stood alone within his room.
He looked up at the starry skies and thought,

Young Man:

"I wonder what is missing in my life?
I have far more than any one I know.
I have all things that money can provide.
And I have never been in want of friends.
But still I feel so useless and alone."

Second Narrator:

And then he heard a quiet voice which said,

Voice:

"Your life seems useless and you feel alone,
Because on either side your neighbors live
In poverty and want—in ignorance—
In deep despair and sick with fear and grief."

Second Narrator:

The young man stood erect and cried aloud,

Young Man:

"How can that be? On either side there lives
A neighbor who has twice my wealth and fame!"

Voice:

"Your neighbor? Tell me who your neighbor is!"

Second Narrator:

The gentle voice was low and clear and sweet.
Again the young man stood erect and said,

Young Man:

"My neighbor is the one who lives next door.
But surely he has all the wealth he needs.
There is no poverty or want within
His costly home. Nor sickness, fear, or grief."

Second Narrator:

The room seemed brighter than before, although
The night was quickly darkening outdoors.
Again the voice was heard in clear, soft tones.

Voice:

"Your neighbor is the Indian who lives
In swampy Everglades and knows of naught
But poverty and sickness and despair.
Your neighbor is the beggar on the street,
The man from crowded tenements downtown,
The Greek who owns the fruit store, and the Jew
Next door. Your neighbor is the Negro boy
Who shines your shoes. He is the Chinaman
Who lives in ignorance because the Word
Of God has never reached his door. He is
The Jap. The Hindu. And the man who lives
In faraway Tibet. He is the man
From Africa or from the frozen North.
If you would lead a useful life, then go
And serve your neighbor now."

Second Narrator:

The young man's eyes
Were wide with questionings. He said,

Young Man:
"My neighbor?
You just told me that he is the one
Who comes from every part of this great world!
How then can I serve such a one as he?"

Second Narrator:

Again the gentle, quiet voice replied.

Voice:

"Go ye therefore, and teach all nations,
Baptizing them in the name of the Father,
and of the Son, and of the Holy Ghost:
Teaching them to observe all things whatsoever
I have commanded you: and, lo, I am with you alway,
even unto the end of the world" (Matthew 28:19, 20).

Offertory Service:

We can not all become missionaries and carry the gospel of Jesus Christ to faraway lands. But we can all serve God and help carry out His Great Commission by bringing our offerings to support such work.

(Play softly "I Love to Tell the Story" while the offering is taken. Conclude with a brief prayer by one of the students.)

(Have the students make the Chinese boy described in *Patterns for 52 Visual Lessons.*)

Benediction.

INDEX TO STORIES

	PAGE
A Dose of Her Own Medicine	66
A Kite, Six Shirts, and a Mud Puddle	62
A Lesson Out of School	179
A Little Dog Speaks	91
Allie Mae's Bible	52
Big-hearted Bess	26
God's Factory	72
God Will Provide	78
Good Habits Speak for Themselves	135
Grandfather Lorey's Will	125
He Who Chooses Right Shall Lead You	175
He Wouldn't Turn Back	149
How Grandmother Taylor Taught the Town	238
How Honesty Paid Mrs. Mulligan	159
How the Tiger Lily and the Onion Came To Be	32
If I Had Not Followed the Star (a Christmas story)	227
I Saw the Star (a Christmas story)	222
It All Began With a Thought	16
Learning the Hard Way	82
Let's Listen to Sally (a temperance play)	129
Love Is a Powerful Thing	184
Mr. Gorizia's Special Load	86
My Mom, a Champion Peacemaker	47
No One Can Take Your Joy	217
Not Ashamed to Work	58
Our Dennis Dillworth	198
Penny Purse	192
Place a Lighted Candle in Your Window (a Christmas story)	233
Right in Her Own Back Yard	145
Serve the Lord With Gladness	212
Share What You Have	8
The Day Good Deeds Came Home	207
The Day Jim Told a Lie	12
The Hurricane That Saved Our Town	140
The Little Bird Who Would Not Give Up	116
The Little Bun Man	203
The Mystery of Oolla-Wakee	96
The Porcelain Vase	111
The Potted Red Geranium	120
The Prize Pile of Scraps	188
The Story of Charles Goodyear	154
The Story of Fanny Crosby	37
The Story of Snubby and Chubby	42
The Sunshine Man	101
Vacation With Aunt Peggy	169
Wanted: A True Friend	106
Winning the Pennant for Madison High	164
Young Timothy, or How Leslie Went to College	22